TURBO C®
PROGRAMMER'S
RESOURCE BOOK

TURBO C®
PROGRAMMER'S
RESOURCE BOOK

Frederick Holtz

TAB BOOKS Inc.
Blue Ridge Summit, PA

FIRST EDITION
SECOND PRINTING

Printed in the United States of America

Reproduction or publication of the content in any manner, without express permission of the publisher, is prohibited. No liability is assumed with respect to the use of the information herein.

Copyright © 1987 by TAB BOOKS Inc.

Library of Congress Cataloging in Publication Data

Holtz, Frederick.
Turbo C programmer's resource book.

Includes index.
1. C (Computer program language) 2. Turbo C (Computer program) 3. Compilers (Computer programs) I. Title.
QA76.73.C15H648 1987   005.13′3   87-18000
ISBN 0-8306-3030-9 (pbk.)

Questions regarding the content of this book should be addressed to:

Reader Inquiry Branch
Editorial Department
TAB BOOKS Inc.
Blue Ridge Summit, PA 17294-0214

Contents

Preface

Borland International has earned a reputation in the software marketplace for offering highly efficient and easy-to-use products at a fraction of the cost of competitive products. It all began with their Turbo Pascal, then Turbo Prolog. This was followed by Turbo BASIC and other examples of Turbo-this and Turbo-that. All of these products have several things in common: they continue to receive excellent reviews from users, they are noted for their efficiency, and they are inexpensive. As a matter of fact, most of Borland's excellent products sell for less than $100.

The last several years have seen a slow but continual drop in the price of software and, optimistically, a rise in software capability and quality. However, in one area of programming, the C language, software has lagged behind many other types, at least in the pricing category.

C, an almost unknown language in the microcomputer field in 1980, has become the most popular programming language for general applications on microcomputers. At the onset, C language programming environments for microcomputers were usually priced in the $400 range, although mail order discount houses were hawking them for around $250. In more recent years, some companies began offering "cut-down" models of C compilers and even C interpreters. Some of these were good, especially for the BASIC programmer who wanted to attain a grasp of C without having to take out a second mortgage. Unfortunately, others were so poor as to be considered more of a detriment to learning C than a help.

The C environments that were inexpensive and good for the beginner had a major shortcoming: the rudimentary environment that had served the student so well was not suited to serious software development, once a good working knowledge of C was obtained. The only alternative was to purchase a developer's package, putting the cost back in the $400 range again.

C language is used mainly in commercial-quality software development. Its portability, compact code, fast execution times, and expressiveness are its strong points. It is used to address many different operating environments. C language compilers now offer a high degree of options that may be called upon to address many different operating situations. For instance, do you want your program to make use of a separate numeric coprocessor? Do you want it to emulate floating point operations in memory? Do you want it to use the coprocessor if it is available and emulate if it is not? Most modern, full-function C compilers offer options that will address any or all of these situations, and several thousand more.

This flexibility, however, has caused the price of C programming environments to remain high. All of this optional flexibility can also create a nightmare for someone new to a C environment who might be making the transition from BASIC.

I can appreciate the plight of the software company that wishes to market a C environment. It's like trying to market an Indianapolis 500 race car that is low in price, easy to use by the beginning race driver, and is able to compete with the best cars on the track. That's an impossible order!

Or is it? Borland International has introduced their long-awaited Turbo C programming package. It retails for less than $100 and beats the high-priced competition in many ways. Most important, it gives up nothing to the long-established C language programming environments. Borland seems to have taken the best of what the market previously offered, then made it better and cheaper.

I know this is beginning to sound like a commercial for Borland and for Turbo C, and in a way it is. In over seven years of programming with dozens of C environments, I have not been as impressed with anything to date as much as I have with Turbo C. It seems to be headed for its place in history, along with some other Borland programming products. Turbo C was my first encounter with this company's products, and what I expected to be a somewhat limited C environment has caused me to recompile some of my commercial software products under Turbo C.

Turbo C is easier to use than most commercial C development packages, compiles faster, runs faster, and costs less. It doesn't take a genius to realize that this is a sure formula for success. At long last, here is the ideal C programming environment, one that is inexpensive enough and offers the user friendliness to appeal to people learning this new language while powerful, fast, and efficient enough for the most serious software development needs. Turbo C is an unqualified winner in every way.

Chapter 1

The C Language
Priesthood

A priesthood, according to Webster, is (1) the office, dignity, or character of a priest, or (2) the whole body of priests. This same source also defines a priest as one who is authorized to perform the sacred rites of a religion, especially as a mandatory agent between man and God. Putting this literal definition aside, however, a popular use of this term refers to a (usually) small and exclusive group of individuals who have chosen to separate themselves from the rest of humanity because of what they know and understand.

Using this definition, priesthoods have been formed by scientists, politicians, hobos, naturalists, and other segments of the human race ad infinitum. This type of priesthood is like the exclusive club or organization that you practically have to be born into to have any chance of membership. All too often, such "clubs" have excluded others in order to emphasize the importance or elitism of the members. Like the college fraternity, the rules for entry into such an organization are often arbitrary and ridiculous. Sometimes, the knowledge that must be had by any prospective new enrollee is jealously guarded by the current membership. "Secret society" is perhaps a better name for such a priesthood.

At this point, you are probably wondering what all of this has to do with the C programming language and, specifically, Borland International's new Turbo C.

The fact is that, until recently, a large number of C language programmers have made up a priesthood with some of the attributes mentioned above. As of late, this priesthood has been opened to general membership with the introduction of C programming tools that are affordable and usable by anyone interested in computer programming. One of the most recent entries in this field is Turbo C, and an important entry it is.

The following is an unsolicited advertisement for Borland's Turbo C: After seven years of programming with most of the popular C environments for microcomputers, Turbo C seems to be the best C language programming package yet offered to a general public that consists of expertise levels from rank amateur to commercial software developer.

That's a firm statement that leaves little room for mitigation, and it has not been made lightly nor in haste. There are other environments that might be more ideal for the beginner. However, when you have reached a moderate level of experience, these environments begin to slow you down, to become less than adequate development tools. At the other end of the experience spectrum, the person or company that develops software for business and/or commercial purposes will find that Turbo C offers everything the other compilers do and more. In a sentence, Turbo C compiles faster, links faster, and runs faster than the most popular C language compilers for microcomputers. Plus, it is easier to use, offers excellent advanced features, and . . . it sells for only $99 retail. This compares with $300 and $400 retail for other compilers. Faster, better, and cheaper! These attributes will guarantee success for Turbo C and will probably cause the competition to try to "go Borland one better." This can only improve the assortment of C language products currently available.

But back to this priesthood thing.

C language was developed in the early seventies by an independent handful of programmers at Bell Laboratories. It was meant to be a portable, simple, and versatile language. While there are various theories about this, I think that C was not originally designed as a language for the programming public, but rather as a "personal" language for the programmers who were writing an operating system that is known today as UNIX. C was a scaled down form of BCPL, hence the name C. Prior to this, another scaled down BCPL model was called B. Even the highly touted UNIX was probably a product of happenstance, rather than a well-planned corporation project. Bell was involved with another company, developing MULTICS, a multiuser operating system. Bell backed out for various reasons, but some of the programmers on the MULTICS project kept playing around with the system's concept. They eventually arrived at UNIX, at first a single-user operating system, offering some scaled-down MULTICS features. It is said that the name, UNIX, was even a tongue-in-cheek moniker. Supposedly, UNIX got its name from the word "eunuch," meaning that this was a castrated form of MULTICS.

Whether this scenario is all true, half-true, has some basis in fact, or is outright garbage is beside the point. One thing is unquestionable. C language was designed by a small group of highly talented programmers. It was designed as a short-hand form of assembly language that offered a high degree of portability and expression. It was a professional programmer's language written

2

by a handful of some of the best programmers in the country. Therefore, its fairly limited use for the decade that was to follow was based on the "professional programming" nature of its development. C was a language for the "best" programmers.

Now, let's take a close look at C. It is a small language, it is a structured language, and it can be used to construct programs that execute very rapidly, sometimes almost as rapidly as programs built from assemblers. One would think that a language with a very small number of statements and a compact set of functions would be easily grasped. Well, it was and it wasn't. Those programmers who had extensive assembly language backgrounds took to it fairly well. The language does have a rather weird syntax and it is quite easy to totally hide a programming sequence from those who are not thoroughly familiar with this syntax. BASIC programmers, therefore, might find C to be, upon first usage, a hostile and alien environment. In fact, a knowledge of BASIC does prepare one to learn C . . . but not until a considerable amount of groundwork and explanation has been provided.

C offered a lot, but most professional software houses were still programming in Assembler. Of course, this meant that if a popular program was to be "brought up" on a different type of computer, the entire program had to be rewritten for the new processor, because assembly language is different for different hardware configurations.

With the coming of the microcomputer "boom" in the late seventies and early eighties, the necessity of portability among hardware configurations became apparent. New computers were being introduced almost monthly, and it was discovered that it was far easier to move a C implementation to a new machine than when the application was written in some other language.

In the early eighties, some software houses began making the switch to C language. Most applications were written in a combination of C and Assembler, the latter being used in program portions that required the fastest execution speed. Efforts were made to write as much of an application in C as possible, so that it might be ported to another machine at some future date with a minimum of rewriting required.

Throughout this period, C compilers for microcomputer environments began to appear. Many of these offered only a subset of the original language developed at Bell Laboratories and were quite poor, being limited to integer-only operations. The sad fact was that some of these did not even work properly. In several instances, the microcomputer public paid outrageous prices of $400 or more for a compiler that had so many bugs as to be all but unusable. I had the misfortune to acquire one of these "duds" as my first C compiler. This was the product I intended to use to learn C. What a laugh. The software company that offered this product shall remain nameless for fear of litigation (I should have sued them), but to make a long story even longer, I spent over $200 in telephone calls to this company; received four more debugged versions of their software in the first month and finally, at the end of another three weeks, got my first C program running on my IBM PC.

I have never before or since known such frustration. I am not alone in saying this. Other authors who write in the C-language field and who had only a knowledge of BASIC before learning C have told identical horror stories. Those of us who were BASIC programmers and who learned (or tried to learn) C during the first two years of the eighties share a common bond of hair-pulling, thoughts of suicide and generalized torture.

It was during this time that the "priesthood" concept appeared in my mind. This exact word, "priesthood," was, years later, used by a professional C programmer whom I was interviewing for a magazine article. You see, in the very early eighties, there were no real tutorials on the C programming language. All we had was Kernighan and Ritchie's *The C Programming Language.* I am not criticizing this book. It is still the major reference source for C and its co-author, Dennis Ritchie, is credited with its design and implementation. However, these authors point out in the opening pages of this text that it is *not* an introductory programming manual. Unfortunately, a "take you by the hand" introductory is what those of us who knew only BASIC really needed.

Where was all of the knowledge about C located? That's easy: among the ranks of the professional programmers. Well, some were more professional than others. It is a fact, however, that some ranks of C programmers carefully guarded the knowledge gained through their experiences. There was a time when those of us who knew only BASIC were looked down on as hopelessly ignorant individuals who were not of adequate mental aptitude to grasp the intricately complex workings of C. Even some members of our BASIC-only ranks tended to agree, because the brunt of the popular microcomputing efforts of the day were devoted to video games, checkbook balancers, novelty programs, etc. To those of us who were desperately trying to learn this new language, there were two groups of programmers: those who knew C (the priesthood), and those who did not.

This might sound like the classical struggle of royalty versus peasants, with royalty never deigning to speak to their social inferiors. However, we "hobbyist" programmers who were not yet programming in a commercial environment might have done just as much to establish that struggle through, if nothing else, the awe in which we held C programmers. Also, it is important to point out that, looking back, most of the C programmers who considered themselves members of that elite priesthood, the ones who would not give an interested amateur the benefit of a few words of advice or even answer a simple question, were probably not in the majority and maybe even a rarity. It seemed to many of us, however, that we were being purposely discriminated against by the C language crowd, including the software companies who wouldn't make us a C compiler that worked and contained a few simple instructions on how to begin using it.

With all of these negative comments, it is important to state that there were some highly professional programmers like Dennis Ritchie and many others who would take the time to give help. Apparently, though, many of my fellow BASIC programmers didn't have the nerve to call Bell Labs and ask to speak to their C guru in order to ask him a few simple questions. I got through to Dennis when he was at the Bell facility in North Carolina. He answered my questions in language that I could understand. For this I will be forever grateful to him. Oh, I had gotten through to a few other C programmers at other companies. Many of them gave quite impressive accounts of just how much they knew and how much I didn't, but when I hung up, I knew no more than I did when I called. The few times I talked to Dennis, I came away with new knowledge and the ability to teach myself a few more things about C.

Throughout this scenario, C language compilers were changing. Lifeboat Associates in New York became the exclusive distributor for the Lattice C Compiler, still the most recognized compiler name in the microcomputer market. When I obtained the Lattice compiler, I also obtained the "trouble number" for Lifeboat Associates. Frankly, I called this department very, very often, not with compiler problems, but with programming problems. The head man at the trouble number was a Fortran programmer, but together, we talked me through quite a few problems. I wish I could recall his name, because he was tremendously helpful and would usually call the Lattice support staff when he couldn't answer a question. Lattice and Lifeboat made it easier for a lot of us to learn C language using the IBM PC as our executing instrument.

Around 1983, true introductory programming guides began to appear. These were literally leapt upon by a small but growing group of hobby programmers who were hungry for C programming knowledge. As we learned more about C language, Kernighan and Ritchie's book was transformed from a collection of ampersands, backslashes, and other hieroglyphs into meaningful and timely information.

Suddenly, C became the "best language for microcomputers." In late 1983, the software industry, overnight it seemed, experienced "C mania." All of the computer magazines were touting C and rating C compilers. C was stacked up against Pascal. People were discovering that C offered programming opportunities. Metropolitan newspapers, normally swamped with computer-related employment advertisements, quickly saw C language programmer positions increase drastically. If you knew how to program in C, this was a plus that might mean the difference between a great job and no job at all. Those who knew even a little bit about programming in C could sometimes compete with more capable programmers who knew more, generally, but who could not program in this one language.

The C priesthood, if there ever really was one, is no more. The ranks of those who program in C are growing monthly. No longer is there a "secret society," and C programs, functions, algorithms, and the like are shared through bulletin boards, magazines, and books.

However, C language still occupies a slot in the "professional programmer" category. We generally hear of C applications that address the needs of the commercial software developers. Are the needs of the so-called hobbyist programmer different? My answer is "not necessarily." The term "hobbyist programmer" is a poor one. It conjures up notions of playing with something. Using a different term, "nonprofessional programmer," is not much better, because this might imply that the output from such a programmer is certainly not professional. I like the term "noncommercial programmer" better, because this simply means someone who is programming for some purpose other than the immediate making of money. I say "immediate" because many programmers in this category are training themselves (sometimes unknowingly) for a future in the commercial programming field.

C is and might always be considered a rather lofty endeavor for noncommercial programmers. Maybe that is as it should be. C is not as easy to learn as some other languages, but it is not as difficult now as it once was, thanks to excellent training manuals and textbooks in conjunction with excellent programming environments. Formerly, the "professional" nature of C language and the limited number of users when compared with languages like BASIC relegated C compilers to the top end of the price spectrum. With the introduction of Turbo C, however, all of this has changed.

Turbo C is a professional C language environment that takes a back seat to no other C compiler generally marketed for the microcomputer environment. At present, Turbo C would seem to be in the driver's seat. Borland International has reported 35,000 advance orders for this product. This figure is astounding to me. A few years ago I visited a group of programmers in a northwestern state and was told that the population of known C programmers had increased by 33% as soon as I entered the state. You see, there were only three known C programmers living in this entire state at the time. I was the fourth and 25% of the total C programmers there at the time.

What makes Turbo C so revolutionary? A combination of things. From the standpoint of popularity, the price of $99 retail is a major part of the success formula. When an executing environment costs two to five times this amount, a noncommercial potential buyer is going to have to think long and hard before making such an investment. At a price of less than one hundred dollars, many, many more programmers will be able to afford to experiment with C.

However, C language compilers have been offered in the past for low prices. One I tried cost only $39 retail. It had surprisingly few limitations and could have been used for some mildly sophisticated development. However, it did not rate as a "professional" C programming environment. To get this kind of performance, the price was in excess of $300 retail, although mail-order houses could usually offer the same package for a little less.

Here is the catch that has plagued the software industry, at least in the area of C programming. If the environment is professional enough, it costs too much to attract a general programming audience. If the product is cheap enough, the features might not be enough to attract that audience. For the most part, C-oriented products were aimed at the commercial and corporate customer, leaving the novice, the person who might like to learn C, in an awkward position. He or she had to make a decision: "Do I buy the less expensive beginners package at first?" If the answer is yes, and the person wants to go further after a grasp of C is obtained, he/she must then spend more money for a professional-level compiler for development. The other choice is to come up with the money for the professional compiler in the first place, thus avoiding the extra expenditure for the novice package. This choice works well if the novice can wade through the masses of files and such contained on the three to eleven diskettes that make up a typical professional C package today. More "wading" is required to even learn how to compile with these packages, because they usually offer ten or more compiling options.

Sadly, a third choice is often made: "I think I'll just forget about it for now."

Turbo C has taken this "between a rock and a hard place" choice out of buying your first C environment. Turbo C is an excellent programming package as far as a professional C environment is concerned, and it will make an almost ideal learning environment. It's not quite as easy to use as one or two other products I can think of, but this is more than made up for by its capabilities. And the novice will, in a matter of days, be past the point where one of these other environments might lend a little more support.

Of the numerous books I have proposed and written for various publishers in the field of popular computing, I am always advised that the publisher wants "a book that is ideal for beginners and yet of a high enough technical nature to be useful to the professional in the field." This is a ridiculous request, on the order of building an automobile that is perfectly suitable for teaching teenagers to drive and yet meets the needs of the professional race driver who desires to win the Indianapolis 500. However, Borland International seems to have accomplished this impossible task with Turbo C. Later chapters will delve into the workings of this excellent C environment, but briefly, it offers an editing/compiling/linking/executing/debugging shell within which programs may be written, compiled, linked, executed, and debugged from a rather typical pull-down window screen. Of course, many of us who write programs for a living frown on these niceties and complain that they often slow us down. Therefore, Turbo C also offers a more conventional means of accomplishing the operations listed above, through a series of separate commands and programs executed under the DOS shell. In this regard, Turbo C satisfies the needs, desires, and prejudices of both the novice and the professional.

Turbo C programs typically are smaller than those obtained from its nearest competitors, compile faster, link faster, and most importantly, execute faster (sometimes 70% faster) than some others that cost so much more. Borland's secret is really no secret at all. They first designed a professional C compiler that would compete with and, generally, outdistance the best C compilers the market previously offered. Having accomplished this, they then built in most of the features a professional programmer would expect of an excellent developmental environment. Once the professional package was complete, they went one step further. They built additional tools and utilities to allow this professional environment to, optionally, be accessed and utilized from a simple menu, one that was universally accepted. Turbo C is *not* a novice environment that can also be utilized by professionals. It is, first and foremost, a professional developer's environment that can also be accessed, via the additional software tools, by the novice.

Borland has built a race car that can win at Indianapolis and can also be driven like a Chevy. All of this is offered for the price of a bicycle.

Chapter 2

Using Turbo C

The opening paragraph of the Borland International Turbo C User's Guide reads:

> "Turbo C is for C programmers who want a fast, efficient compiler; for Turbo Pascal programmers who want to learn C with all the 'Turbo' advantages; and for anyone just learning C who wants to start with a fast, easy-to-use implementation."

These are appropriate words, indeed. However, the term "fast, easy-to-use implementation" might lead one to conclude that Turbo C is a nice "starter" package, but might leave something to be desired for true, systems programming. The reason for this assumption lies in the fact that C environments have, traditionally, been either easy-to-use and inappropriate for efficient complex programming tasks, or they have been highly efficient and notoriously difficult to use.

- Fact: The Turbo C Compiler is fast.
- Fact: The Turbo C Compiler is easy to use.
- Fact: The Turbo C Compiler gives up nothing in program efficiency to the major competitive C programming environments for microcomputers.
- Fact: Turbo C retails for less than $100, compared with $350 to $400 for its closest competition.

These facts are not idealistic "imaginings" from someone who is paid to write appealing advertisements for a product. They are the results of hundreds of hours of testing thousands of C programs using Turbo C and comparing it with all of the most popular C compilers for MS-DOS machines. I am highly impressed with Turbo C and make no apologies, because this enthusiasm has been earned.

THE TURBO C PACKAGE

Borland's Turbo C consists of four distribution disks and two manuals. The Turbo C User's Manual contains approximately 300 pages, while the Turbo C Reference Manual is nearly 400 pages in length. The User's Manual provides an excellent step-by-step introduction to setting up and using Turbo C. New users of C language will appreciate this type of introduction, as will more experienced users who are accustomed to the traditional "hashing out" procedure often required when starting out with new C environments. This manual also provides some good background information about programming in C language in general. While certainly not a tutorial on the entire C language, this section might prove to be a convenient reference source for beginners.

The manual does leave a bit to be desired when explaining some of the more elaborate features of Turbo C. Beginners will probably get bogged down by some of the terminology. However, many of these features won't be used immediately by these beginners. By the time their C experience has reached the level where advanced features can be used, their grasp of C "language" should enable them to pick up on most of the industry buzz words.

One point to remember is that Turbo C is not just a basic C programming environment. It offers an interactive user's menu that grizzled, dyed-in-the-wool oldtimers love to hate. Such a menu, however, is an ideal learning environment for newcomers to C. Turbo C satisfies both parties. The use of the menu is optional. Alternate compiling methods which follow the more traditional "command line" approach should make those programmers who shun menus quite happy.

From my standpoint, I almost always use the menu. Oh, I have written four or five batch files to take care of some specialized needs, but the menu suffices 95% of the time. Sometimes, I think there is a tendency on the part of long-time C programmers to purposely stop the march of progress in the area of "easier-to-use." This might be compared to the homeowner who still prefers to cut his lawn with a scythe, shunning the power lawn mower. Such people are said to be "colorful" or "eccentric" (if they have money), or "crazy" (if they don't).

In C programming, good arguments can be made for interactive menus, and arguments that are just as good can be made against them. If the truth be known, there are times when the menu is a big help, and others when it gets in the way. Turbo C programmers may use either the menu or command-line methods, or both, when interfacing with this C compiler.

In a nut shell, Turbo C contains a *complete* C compiler. This is not a subset of the original language. Rather, it is a superset, containing all the original C language offered, and a lot more. Most of the functions and statements available to the programmer in Turbo C will be familiar to users of Lattice C, Microsoft C, and Mark Williams C.

Microsoft C (Version 4.0) is probably the closest match to Turbo C in regard to lists of functions and general usage. This is a qualified statement, because all of the excellent compilers mentioned are closely aligned, and it is usually a simple matter to modify a program written for one to enable it to be compiled under any one of the others. This fact indicates that, from a programming standpoint, all of these compilers are very similar. Therefore, it might be most appropriate to state that Turbo C fits right in with all of these other compilers (the former Big Three) from the programmer's point of view.

The programmers who designed Turbo C, however, obviously must have taken a close, hard look at the most popular C compilers for MS-DOS machines, and decided to take what was best from each one. Turbo C functions seem to be a composite of the functions in these three other compilers. For instance, Microsoft C offers programmable far pointers for mixed memory model operations and several functions that can move data anywhere in RAM. On the other hand, it does not offer a PEEK or POKE function, as such. Certainly, you can easily PEEK and POKE from the small model compiler using far pointers, movedata( ), or other functions. The Lattice C compiler, on the other hand, offers discrete peek( ) and poke( ) functions to be used within the small memory models. So does Turbo C. Of course, Turbo C conforms closely to the new ANSI standard for the C programming language. All compiler models are drifting in this direction, some more than others.

Turbo C also offers some new functions that address text handling, memory management, interface with DOS files, etc., creating a new and exciting C programming environment that really offers no unpleasant surprises for those of us who have used other compilers. Several pleasant surprises are in store for the experienced user, and this chapter highlights some of them.

If you are a newcomer to C who has chosen the Turbo C Compiler, then your choice is a wise one. I am unaware of any other full-featured C programming environment that offers the user-friendliness of Turbo C. In my opinion, the most friendly C programming environment for BASIC programmers today is the RUN/C Interpreter, which offers several built-in BASIC-like functions, such as cls( ) and locate( ), and others not found in most C packages. However, this interpreter cannot match the speed of a compiler, and a compiler will eventually be necessary for serious program development.

Of special importance is the fact that the Turbo C package compiles programs very rapidly. This is a decided plus, because your programs can be up and running in seconds, instead of minutes as with several other good compilers. This also means that programs which contain errors will be detected faster during the rapid compile and linking stages offered by Turbo C.

The advantage of an interpreter lies in its ability to immediately begin running source code without going through a compiling stage. The disadvantage is the slow execution speed, an inherent by-product. Turbo C is as fast as any of the popular compilers on the market. In fact, it is faster. And, it compiles faster too. Although you can't run a source program immediately, you can run it within 25 to 45 seconds if the program is small. This is a good trade-off: fast compile times combined with extremely fast execution. This trade-off allows the Turbo C programming package to be a good training environment for newcomers, and is perfectly adequate to take care of professional programming needs as these newcomers become proficient in C.

Turbo C is that rare programming package that grows with the experience level of the programmer. I can think of no reason why the person who learns C using Turbo C would need to switch to another compiler after he/she has gone beyond student status in search of more power. Turbo C is a good investment.

SYSTEM REQUIREMENTS

Turbo C is designed to operate on the IBM PC family of microcomputers and all close compatibles running DOS 2.0 and higher. This includes a group of hundreds of microcomputers including the IBM PC, XT, AT, and almost every other machine that is MS-DOS compatible. Each system must be equipped with a minimum of 384K RAM and one 360K disk drive.

Those are the minimum requirements, but let me assure you that using Turbo C with such minimums will be pure Hell. The same can probably be said of any other serious development package in C or any other language.

To really get the full benefit out of Turbo C, your machine should contain at least 512K memory, and 640K is even better. You should have two disk drives at a minimum, although a hard disk is really to be preferred, and is required if you don't want to be pulling your hair out over diskette changes at critical times. The IBM monochrome display, I feel, provides a better programming "window" than does the color display, at least for easily deciphering all of those characters that tend to run together when long hours are spent programming in C.

The system used as the research model for programs in this book is a standard IBM PC with the 4.77 MHz clock, 640K RAM, IBM monochrome display, monochrome display adapter, Princeton Graphic Systems HX-10 RGB color monitor, IBM color card, and an 8087 math coprocessor. As far as disk drives are concerned, my system contains two 360K diskette drives and two 27 megabyte hard disks. This somewhat over-engineered "standard" PC was designed to allow me to test software packages in an environment that would roughly reflect several different "minimum" systems that might be had by the typical user, while not restricting me unnecessarily. The processing speed of this computer is no different from any other IBM PC, and even slower than many clones. I can disregard the hard drives and use one or two diskette drives. I can even configure the machine so that it operates from a single drive and "thinks" it has far less memory than is really on-board. I can also crank in a Turbo board that will triple the processing speed.

Turbo C was run under PC-DOS Version 2.1 for most of the research on this book. On a few occasions, I switched to DOS 3.2 in order to test some

Turbo C functions that are operable only under this system. Most of my commercial software development is done under DOS 2.1 to assure compatibility with the thousands and thousands of PC users who are still operating under earlier versions. Naturally, programs developed under DOS 2.1 work just fine when run in a higher version.

I have tested Turbo C in many configurations, and find that a practical minimum, for me, is 512K, a single hard disk, a single floppy disk, and the monochrome display. Other users might find these minimums very conservative or extremely radical. It all depends on what you want to do, how fast you want to do it, and how much inconvenience you can tolerate. For me, using anything but a hard disk with its rapid read/write capabilities is a severe handicap. A Turbo processor board is a nice addition, but I find the 4.77 MHz speed of the stock IBM PC to be perfectly comfortable in working with Turbo C, because of its rapid compile times. Of course, Turbo boards make the entire package fly.

IBM PC-AT machines and clones provide an ideal setting for Turbo C. While I have not tested this programming package on any of the new 386 machines, I am sure these will offer far greater advantages. As a matter of fact, a 10, 12, or even 16 MHz PC-AT clone or 386 machine would probably allow Turbo C to act almost like an interpreter for relatively small programs. The compile and linking stages would be handled in just a few seconds, and the program could be run almost immediately. Turbo C compiles and links quickly because intermediate files are written to memory, not to the disk drive. This brings about a speed increase that can be described as highly significant.

GETTING STARTED

The Turbo C User's Manual contains a lot of detailed instructions for copying the original Turbo C diskettes and getting "geared up" for Turbo C. Instead of rehashing what this manual already contains, I will tell you how I installed Turbo C on my system.

The entire Turbo C programming package is contained on four floppy disks. Disk 1 contains the TC.EXE file, which is the Turbo C integrated environment; TCHELP.TCH, the Turbo C Help file; README.COM, and README, a last-minute update file that presumably will contain the latest "bug" reports. README.COM is the executable file that simply reads the file information in README.

Disk 2 contains TCC.EXE, the command line version of Turbo C; TCLINK.EXE, the Turbo C linker; CPP.EXE, the C preprocessor; and several utility programs.

Disk 3 contains all of the #include (header) files and the runtime libraries for several of the compiler memory models. The start-up object files are found on this disk as well.

Disk 4 contains more libraries and object files for other memory models. There are also several miscellaneous files on this disk.

In my installation, I created a directory on hard disk named \ *turboc*. Within this directory, I created two subdirectories, \ *turboc* \ *include* and \ *turboc* \ *lib*. The entire contents of Disk 1 was copied to \ turboc. Next, all files on Disk

2 were copied to the same directory. After this transfer was complete, Disk 3 was placed in drive A:, and I changed directories on the hard disk to \turboc\include. I then typed the DOS command:

```
copy a: *.h
```

With Disk 3 in drive A:, all of the header files (those with the .h extension) were copied from this disk to the subdirectory. I then switched to \turboc\lib and, with Disk 3 still in drive A:, entered:

```
copy a: *.lib
```

When all of the library files were copied, another DOS command was input:

```
copy a: *.obj
```

This command copied all of the object files from Disk 3. Next, Disk 4 was inserted in drive A:, and all files were copied from this disk to the same directory on the hard drive.

My installation was now complete. All of the executable files and their support files were contained in the \turboc directory. All header files were contained in \turboc\include, and all library and object files were in \turboc\lib. This installation was done, admittedly, without reading any of the User's Manual instructions, as some of us who are in a hurry to be up and running are apt to do. Fortunately, I later discovered that this is exactly the installation the manual recommends. It would seem to be the logical way most C programmers would make such an installation.

If you are not blessed with a hard disk drive, then I recommend you get one if at all possible. Without it, you are going to be slowed up with the "mechanics" of your system, when this attention might be better put toward the mechanics of C programming. Of course, it's an easy thing to say, "Go out and buy a $600 hard disk," and another thing to do it. You can get by with two floppy drives or even one, but "getting by" is all you'll be doing. The key to needing the hard disk is mainly the storage capacity, and not necessarily the increased speed of access, although the latter is quite a boon as well. Even a cheap and slow 5 or 10 megabyte drive with 80 millisecond access time is better than a floppy. Such "obsolete" hard disks can now be had for a few hundred dollars, and would be a worthwhile investment.

If my recommendations for the "minimum" C programming system for use with Turbo C are not within your reach, take heart! The User's Manual explains the best method for using this software on just about every common configuration of PCs and disk drives.

WRITING AND RUNNING A FIRST PROGRAM

All that is necessary to begin working with Turbo C is to be in your working directory, which from my installation notes would be \turboc. Those persons without a hard disk can think of the three directories I described earlier as three separate floppies named *turboc, turbocinclude* and *turboclib*. From this point on, I will make reference only to the directories and subdirectories I initially established on my working model.

In the master directory there is a file named TC.EXE, which is the Turbo C Integrated Programming Environment. It contains the working menu that accesses the compiler, linker, editor, and everything else Turbo C makes use of. To gain access to it, type:

TC <return>

Shortly, the menu will appear on your screen. If you are using a color monitor, then the menu will be multicolored for best visual clarity. The menu "frame" will be in dark and light blue, while the text editor will write in amber on a black window.

THE MAIN MENU

It is from this menu that all programs may be written, compiled, linked, and executed. You may also access many other options, such as changing the compiler models, debugging, etc. This is a complete interactive environment, allowing you to access nearly all of the possible uses of the Turbo C programming package. There are very few things that can be accomplished with the command-line method of compiling programs under Turbo C that cannot also be handled with more convenience from the menu.

There are seven pull-down windows in the Main menu, plus an on-line HELP utility that is accessed by pressing the F1 function key. The various options are accessed by simultaneously pressing the ALT key and the key that represents the first letter of the option you want. For instance, to access the pull-down File menu, you would use the following combination:

ALT + F

This window will be opened and several options may be chosen by moving the highlight bar via the cursor movement keys.

The Main menu options are as follows:

File. This menu provides options to load, save, pick, create, or write to a disk. From this menu you may also list and change directories, temporarily revert to DOS control, or exit the Turbo C Main menu entirely.

Edit. Striking ALT + E invokes the screen editor, and allows source programs to be created or edited.

Run. The ALT + R combination causes a source program to be compiled, linked, and run in one operation.

Compile. The Compile menu provides options to compile and link a source program. Some of these options include compiling and linking, compiling only, or linking only.

Project. The Project menu allows programmers to name all of the files that are associated with a particular program so that this program may be compiled as a single project.

Options. The Options menu allows the programmer to select all of the many options offered by the Turbo C package. These options include choosing one of many memory models, compile-time switches, defining macros, and specifying where the header and library files are to be found.

Debug. The ALT + D key combination allows errors to be tracked.

The following discussions center around the features offered in each of these menus.

File

The File menu allows the user to select from several choices that involve loading, editing, and saving files. Other choices will allow you to return to the DOS shell (temporarily leaving the Turbo C interactive environment), and to display the files in a directory.

The options are chosen by stepping down each selection with the cursor control keys on the numeric keypad. Each selection is highlighted as it is scanned.

Load. The first selection is "Load F3." This can also be immediately accessed by pressing the F3 function key. When this option is chosen, it means that a file is to be loaded into the editor. A window appears on the screen and you may input the name of an existing file to load. If the file does not exist, then this is the name of a new file that may be written and saved. After this choice, Turbo C puts you into the edit window. This full-screen editor allows you to begin to write a new program immediately, or to edit a program that was just loaded.

Pick. The Pick option in the File menu allows you to pick from a list of the last eight files loaded into the editor. If you select one of these, it is loaded into the editor and the cursor is placed at the point where you last left the file. This is very convenient when various programs must be written simultaneously.

New. This option means that the file is a new one and has not been previously named. The file is identified as NONAME.C, and will be saved as such unless it is renamed using another option from this menu.

Save. This option saves the current file in the editor to the disk. If the current file is NONAME.C, a window will appear in the editor asking you if you want to change the name. You may do so by simply typing the new name, or you may save it as NONAME.C. Whether or not the file has any other name, it is saved immediately under this new name, overwriting any other files of the same name.

Write to. This option allows you to write a file contained in the editor as a new name. The new name is given when the window prompt appears.

Directory. As its name implies, the Directory option allows you to get a listing of the contents of any DOS directory. If you press <return> after selecting this option, the current directory appears in its own window.

Change dir. This option displays the current directory and then prompts for the name of another drive and/or directory. When this information is provided by the user, the new directory is written to the window.

OS shell. This option allows you to temporarily exit the Turbo C interactive menu and reenter DOS control. You may use the DOS commands as you normally would, but remember that Turbo C stays resident, so you won't have as much memory to work with as before. To return to the Turbo C environment, enter the following at the DOS prompt:

exit <return>

Quit. The Quit option allows you to permanently leave the Turbo C interactive menu. If a file is currently contained in the editor that has not been saved to disk, you will be asked if you want to save it before the exit is made. If your response is positive, then the file is saved and the exit is made. If you answer no, then the exit is made immediately, and the program in the editor is lost.

Edit

The Edit command is invoked from the main menu by the ALT+E keypress combination. This puts you into the full-screen editor window and allows you to begin writing or editing a loaded program immediately. The Editor menu offers no further options, but the screen editor is discussed in more detail later in this chapter.

Run

The Run command invokes Project-Make, then runs the program in the editor using the arguments given in Options/Args. Project-Make is a program building tool that will be overviewed later in this chapter.

Compile

The Compile menu offers several options that can produce an object module from the source code in the editor or an EXE file. You can also elect to link a series of object files already in existence with the appropriate library files.

Compile to OBJ. The Compile to OBJ option is the one to choose if you just wish to compile the source code in the editor. The source code is run through the compiler, the object file is produced, and control is returned to you. The name of the object file will be the same as the source file, only it will have an .OBJ extension.

Make EXE File. This option calls Project-Make. Generally, it takes a program from the editor, compiles it if necessary, and then links it with the appropriate files. The result is an executable version of the source program in the editor.

Link EXE. The Link EXE option accesses the current object and library files and links them without producing a new EXE file.

Build All. This option unconditionally rebuilds all of the files in a project, regardless of whether or not they are out of date. Unlike Make EXE File, which rebuilds only those files that are not current, this option rebuilds all of them.

Primary C File. This option is chosen to specify which source file (.C extension) will be compiled to .OBJ files.

Project

The Project menu allows the user to combine multiple source files and object files to create finished programs. This is useful when many source and object files are involved in arriving at a master executable program.

Project Name. The Project Name option allows you to select or change the name of a project file. Such a file contains the names of source files to be compiled or linked. This project name will also be the name given to the executable file when it is created.

Break Make On. This option allows you to specify what types of conditions warrant halting the Make operation. You may specify a stop after compiling a file that has warnings, errors, fatal errors, or, as a safety routine, before linking.

Clear Project. This option allows you to clear the current project and replace it with another if desired.

Options

The Options menu is accessed via the ALT + O combination. This is probably the first menu you will access upon entering Turbo C for the first time. This menu contains settings that determine how the Turbo C environment will interact with your system configuration. It also allows you to select a set of *default criteria,* such as computer memory model, code generation, and optimization. In fact, each of the options in this menu offers further options that determine just how Turbo C will compile code, where it will search for library files, whether it is to use register variables, etc.

Compiler. Seven options are available when the Compiler option is accessed. The following list briefly describes six. The seventh, Names, should be used only by advanced programmers.

- *Model* is an option that allows you to select from one of six memory models available in Turbo C. The "Small" memory model is the default. Other models include "Tiny," "Medium," "Compact," "Large," and "Huge."
- The *Defines* option allows you to specify macro definitions that are always to be a part of any program you compile. Multiple definitions may be input, and should be separated by semicolons.
- The *Code Generation* option offers ten suboptions that cause the compiler to generate either a C language calling sequence or a Pascal calling sequence for function calls. For all but expert applications, this should be left in the default of C. Another suboption allows you to specify the instruction set in order to target a specific microprocessor. The default here is 8088/8086, but this can be changed to 80186/80286. Yet another suboption allows you to determine

how floating-point code is generated. You can choose from code that provides floating-point emulation, code that is targeted toward a math coprocessor, and code that uses the coprocessor if available or emulates if it is not.

• *Optimization* is an option that you pretty much have to experiment with. It allows you to select the manner in which Turbo C will optimize the code it produces. You can toggle between optimizing for size and optimizing for speed. You can also toggle between using register variables or not. Register optimization can be turned on or off, and jump optimization, when selected, reduces the code size by reorganizing loops and eliminating redundant jumps. More on this later in this chapter.

• The *Source* option determines how the compiler handles the source code during the start-up phases of compilation. One option allows you to alter the length of identifier names within the range of 1 to 32 characters. Default is 32 characters. You can turn the nested comments option on or off. When it's off, nested comments are not permitted, in keeping with the Kernighan and Ritchie standard. The last option in this section toggles the ANSI keyword option. When on, the compiler will recognize only ANSI keywords and will treat Turbo C extension keywords as normal identifiers.

• *Errors* is an option that determines how the compiler will deal with diagnostic messages. You may specify a halt in compilation after a certain number of errors or warnings have been reported. You can also specify whether or not messages are to be displayed.

Linker. The items in the Linker menu deal with establishing various options for the linker. From this menu, you can select the type of map file to be produced, specify default libraries, disable stack warning messages, and determine whether or not the linker will be case-sensitive.

Environment. The Environment menu allows the Turbo C environment to interact with your system. From this menu, you tell Turbo C where to find the #include files, the library files, and even where to write the output files. You also specify where the Turbo C directory is, so that the environment can locate its own help and configuration files. The Auto Save Edit option helps prevent loss of source files by automatically saving a file being edited when you select RUN or temporarily exit to the DOS shell. Several other options allow for custom-tailoring of the Turbo C package to your computer and disk drive configuration.

Debug

The final Main menu selection is Debug, which offers three options. The first affects the way Turbo C highlights possible problem areas in a source file that has resulted in error or warning messages after compilation. You can specify whether these messages are to be retained from edit to edit. You can even turn the message window off completely. A bonus within the Debug window is the listing of the amount of available memory. This is the memory that is not currently being used by Turbo C to maintain the environment.

This discussion on the main menu has entailed the briefest of overviews. Fortunately, highly detailed information is provided in the excellent Turbo C User's Guide. It is hoped that this overview is adequate to present a fair description of Turbo C to those readers who have not yet purchased or used this package but might be considering it for their C programming environment.

USING TURBO C

The documentation included in the Turbo C User's Manual and the Turbo C Reference Guide is probably worth the price of the entire package. While this book is meant to be instructive, it is certainly belaboring the point to list each and every function and each and every operation that makes up the Turbo C package. The nature of this book involves making the reader more familiar with Turbo C programming by presenting sample programs (about 200, in fact) along with understandable explanations. Suffice it to say that if you elect to go with Turbo C, you won't be lacking in documentation on how to interact with this excellent programming system. The following discussions are an overview of my initial reactions to Turbo C as a programming environment and my continuing experiences working in this realm.

Programmers who are accustomed to C language environments will have little or no problem adapting to Turbo C. Previously, I described how I loaded various Turbo C files into the Turbo C directory and into several subdirectories. At this point, I activated the Turbo C integrated environment by executing the file TC.EXE. This invoked the menu just discussed.

Fortunately, the default settings for this menu require very few changes to begin programming in this environment. The first menu I selected was OPTIONS. Here, I specified that the include directory could be found in \turboc\include. I also indicated the location of the library directory, which is \turboc\lib. Everything else was left in the default mode.

The first job is to write a C program. I did this by entering the ALT + E combination at the keyboard. This immediately opened the screen editor, and I quickly hacked out Kernighan and Ritchie's "hello, world" program. I then entered ALT + C and chose the Make option. In short order, I had a program named NONAME.EXE. I chose to reenter the DOS shell to execute the program. There were no surprises; the program ran as intended.

After several months of using Turbo C, I have developed my own personal habits and routines for writing, compiling, and executing code. I normally write the source code and then enter the Make utility via the F9 function key. If I've done my job, this produces an executable file. Rarely do I use the RUN command from the menu. I usually exit temporarily to DOS, test the program, and then reenter Turbo C to make changes or add more code.

The editor is not some fantastically new and modern fifth-generation wonder. If you've used the Turbo Pascal or SideKick editor, or even MicroPro's WordStar, then you are already familiar with the Turbo C editor. It's an easy editor to use and very easy to learn. It is far superior, in my opinion, to most other editors used for writing programs.

COMPARING TURBO C

As a person who makes his living writing programs in C and writing about programming in C, it is understandable that I would have a significant amount of compilers, libraries, and the general gamut of C programming environments on hand. I do, and I have one or two that I use for the brunt of all my commercial programming endeavors. As of this writing, Turbo C is my programming environment of choice. I have made comparisons of Turbo C with the best compilers the market previously offered. Turbo C seems to come out on top, at least in regard to the properties I feel are important. As has been stated elsewhere in this book, programs written in Turbo C compile faster, link faster, and run faster than when compiled and linked in these other environments. I'm not specifically naming these others at this time because without a doubt they too will be improving their products in order to compete with Turbo C and each other. While a program compiled under Turbo C might run 50 percent faster than one compiled under another environment today, by the time you read this, the slower environment might have been improved to closely match or even exceed what Turbo C can do today. Such are the trends in today's programming environment marketplace.

There is one area, however, that is going to be difficult for the suppliers of these other products to beat. This has to do with the cost of the package itself. Turbo C retails for less than $100 and is being hawked by the mail-order houses for less than $70. As mentioned previously, most of the high-level compilers for MS-DOS machines are priced between $350 and $400 retail. Turbo C will probably change this trend toward high-priced C language environments. Just as this book is going to press, Microsoft Corporation announced a new C language package that sells for less than $100. Certainly, others will follow suit. This will be good for the thousands of hobbyist programmers who have not been able to "sink their teeth into" C because of price.

When I first began writing this book, I elected to use a standard IBM PC for most testing, because this environment represents a reasonable configuration. Compared with other professional compilers, Turbo C compiled and linked my programs at what seemed like lightning speed. For my professional development work, I use a PC AT with an 8 MHz clock. Turbo C really flies in this environment.

My real surprise came when I noticed the tremendous speed increases I was gaining with Turbo C. Some programs ran as much as 70 percent faster than with a nonoptimizing, competitive compiler, and 30 percent faster than with another optimizing environment. This made the old IBM PC seem like one of the fast, new machines. When run on the fast, new machines, the results were even more apparent.

Something that impresses me even more is the friendliness of this package. It is an extremely easy environment to become accustomed to and to depend on. After using it for three months, I have no harsh criticisms.

COMPILER MEMORY MODELS

Turbo C, like most modern C compilers, offers several different memory models that may be selected by the user. In fact, Turbo C offers six memory models, which is more than most. Each memory model has its own set of libraries and start-up object files. The model you choose to program in is determined by a number of factors, including source code size, object code size, the amount of data storage needed, and execution speed. Of the six memory models offered, the default is the "Small" model. This is the one that I have the most experience with, and the one I target for all of my commercial work if at all possible and practical.

Tiny. The Tiny memory model is the smallest of the six offered. It offers a total of 64K for all code, data, and arrays. This model uses only near pointers, and programs compiled under this model can be converted to .COM format, which allows for faster loading and start-up execution of the file. Most small programs will fit the Tiny model if it is not necessary to declare a large number of arrays or arrays with very large subscripts.

Small. The Small memory model is similar to the Tiny model, in that near pointers are always used. However, code and data segments are separated and do not overlap. The Tiny model allows a total of 64K for code and data, while the Small model offers 64K for each, giving a total size of 128K. In the Small memory model, the stack and extra segments start at the same address as the data segment. Borland states that this is a good memory model size for average applications. It can also be used for some of the moderately large applications by using highly efficient programming techniques. I have written several moderately large applications and compiled them under the Small memory model with excellent results. Because both the Tiny and Small models use near pointers for all operations, these 2-byte entities offer the fastest execution times. Turbo C also offers the advantage of explicitly programming far pointers from these smaller models, which is also a bonus. In such instances, near and far pointers are intermixed within the same memory model.

Medium. In the Medium model, the data segment is limited to a 64K area, but code can occupy up to 1 Mb. Far pointers are used, so execution speed will be slower than with the Tiny and Small models. The Medium model, however, would be used only when the smaller models would not suffice. The Medium model is best for large programs that don't store a lot of data in memory.

Compact. The Small and Medium memory models are fairly standard in most modern C compilers. You don't see Tiny models as often, nor do you see a lot of models that are labeled Compact. In the Turbo C implementation, the Compact model is the reverse of the Medium model. The Compact model uses far pointers for data, but uses near pointers for code. (In the Medium memory model, far pointers are used for code, but not for data.) The code is limited to a 64K area, while data has a 1 Mb range. The Compact model might be chosen when program code is small, but it must access a large amount of data.

Large. The Large memory model of the Turbo C compiler sets aside 1 Mb for code and 1 Mb for data. Only far pointers are used for access, so this model will execute code more slowly than the previous models, due to the 4-byte pointer operations involved. The Large memory model should be reserved for very large programs that access an equally large amount of data.

Huge. The Huge memory model is quite similar to the Large model, in that it uses far pointers for both code and data. However, all of the previous models limit the size of all static data to 64K. In the Huge memory model, static data can occupy more than 64K. The total amount is determined by the memory configuration of your computer.

To change memory models, all that is required is to reset the Compiler option in the Options menu. If all of your library files and object code start-up files are in one directory, making this compiler change will be a one-step operation. It is for this reason that I explained in some detail how the Turbo C files were installed on my hard disk. If you're operating without a hard disk, you might have a considerable amount of disk-swapping operations to perform when switching to a different memory model.

If you are not a highly experienced C programmer and are just becoming adjusted to Turbo C, it is my recommendation that you start under the Small memory model. This should pose no limitations at all. Most professional programmers who write code for MS-DOS machines try to stay within the roomy confines of models that use the 2-byte pointers.

LEAVING THE INTEGRATED ENVIRONMENT

All of the discussion thus far has centered around the use of Turbo C from the Integrated Development Environment. This is far different than the command-line method many C programmers are accustomed to, in which all commands are issued under DOS via executable files that accept arguments as they are invoked.

Traditionally, professional programmers hate integrated and interactive environments that include everything from handy pulldown menus to garbage can icons. Some programmers complain that the integrated environment slows them down, while others just don't like adapting to a new and often better way of doing things. In any event, Turbo C gives you a choice of environments. If you don't want to use the integrated system with all of its convenient menus and other built-in features, you can go the command-line route and invoke the compiler and linker via arguments from DOS.

I had occasion to leave the Integrated Development Environment and pursue the command-line route a few hours after getting into Turbo C. The only real problem with the interactive system lies in the fact that it requires a fair amount of memory for its own purposes. When you compile programs, no intermediate files are written to disk. They are all written to memory. This is another reason for the fast compile and link times exhibited by Turbo C. However, using memory to hold these intermediate files consumes more of your precious RAM.

My initial test machine was equipped with 512K RAM. This was more than sufficient for the compilation and linking of some fairly large applications that ran to several thousand lines of C source code. However, one particularly long and complex program could not be compiled within the integrated

22

environment. Too much memory was consumed by the environment and the intermediate file that was written to memory.

Turbo C is quite kind to you when you run out of memory in this manner. It simply stops the compiling process and issues an error message stating that it has run out of memory.

Out of necessity, I exited the environment and invoked the command-line options to compile and link this program. The procedure took place with no problems at all. Several batch files were later written to allow for similarly large and complex programs to be compiled and linked in the same manner.

TCC

The command-line version of Turbo C is contained in the file TCC.EXE. The Turbo Linker program is contained in TLINK.EXE. The command-line utilities also include versions of Make, Touch, and similar utilities that can be invoked from the integrated environment. Table 2-1 shows the various command-line options that are invoked when TCC is called.

Table 2-1. Command Line Options in the Form of: TCC option [file/occurrence].

Option	Meaning	Option	Meaning
-1	80186/286 instructions	-A	Disable nonANSI extensions
-B	Compile via assembly	-C	Allow nested comments
-Dxxx	Define macro	-G	Generate for speed
-Ixxx	Include files directory	-K	Default char is unsigned
-Lxxx	Libraries directory	-M	Generate link map
-N	Check stack overflow	-O	Optimize jumps
-S	Produce assembly output	-Uxxx	Undefine macro
-Z	Optimize register usage	-a	Generate word alignment
-c	Compile only	-d	Merge duplicate strings
-exxx	Executable filename	-f	*Floating point emulator
-f87	8087 floating point	-f-	No floating point
-gnnn	Stop after nnn warnings	-innn	Maximum identifier length nnn
-jnnn	Stop after nnn errors	-k	Standard stack frame
-mc	Compact model	-mh	Huge model
-ml	Large model	-mm	Medium model
-ms	*Small model	-mt	Tiny model
-nxxx	Output file directory	-oxxx	Object filename
-p	Pascal calls	-r	*Register variables
-u	*Underscores on externs	-w	Enable all warnings
-wxxx	Enable warning xxx	-w-xxx	Disable warning xxx
-y	Produce line number info	-zxxx	Set segment names

xxx	=	file
nnn	=	number of occurrences
*	=	default
-option-	=	turn option off

This list of options is quite complete, and allows you to do anything from the command-line environment that you can do from the integrated environment. In fact, you can do a little more from the command line. If you intend to use assembly language routines with your C code (in other words, call assembly language modules from C), you will have to invoke the -B option from the command-line version of Turbo C. This can't be done from the integrated menu.

The following shows the contents of a batch file I quickly produced to perform a simple compilation using TCC:

```
tcc  − I \ turboc \ include  − ms  − c %1
```

This line invokes the − I option to tell the compiler where to find the header files. The − ms option is the default, and does not need to be invoked, but it is done here for the sake of clarity. This tells the command-line version of Turbo C to use the Small memory model compiler. The − c option is a signal to only compile the target program that is represented here as %1.

The next batch file invokes TLINK.EXE, the command line linker:

```
tlink  \ turboc \ lib \ c0s + %1,%1,,  \ turboc \ lib \ emu + \ turboc \ lib \ cs
```

The arguments to TLINK are the same as the arguments to the MS-DOS linker, LINK.EXE. In this usage, the c0s.OBJ start-up module for the Small memory model is found in the \ turboc \ lib directory of my hard disk. This module is coupled with the name of the object file that is output by the compiler. The second %1 tells the linker to give the EXE file the same name as the program object file. The final sequence tells the linker to access EMU.LIB and CS.LIB from the \ turboc \ lib directory on the default drive.

Compilation and linking are just as rapid when invoked from the command-line version of Turbo C. I only use the command-line version when it is not possible to compile or link programs because of their size or lack of on-board RAM. Speaking as one who has always operated on a command-line basis with C environments, I find the integrated environment to be quicker and more convenient. I have enjoyed making the switch.

OPTIMIZATION

As was pointed out earlier in this chapter, the user has several optimization choices when using Turbo C. Various types and stages of optimization can be selected via the Options menu within the integrated environment.

You can toggle between optimizing for size and optimizing for speed. What does this mean? Supposedly, when you optimize for size, the compiler chooses the smallest code sequence possible. When this option is toggled for speed, the compiler chooses the fastest sequence for a given task. At least this is what the manual says. In fact, a best guess is made in both situations. The guess is sometimes right, but it's often wrong. Sometimes, when you optimize for size, you might get a larger program than if you had optimized for speed.

Sometimes, optimizing for speed will result in a slower program than if it had been optimized for size. Just as often, the program will be the same size and will run at the same speed regardless of which optimization method you chose. This is not a criticism of the Turbo C compiler. It just means that a best guess is just that—a guess at what method is best to pursue in arriving at the goal of smaller size or increased speed.

I talked with several of the key people in the Turbo C project at Borland, and was told that the best thing to do is compile programs that might be size- or speed-critical under both options, and then choose the one that yields the best results. I compiled a very large and complex commercial program initially for size, and received a very impressive run in regard to execution speed. Then I recompiled it for speed. The code size was about the same, but it ran more slowly by a few percentage points. Obviously, the optimization for size resulted in the best overall performance of the program, and this was the optimization that was finally chosen.

Another optimization selection that you can make involves whether or not *register variables* are to be used. This selection is normally turned on, and in this state, register variables will automatically be assigned. When it's off, the compiler will not use any register variables. Again, a best guess is made as to which variables should be register variables, but this option usually results in faster execution times (often marginal) without an increase in code size. With this feature toggled off, even the declaration of variables as type register will have no effect.

Two other optimization options, register optimization and jump optimization, are normally off. The first suppresses redundant load operations by retaining register values and reusing them where possible. I don't use this option very often because the compiler can't tell when a register has been changed indirectly through the use of a pointer. If this occurs, crashes are sure to follow.

Although the jump optimization is defaulted to off, I usually toggle it on. The programmers at Borland have told me they generally use this optimization as well. It reduces code size and increases speed, mainly by reorganizing loops and switch statements.

Don't expect any of these optimizations to make a tremendous amount of difference in either code size or code speed, however. I certainly urge you to try various combinations and perhaps a significant performance increase will be had with certain program constructs. These optimizing options are just another aspect of Turbo C that offers the user more control over the programs he or she authors.

HOW TURBO C DIFFERS FROM CLASSIC C

Borland's Turbo C is a C implementation that adheres closely to the new ANSI standard. The original C programming language was not really developed to any independent standard, so this job was left to the American National Standards Institute. Kernighan and Ritchie described a minimum standard for C in their book, *The C Programming Language.* Turbo C adheres to this standard, but also offers the ANSI extensions, which are a great boon to all C programmers. Turbo C represents an effort to improve the traditional C programming language by adding new features and increasing the power and flexibility of older features.

This section is written especially for people who have a fair amount of experience programming in earlier versions of C. The discussion in this section focuses on some of the differences incorporated in the ANSI standard and, more importantly, on the special new features that can be a great aid in increasing programmer productivity.

Identifiers

In the original version of C, identifiers could consist of all of the letters in the alphabet (uppercase and lowercase) and the digits zero to nine. The underscore character was also supported. Turbo C allows the use of all of these, and the dollar sign ($) as well. An identifier is simply the name you would give to a C language variable, function, etc. All of the characters mentioned above may be included in these names. However, all identifiers must begin with a letter or the underscore character. They cannot begin with a number or the dollar sign.

While identifiers can be as long as you like, only the first 32 characters are applicable under Turbo C. It is difficult to imagine an identifier that would even be half this long, so the 32-character limitation should be more than adequate. There is a compiler switch that allows you to modify the effective identifier length of from 1 to 32.

The *case* of alphabetic characters is a distinguishing feature. In other words, "A" and "a" are two different characters. This has always been true within C, even from its inception. However, the MS-DOS linker has traditionally been unable to differentiate between function names in uppercase and lowercase. The traditional linker treated both as one and the same. The Turbo C linker, TLINK, is case-sensitive, although this can be turned off with a command line switch.

Constants

All of the constant types that were legal in the original C language are also legal in Turbo C, and there are a few worthwhile extensions that most programmers will immediately put to use. Constants with a value range of from 0 to 4294967295 are allowed, and negative constants are simply unsigned constants with the minus operator preceding them. As is customary, octal and hexadecimal numbers are as acceptable as decimal values. C programmers have long been aware of the L suffix (also l), which may be appended to any constant, forcing it to type long. In Turbo C, the U or u suffix may also be used to force a constant to be of an unsigned quantity. If the constant is greater than 65535, the U suffix forces it to be an unsigned long type. You may even use a combination of suffixes, as in the following:

8486UL

This forces a value to *unsigned long*. The unsigned long data type might be new to many C programmers who have had no experience with C compilers written to close ANSI standards. A long integer value may have a range of -2147483647 to $+2147483647$. An unsigned long will have no negative component and can therefore represent twice the positive range within the same four bytes. The range of an unsigned long integer would be from 0 to 4294967295. This is also the maximum value that is allowed in Turbo C.

Character Constants

Turbo C supports two-character constants, for example, DS, \n\t, and \007\007. These constants are represented as 16-bit integer (int) values with the first character in the low-order byte and the second character in the high-order byte. However, these constants are not portable (presently) to other C compilers.

Single character constants like E, \n, and \033 are also represented as 16-bit int values. Here, the low-order byte is *sign extended* into the high byte; that is, if the value is greater than 127 (base 10), the upper byte is set to -1. This can be disabled by declaring the default character (char) type to be unsigned. This forces the high byte to be zero regardless of the value of the low byte.

Turbo C supports the ANSI extension of allowing hexadecimal representation of character codes, such as \x1F, \x82, and so on. Either x or X is allowed, and you may have one to three digits. Turbo C also supports the other ANSI extensions to the list of allowed *escape sequences*. Escape sequences are values inserted into character and string constants, preceded by a backslash (\ ).

Floating Constants

As was true with the original C programming language, all floating-point constants are really doubles. There used to be no such thing as a single-precision floating-point constant. However, Turbo C allows such an entity to be created (forced) by tacking on an F suffix in the same manner one would add the L suffix to force a value to be of type long.

String Constants

In the original C language, a string constant is a series of characters surrounded by double quotation marks. The backslash character had to be used as a continuation character when string constants were so long as to extend beyond the boundary of a single line. This is not necessary in Turbo C; multiple-string units are acceptable to the compiler. The following is an example of how this feature can be effectively used:

```
main()
{
```

```
        char *a;

        a = "Now is the time for all good men"
            "to come to the aid of their party.";

        puts(a);

    }
```

This program will display this line:

Now is the time for all good men to come to the aid of their party.

HARDWARE SPECIFICS

The storage requirements of various data types are very machine- and implementation-specific. Most MS-DOS machines, and the C compilers for these machines, observe the same storage rules for the various data types. Turbo C brings some new data types, such as long double and unsigned long and even unsigned short and unsigned char. However, the byte size allocated for each of these types is standardized.

As with most implementations, an int is a two-byte quantity. *Shorts,* or short ints, are of the same size, and can represent the same range of values. Char variables are one-byte entities, as are unsigned char variables. Unsigned ints consume two bytes of storage space, while longs and unsigned longs are allotted four bytes. The same four bytes are also allotted for floats. Double variables are allocated eight storage bytes. The *long double* type is the same length as a double, and represents the same range of values.

Turbo C offers two types of pointers that can be generally categorized as *near* and *far* types. Near pointers are allotted two bytes for address storage, while far pointers (and huge pointers, too) are allotted four bytes.

In Turbo C, different pointers in your program may be of different sizes, depending upon the memory model or pointer type modifiers you use. For example, when you compile your program in a particular memory model, the addressing modifiers (near, far, huge, __cs, __ds, __es, __ss) in your source code can override the pointer size given by that memory model.

A pointer must be declared as pointing to some particular type, even if that type is void (which really means a pointer to anything). However, having been declared, that pointer can point to an object of any other type. Turbo C allows you to reassign pointers like this, but the compiler will warn you when pointer reassignment happens unless the pointer was originally declared to be of type void. However, pointers to data types cannot be converted to pointers to functions, and vice versa.

TYPE SPECIFIERS AND MODIFIERS

Turbo C supports the following basic types not found in the original version of C:

```
unsigned char
unsigned short
unsigned long
long double
enumeration
void
```

The first three basic types in this list are self-explanatory; the fourth is equivalent to the type double. The types int and short are equivalent in Turbo C, both being 16-bit entities.

Enum

Turbo C implements enumerated types as found in the ANSI standard. An enumerated data type is used to describe a discrete set of integer values. For example, you could declare the following:

```
enum days { sun, mon, tues, wed, thur, fri, sat };
```

The names listed in days are integer constants with the first (sun) being automatically set to zero, and each succeeding name being one more than the preceding one (mon = 1, tues = 2, and so on). You can also set a name to a specific value; the names without specified values that follow it will then increase by one, as before. For example, consider the following:

```
enum coins { penny = 1, nickle = 5, dime = 10, quarter = 25 };
```

A variable of an enumerated type can be assigned any value of type int. No type checking beyond that is enforced.

Void

In standard C, every function returns a value. If no type is declared, then the function is of type int. Turbo C supports the type void as defined in the ANSI standard. This is used to explicitly document a function that does not return a value. Likewise, an empty parameter list can be documented with the reserved word void. For example, consider the following program:

```
main()
{
    putmsg();
}

void putmsg(void)
{
    printf("Hello, world\n");
}
```

As a special construct, you may cast (coerce) an expression to void in order to explicitly indicate that you're ignoring the value returned by a function. For example, if you want to pause until the user presses a key but ignore what is typed, you might use this:

```
(void)  getch( );
```

Finally, you can declare a pointer to void. This doesn't create a pointer to nothing; it creates a pointer to any kind of data object, the type of which is not necessarily known. You can assign any pointer to a void pointer (and vice versa) without a cast. However, you cannot use the indirection operator (*) with a void pointer, because the underlying type is undefined.

The Signed Modifier

In addition to the three type adjectives defined by Kernighan and Ritchie—long, short, and unsigned—Turbo C supports three more: signed, const, and volatile, all of which are defined in the ANSI standard.

The signed modifier is the opposite of unsigned, and explicitly says that the value is stored as a signed (two's complement) value. This is done primarily for documentation and completeness. However, if you compile with the default char type unsigned (instead of signed), you must use the signed modifier in order to define a variable or function of type signed char. The signed modifier used by itself signifies signed int, just as unsigned by itself means unsigned int.

The Volatile Modifier

The volatile modifier, also defined by the ANSI standard, is almost the opposite of const. It indicates that the object may be modified, not only by you, but also by something outside of your program, such as an interrupt routine or an I/O port. Declaring an object to be volatile warns the compiler not to make assumptions concerning the value of the object while evaluating expressions containing it, because the value could (in theory) change at any moment. It also prevents the compiler from making the variable a register variable.

The Const Modifier

The const modifier, as defined in the ANSI standard, prevents any assignments to the object or any other side effects, such as increment or decrement. A const pointer cannot be modified, though the object to which it points can be. Note that the const modifier used by itself is equivalent to const int. Consider the following examples:

```
const float pi = 3.1415926;
const min = −32768;
const *char str = "Turbo C";
```

Given these, the following statements are illegal:

```
pi = 3.0  /* Assigns a value to a const */
i = ++min;  /* Increments a const */
str = "TLINK";  /* Points str to something else */
```

FUNCTIONS AND FUNCTION PROTOTYPES

Turbo C was designed to adhere very closely to the new ANSI standard for the C programming language. For the most part, the ANSI standard complies with the original Kernighan and Ritchie standard, but offers a lot more. When writing functions under the old C standard, functions were declared by specifying the name and the data type that was returned. The default was an integer return, which did not need to be declared. Functions throughout this text adhere to the old standard, but Turbo C also offers some new methods of writing functions that are sure to be more and more widely used as more and more C compilers adhere to the ANSI standard.

The classic way of writing a C function is shown in the following source code:

```
int mult(x, y)
int x, y;
{

    return(x * y);

}
```

However, the ANSI standard adopted by Turbo C allows for a new method, which is illustrated below:

```
int mult(int x, int y)
{

    return(x * y);

}
```

This new style defines the content of arguments to the function within the definition line itself. This new style also allows for prototypes to be used. This is a *function declarator* that looks just like the top line of the above function. However, this declarator causes the arguments to the function to be coerced to the type specified in the prototype. This was not true of the Kernighan and Ritchie standard.

There are many complex mathematical functions that are now a part of the C language function set which require arguments that are of type double. If integer arguments are supplied here, the function will not return the proper value. However, the use of a prototype will automatically cause the integer arguments to be coerced to type double. The following program shows an example of such a function (one requiring a double-precision argument) written in two different styles, the old and the new:

```
main()
{

        double mult();
        printf("%lf\n", mult(2, 4));
}

double mult(x, y)
double x, y;
{

        return(x * y);

}


double mult(double x, double y);
main()
{

        printf("%lf\n", mult(2, 4));

}

double mult(double x, double y)
{

        return(x * y);

}
```

OLD STYLE

NEW STYLE

The first example will return an incorrect value from the function that is designed to simply multiply one double argument by the other double argument and return the double-precision value. In keeping with the Kernighan and Ritchie standard the function itself is declared double within the calling program and also in the definition line of the function proper. An incorrect value is returned, however, because this function is given integer constants for arguments. The function definition calls for double arguments. Again, this function is written correctly according to the old style, but it has been handed incorrect arguments and an erroneous return will result.

The second example uses a function that is written in the new style. Outside the body of the calling program, a global prototype is used. This is the line prior to the call to main( ), which declares mult( ) to be a function that returns a double-precision value containing two arguments, each of which are also

32

doubles. Notice that the function definition begins in exactly the same manner using the same style prescribed by ANSI. In this case, however, it is not necessary to declare mult( ) to be double within the calling program, because this has already been done globally by the prototype. The same integer argument constants are fed to mult( ) in this second program. However, this one will return the correct value because these integers have been coerced (cast) to type double. This means that any numeric argument will suffice here, due to the coercion enforced by prototyping.

Prototypes for all of the complex mathematical functions, and many others, are contained in the various header files supplied with Turbo C. It is not mandatory that prototyping be used, and generally, I have chosen not to use prototyping for most of the discussions in the remainder of this text. Prototyping is a very powerful attribute of Turbo C, but if you're just beginning to learn C language, prototypes provide the type of protection that can cause students to become sloppy about the arguments supplied to functions. I prefer to teach C using the Kernighan and Ritchie standard for functions. Once the language has been grasped, the programmer can then more easily determine when and where prototyping can be used to best advantage.

The modern style of writing functions (declaring the argument types within the definition line) increases the error-checking performed, even when function prototypes are not used. The use of prototypes with functions written in the modern style will cause the compiler to double-check your arguments and coerce them to the proper values if necessary. More about prototyping is included in Chapter 3.

SUMMARY

In the making of a major motion picture, the filming sequence does not always follow the story line. In such instances, it is not unusual for the opening scenes of a movie to be filmed after the rest of the picture is "in the can." In a similar way, I elected to write this descriptive chapter about Turbo C just prior to going to press. This chapter includes some general overviews about the environment, as well as some highly prejudiced opinions of my own that are based on three months of almost continuous usage.

The reader should consider the thousands of aspects of Turbo C that have not been mentioned in this chapter, not just the briefest of highlights that have been covered. I am extremely impressed with the huge amount of options, operations, and services that this inexpensive package provides to the user. In fact, I am still somewhat overwhelmed by the sheer numbers of things I still want to try within the Turbo C environment.

I feel that Turbo C is unique in its ability to provide the professional programmer with the necessary tools of the trade, while at the same time providing the user-friendly environment that is mandatory for the student being exposed to C for the first time. To me, Turbo C brings with it a new era, or even a new generation, of C language software capabilities that are bound to become the "requirements" for successful competing C environments in the future.

When new products are released, there is a fairly large faction of researchers, writers, and others who take delight in tearing these new additions to the market to shreds. Many in this crowd delight in finding fault, and are certainly not shy about expressing such views to anyone who will listen. While writing this book, I have had the opportunity to speak with many, many individuals within the C language culture and marketplace. In three months of doing research in this area, I have not heard a serious complaint about Turbo C. Certainly, I have heard people say they wish it contained this, or didn't contain that, but these have been minor points like "they should have put the Options menu at the left of the screen instead of the right." Companies like Lifeboat Associates in Tarrytown, New York, at one time a supplier of only a single C compiler, are now actively promoting their distributorship of Turbo C. Other companies are gearing up to do likewise.

Borland International has long had a reputation in the software marketplace for quality, affordable products. This company has not only lived up to its reputation by offering Turbo C, but has elevated itself to an even higher position. I can pay them and Turbo C no higher compliment.

Chapter 3

Turbo C
Arithmetic Operations

Simple mathematical operations are often a beginning step to becoming comfortable with any new, arithmetic-based computer language. C is such a language, and newcomers will have little difficulty with most direct mathematical operations using Turbo C. BASIC programmers will be glad to know that C language math operations and program presentation are very similar to those found in BASIC. Many of the math functions common to one language are also common to the other. The main difference lies in the fact that the C programmer must know what types of numeric variables are required and what types of numeric values will be returned by the various operations.

Knowing the different types of arithmetic variables and constants is a prerequisite to C programming. In languages like BASIC, a number's precision is not terribly important for many operations, because the BASIC interpreter environment offers many automatic conversions and built-in protections. In C, it is all-important, and can mean the difference between a successful program run, one that doesn't run at all, or, in the worst case, one that runs but returns erroneous information.

C language is oriented toward integer values. This will come as no surprise to anyone familiar with computer languages. The only math your computer can perform is integer-based. All floating-point operations are carried out in software or in a math coprocessor if one is installed. C language, generally, assumes that a value is an integer unless there is some indication to the contrary. It also assumes that functions return an integer value unless told otherwise.

Some of the earlier C compilers made for microcomputers were integer-only, and would not support any floating-point operations. Fortunately, these are a thing of the past, but C language is still heavily oriented toward the integer, and to integer mathematical operations.

C language offers the common mathematical operators +, −, *, and / which are used to add, subtract, multiply, and divide respectively. All but one of these common operators works in the same manner as the equivalent BASIC math operators. The following program adds, subtracts, multiplies, and divides various values:

```
main()
{

        int x, y, z;

        x = 10;
        y = 3;

        z = x + y;
        printf("%d\n", z);

        z = x - y;
        printf("%d\n", z);

        z = x * y;
        printf("%d\n", z);

        z =  x / y;
        printf("%d\n", z);

}
```

There should be no surprises here to learn that this program displays the values 13, 7, 30, and 3 on the screen. These are the integer results of the add, subtract, multiply, and divide operations that are invoked in this program.

As was mentioned earlier, all of these operators perform as they would in BASIC, with one exception. This is the divide operator. Although, it seems to perform like the divide operator in BASIC, the C compiler environment is integer-oriented. Therefore, some divide operations won't come out the way you expect. The operation in the program shown above results in a displayed value of 3, the integer result of dividing 10 by 3. Suppose you wanted to divide two integers and display the result as a floating point value. Study the following program:

```
main()
{

        int x, y;
        float z;

        x = 10;
        y = 3;
```

```
        z = x / y;

        printf("%f\n", z);

}
```

This program should display the value 3.333333, right? Wrong!!! This program will display 3.000000, the floating-point expression of an integer value. What went wrong? The answer is "nothing." The C compiler assumed that you wanted the integer result of x divided by y. This is what was assigned to z, the integer value 3. When this was displayed, zeros were used to fill in the vacant decimal positions. In BASIC and other languages, division of two integers can and will result in a floating-point value. In C, the division of integers results in an integer value. There is nothing you can do to change this rule, but there is plenty you can do to work within it to your best advantage.

If you want to divide integers and end up with a floating-point result, then don't divide integers, divide floating point values. How can this be done? Simply by converting the integer values to floating-point equivalents. The above program will run successfully when it is rewritten as the following:

```
        main()
        {

            int x, y;
            float z;

            x = 10;
            y = 3;
            z = (float) x / (float) y;

            printf("%f\n", z);

}
```

Now this program properly displays the value 3.333333. The reason for this involves the *cast* operators in the division line. These operators coerce the values or variables that follow them to the specified cast. The contents of variables x and y are not changed, but the cast operators cause their respective values to be returned as floats. It was stated earlier that the C environment returns an integer value when two integers are divided. In this case, two integer values were converted to float values and then divided. Therefore, the result was a floating-point value that was assigned to z.

Actually, it was not necessary to use the cast operator on both "sides" of the division operation. The program would have been successful with:

```
        z = (float) x / y;
```

or

```
        z = x / (float) y;
```

Either of these methods would also have resulted in the intended operation.

All of this has to do with arithmetic conversions in C, and there are a few simple rules that will guide you through these conversions. Remember, in C it is usually necessary to know exactly what type of numbers you are dealing with. This is especially true when the results of a mathematical operation are to be given to printf( ) for display to the screen. The conversion specification that serves as a part of the control string argument to this function must match the mathematical return of an expression. If not, erroneous information will be displayed. Also, certain other functions in C require specific types of arguments. If the wrong type of numeric quantity is supplied, then the return from such a function might be in error.

NUMERIC TYPES

In this discussion, a "type" is a classification of numbers and of variables that represent numbers in C. A variable type is declared, while a constant type will depend on the size of the number, whether or not it has a fractional component, and what (if any) modifiers are used in expressing it. In C, there are two basic numeric types: integers, and floating-point or "real" numbers. Integers consist of whole numbers, and have no fractional component. Floating-point values always have a fractional or decimal component, even when this component is zero. It takes more storage space to represent the value of a floating-point number than it does to represent the value of a standard integer. For this reason, integer operations are faster than floating-point operations. Each of these two basic numeric types can be, and is, divided into several more subtypes, most of which deal with numeric precision. Precision is the accuracy that can be represented. This deals directly with the number of numeric places that can be contained by any one type.

Integers

In C, integer types are normally divided into categories of char, short, int, unsigned, and long. These may also be expressed as char, short int, int, unsigned int, and long int. Some C programmers may object to my listing char as a numeric type, but it is, and stores a single byte with a value ranging from 0 to 255. (Note: Turbo C defaults to unsigned char which may range from 0 to 255. There is also a new data type under ANSI, signed char, which has a range of −128 to 127.)

Generally speaking, the size of short, unsigned, and long are referenced against the basic numeric unit, the *int*. An int is an integer type that usually reflects the normal integer size for the host machine. In plain language, an int on MS-DOS machines is a whole number ranging from −32768 to +32767. This is the largest numeric range that can be expressed in two bytes, the normal space allotted for standard integer values.

Using this as a reference, how large is a short or short int? There are no guarantees about the specific size of a short int, save that it will never be larger than an int. Typically, short ints on MS-DOS machines are the same size as ints, that is, two bytes for a range of −32767 to +32768. Occasionally, on larger machines, a short will be half the size of an int as far as storage is concerned, and at least twice the size of a char. In Turbo C implementations, a char is a single byte long, a short is two bytes long, and the same length applies to ints. Therefore, there is no difference between an int and a short, either in regard to storage space or in the value range that can be represented. This is common with most C implementations on microcomputers. For this reason, you will very rarely see shorts used.

An int requires a minimum of two bytes for several reasons. First of all, the maximum value that can be represented in one byte is 255. The minimum value is zero. This happens to describe the range of values that make up the ASCII character set. However, two bytes may be used to describe a value equal to (256*256)/2 or −32768 to 32767.

Assume that x is declared an int in a C program. Assume further that two bytes are set aside for storage to this variable, at memory positions 10 and 11. These two bytes will be used to represent any value assigned to x. If x is initially assigned a value of 210, then byte 10 will be equal to 210 and byte 11 will be equal to 0. The sequence 210-0 is the two-byte representation of the value 210. If x is assigned a value of 255, then the sequence will be 255-0, the two-byte representation of decimal 255. Up to this point, the second byte has remained at zero, because one byte (the first one) is all that is necessary to represent values of from 0 to 255. Increasing the value of x to 256, however, causes the second byte to become active. The two-byte sequence will now be 0-1, the two-byte representation of 256. The sequence 1-1 is 257, and 2-1 is 258. When x is equal to 511, the sequence is 255-1, so a value of 258 causes the second byte to be incremented by one. This value is represented by 0-2. The formula for calculating the value of a positive integer based upon two-byte values is shown below:

$$value = byte2 * 256 + byte1$$

This is the way integer values of from 0 to 32767 are stored in two bytes. If you try this formula, you will soon discover that a maximum value of 255*256+255, or 65535, can be represented by two bytes. This is true, but an int must also represent negative values. For this reason, the maximum value the second byte may contain is 127, while the first byte will be equal to 255. This is the maximum positive integer value of 32767.

When the second byte contains a value of 128 or more, this signifies a negative value. For instance, a value of −1 is represented by the byte sequence 255-255. The value −2 is represented by 254-255. The formula for calculating a negative integer value based upon a two byte sequence is as follows:

$$byte2 * 256 + byte1 − 65536$$

Remember, if the second byte is equal to or more than 128, then a negative value is represented. If it is less than 128, then the two-byte sequence is representing a positive value. This is the way standard integer values are stored on the IBM PC and most other MS-DOS machines.

It was noted earlier that if each of the two bytes could reach a maximum value of 255, then a maximum value of 65535 could be represented in two bytes. There is a numeric data type that does just this. The *unsigned int* is assigned two bytes of storage when it is declared, and it may represent integer values from 0 to 65535. No negative values may be represented by an unsigned int.

To represent values above 65535 or values outside of the normal integer range of −32768 to +32767, it is necessary to allocate more bytes of storage. This is exactly what occurs when a *long int* is declared. In most MS-DOS implementations of C, including Turbo C, a long integer is 4 bytes long. This means that values from −2147483648 to +2147483647 can be represented.

In Turbo C, and nearly all other MS-DOS implementations of C, a short is the same length as an int, and it represents the same value range as an int. Also, an unsigned int is the same length as an int. It represents positive values only, in the range of 0 to 65535.

Real Numbers

Real numbers, also known as floating-point numbers, require at least twice the storage of equivalent integers. The storage format follows the same principles as integer storage, but is more complex. In C language, there are normally only two floating-point subcategories. These are *float* and *double*. A float is a single-precision floating-point value, while a double is a double-precision floating-point value. Due to the large quantities involved, it becomes impractical to state the range of values that can be represented by each in standard decimal form. Scientific notation is used to avoid very long strings of numbers. In MS-DOS implementations of C, a float is usually in the range of 3.4E−38 to 3.4E+38, while a double covers the range of 1.7E−308 to 1.7E+308. In Turbo C, storage of floats and doubles follows the standard MS-DOS format of 4 bytes for floats and 8 bytes for doubles.

GOING FURTHER

The previous discussion on integer and floating-point values is pretty much standard for all MS-DOS implementations of C. However, Turbo C differs from some of the earlier implementations in that there are a few additions. It was stated that a char variable can be used to represent only positive values from 0 to 255. In Turbo C, this has been changed. There are now two types of char variables that can be declared: *signed* and *unsigned*. A standard char variable is signed, which means that it can represent both positive and negative values of from −128 to +127. The unsigned char, the one that used to be standard with the C environment, can be assigned values from 0 to 255.

In the past, all char declarations were of the unsigned type, because the signed char did not exist. This new type will undoubtedly add to the programming versatility of C, but this feature has not been universally adopted by all C environments, and programs written before the advent of the signed char will create compilation conflicts. For this reason, the Turbo C interactive environment automatically defaults to the unsigned char convention unless instructed to do otherwise. This means that all char declarations will default to unsigned char unless the environment is instructed otherwise. This default should avoid any compatibility problems with other programs that were written outside of Turbo C.

Other data types that were not a part of the original C language include unsigned short, unsigned long, and long double. These are quickly explained. An unsigned short is the same as an unsigned int in this MS-DOS implementation. This stands to reason, because an int and a short are the same length. An unsigned short may represent values in the range of 0 to 65535.

The unsigned long is the long equivalent of the unsigned int. This type of value must always be zero or positive, and may have a top positive value of 4294967295. This data type means that positive values of twice those of standard longs may be represented within the same 4 bytes.

Finally, a long double in Turbo C is simply a double. This data type will allow Turbo C to remain compatible with programs that might use this data type in the future. However, in this implementation, there is no difference, in terms of bytes, between a double and a long double.

While on the subject of data types and sizes, I should mention that the Turbo C compiler utilizes two basic types of pointers. The smaller memory models use near pointers, while the medium, large, and huge models use far pointers. A near pointer is allocated 2 bytes to store addresses, and the far pointer is allocated 4 bytes. Because of the difference in size and the bytes that must be read and/or manipulated, near pointers execute faster than do far pointers. For this reason, programmers who are involved in speed-critical applications usually opt for the small memory models using near pointers where this is practical.

DATA CONVERSIONS

When C language mathematics is performed, it is necessary for the environment to convert the operands in the expression to a predetermined format. This allows for the speediest and most accurate mathematical operations. While these conversions are done for us by the environment, speed-critical programs will run faster when such conversions are done by the programmer. Each internal conversion consumes time, causing the program to take longer to run.

The arithmetic conversions that pertain to C are as follows:

- All char or short values are converted to ints.
- All float values are converted to double.
- If either operand is of type double, then all other operands are also converted to doubles.
- Else, if either operand is an unsigned long, then the other operand is converted to an unsigned long.
- Else, if either operand is a long, then the other operand is converted to long.
- Else, if either operand is an unsigned int, then the other is converted to

unsigned int.
• If none of the above are involved, then int operands are involved and the result is int.

While these rules might sound odd, they do tell us a lot about how C language handles numbers. First, the conversions that always take place are float to double and char, or short to int. This means that any value assigned to a float variable will be converted to double before the mathematical operation takes place. Therefore, if a and b have been declared floats and each is assigned a value of 4.0, adding the two values will cause them to be converted to double-precision floating-point entities, and the result will be double. It is for this reason that few C language programs use float types.

The only advantage to declaring a float variable is in the area of memory allocation. A float variable is allocated four bytes for storage, while a double is allocated eight bytes. If a program is pushing the limits of available memory, then memory conservation might be more important than execution speed. However, if there is more than adequate memory, there is no reason to use float variables (at least this has always been the theory).

Doubles should always be used when memory allocation is not critical. I say this because mathematical operations using doubles should execute faster than the same operations that use floats. Beginners to C might raise a few eyebrows at this remark, because we have all had it drummed into us that "longer" numbers execute more slowly than "shorter" numbers. This is true, always. However, no mathematical operations in C are performed with float values. All floating-point math involves doubles and doubles only. A float is always converted to double before the operation takes place. It is this conversion that eats up execution time. If the value were a double to start with, then the conversion would not be necessary at all and this time would be saved. Or is this really correct?

The previous several paragraphs of this chapter have preached what has been true in the past about most C compilers, but none of it is true with the Turbo C compiler. I don't know why, but float operations are executed slightly faster than those same operations that use doubles! This doesn't make sense at first glance, because all floats must be converted to doubles. In all of the C environments I have used in the past, mathematical operations involving doubles often executed twice as fast as those that used floats.

I was quite astounded by these results, so I called the technical hotline at Borland International. The technical representative I talked to was quite surprised to learn that floats were faster than doubles in Turbo C. I was referred to the head of the Turbo C project, and he too was surprised. He suggested that it might be the presence of my 8087 math coprocessor that was creating this condition. I switched out the coprocessor via software and recompiled my benchmark programs. Again, the floats were slightly faster than doubles. No one at Borland seemed to know why this was so, and no one had figured out an answer by the time this book was going to press.

As a further attempt to sort out the answer, I tried the same benchmarks on a newly acquired copy of Microsoft C (Version 4.0). At the time, I had not used this environment very much, but I was aware that Microsoft C and Turbo C are supposedly object-code compatible.

Upon running the Turbo C benchmarks under Microsoft C, I found a connection. Floats also ran faster under Microsoft C than did doubles. I don't know what the answer is regarding why doubles are not faster than floats, but, theoretically, they should be. All floats are converted to doubles and mathematical operations are performed on these doubles. Some quirk (intentional or otherwise) in the code causes floats to be slightly faster. This is certainly no problem at all, because the difference in the two execution times is negligible. It is an interesting aspect of Turbo C (and Microsoft C) however, and a question I hope to have the answer for eventually.

I tried other benchmarks that tested for any speed differences between mathematical operations handled as char values and as int values. Here, the results yielded no surprises. All char values must be converted to ints, so they execute slightly more slowly than do programmed int values that require no conversion. One benchmark that ran in 12.4 seconds using char values completed execution in 10.0 seconds when the char variables were changed to ints. This is the way it should be when going from floats to doubles. Why it doesn't hold for this latter conversion, I do not know. However, I seem to be in good company, because no one else seems to know either.

Generally speaking, C language mathematical operations are closely aligned with those same operations in BASIC. There are some exceptions, however, and these deal more with the protection that the BASIC environment affords which the C environment does not. This also speaks to the differences between an interpreter and a compiler. Trouble can often occur in C when a mathematical operation results in a value that does not fit the type of variable used to represent it. It is mandatory that a variable used to represent the result of a mathematical operation be of the data type that is capable of containing the mathematical return. For instance, consider the following operation:

$$i = 30100 * 3;$$

This will cause problems if i is declared an int, because an int variable can only be used to represent values that range from -32768 to $+32767$. Although 30100 is an int value and 3 is an int value, $30100 * 3$ is not. The result of this mathematical operation is 64000. This value would be an integer, but would lie outside of the range of a standard int. If y had been declared unsigned (range 0-65535) or long, there would be no problem. This illustrates that the result of common mathematical operations involving standard integers might not be standard integer values.

It is in this area of possible confusion that C language programmers have to be on guard. It is not enough to know the types of values that are being used to perform mathematical operations. We must also know what types of results these mathematical expressions yield. It is perfectly acceptable to assign an integer variable a floating-point value, as long as that value falls within the acceptable range of that variable. The following program demonstrates this:

```
main()
{

    int x;
    double y;

    y = 38000.442;
    x = y / 2;

    printf("%d\n", x);

}
```

This program declares two variables, one an int type and the other a double. Double variable y is assigned a value that lies outside of the signed int range. In the next line, int variable x is assigned the value of y divided by two, which equals 19000.221. However, x is an int variable, and cannot represent a fractional component. Therefore, this floating-point value is converted to an integer by truncation. This means that the fractional portion is simply lopped off. No rounding takes place. The end result of this program is to assign x the integer value of 19000.

In this instance, the double-precision floating-point value was within the range of values that may be represented by a standard (signed) int variable. However, if the value of y had been initially set at 100000.8, then the mathematical expression would have yielded a value of 50000.4. This is outside of the allowable range of a standard int. In this case, x would be assigned a value of − 15536, not the 50000 that a beginning C programmer might expect. If you subtract 15536 from 65536 you arrive at 50000. This is what happens when you ask a variable to hold a value that is an illegal quantity.

When programming errors like this are made in the midst of a long and complex routine, debugging can be very, very difficult, because no obvious errors are reported. The variable is assigned a legal value, although an erroneous one. This is what happens when the programmer has lost all idea of what types of values are being dealt with. C programmers quickly become very conscious of numeric types, values, and conversions. This is mandatory to successful programming in this language. Unlike BASIC, there is not a large bevy of error-detection routines and error messages to "babysit" your programming efforts.

COMPLEX MATH FUNCTIONS

Fortunately, today's modern C compilers are well equipped with the complex functions necessary for most of the common mathematical operations. This was not so at the beginning of this decade. Many of the C compilers for microcomputers didn't even offer floating-point operations at all. This was a tremendous restriction on many programmers who were trying to learn C and had come from a more "friendly" environment, such as BASIC.

Even when C compilers became stocked with more features, the complex math functions like pow( ), exp( ), sqrt( ) were not a part of the standard function set. Indeed, these functions were a part of the UNIX operating system, the normalized host system for C language. The UNIX math functions were called from UNIX, just like MS-DOS functions are now called from C programs. During the second quarter of this decade, these complex functions began appearing in the better compilers. Today, the idea of a C compiler for microcomputers that does not contain a large bevy of complex math functions is laughable.

Most of the complex math functions discussed in this section return double-precision floating-point values, also known as doubles. A great many of these also require arguments that are of type double. The Turbo C compiler offers a convenience for C programmers in regard to these math functions. Designed to ANSI standards, this compiler contains a header file that may be #*included* with any program that calls these functions. This header file contains prototypes that declare such functions as doubles (or longs, or whatever is appropriate for an individual function). These prototypes will also coerce any arguments to these functions to the required type. These prototypes will make the correct declarations of math functions, and will see that all arguments to them are coerced to the proper type.

It can, however, be argued that such safeguards as prototypes and header files also have their disadvantages, especially when it comes to actually learning C. First, programs that use them produce slightly larger object modules than would be the case without them. Second, many programs might not execute quite as fast as when traditional methods of using these complex functions are incorporated.

To illustrate this point, we will use the pow( ) function as an example. This function is used in a format of:

pow(x, y)

where pow( ), x, and y are all declared doubles. The following program shows how pow( ) might be used in a program:

```
main()  /* Raise x to the y power */
{

        double pow(), x, y;

        x = 3.3;
        y = 2.0;

        printf("%lf\n", pow(x, y));

}
```

For pow( ) and all functions that return double values, it is mandatory that the function itself be declared double. This lets the executing environment know to expect a double-precision value from this function, rather than an integer. Also, it is mandatory that the arguments to pow( ) be double-precision values. If any one of these steps is left undone, the function will return an erroneous value.

If you wanted to insert variables or constants that are not doubles as arguments to pow( ), it is mandatory that these be coerced to double-precision values via the *cast* operator, or by specifying integer constants as floating-point values. This last directive might sound strange, but it simply means to tack on a decimal point and a zero following the former integer value. Both of these methods are demonstrated in the following program:

```
main()
{

        double pow(), f;
        int x, y;

        x = 2;
        y = 3;

        f = pow((double) x, (double) y);

        printf("%lf  %lf\n", f, pow(3.0, 2.0));

}
```

Notice that pow( ) has been declared a double, as has the variable f. Two integer variables are also declared, and assigned values of two and three, respectively. Next, pow( ) is called, with x and y as its arguments. These are integer variables, however, and illegal as arguments to this function. Therefore, the double cast operator is used to coerce these two integer values to double-precision types. The return from pow( ) is assigned to the double variable f. Next, the printf( ) function is called to display the contents of f and to display the return from another call to pow( ).

Within the control string of the printf( ) function, you will notice that %lf conversion specifiers are used, which indicate a double-precision argument. The call to pow( ) uses constants for arguments. These are expressed in floating-point format using the decimal point and a zero fractional component. This is the way such constants must be expressed. Although they contain no fractional component, they are still floating-point values and, as such, legal arguments to pow( ).

If either of the previous two programs had #included the math.h header file, it would not have been necessary to have declared pow( ) as type double. The header file would have done this for you. Also, it would not have been necessary to worry about the type of numeric values handed to the function. The header file declares the type of arguments this function is to expect, and coerces them to type double if they are other than double.

So why go through all of that extra trouble with the method shown in the two examples when the header file can more or less normalize this function for us?

The ability to include prototypes with a C program to handle such declarations and coercions is new, having arrived with the ANSI standard. Previous C environments did not support prototyping. There might be a tendency on the part of many programmers, who have come up through C language the hard way to spurn such new innovations as prototyping, calling them babysitters for bad programmers. I am not one of those who is knocking the ANSI standard. As a matter of fact, I welcome these new innovations. However, prototyping can be misused. And I feel it is still very important to understand how to program without these safety features, because there might come a time when the absolute n^{th} degree of execution speed or program compactness is necessary. In such a situation, it might be necessary to avoid using prototypes in favor of a slight code size decrease or, possibly, a speed advantage. The great majority of C programs that are written by people learning C and those of us who make a living programming in this language, however, will run with the same relative efficiency whether prototypes are used or not. Prototyping is a programming convenience that can take a lot of the frustration out of learning C and out of utilizing this language.

There is a possibility, however, that prototyping might allow C students to get away with programming habits that could be considered "bad." The danger I see in the "automatic" inclusion of math.h in any program that calls the complex math functions is that such a practice might cause the person learning C to be relatively oblivious to the types of values that such functions require for their arguments. The best speed can often be obtained when these functions are given the proper arguments that are programmer-supplied or programmer-typed, as opposed to other argument types that must be coerced. One major difficulty that newcomers to C often have is the recognition of the many data types involved, the necessary argument types, and the argument return types.

The point I am making is against the "automatic" inclusion of files containing prototypes. There are times when they are advantageous, and times when they are not. Don't get in the habit of #including extraneous files in your program when, perhaps, more efficiency can be gained by typing a few more source lines yourself. Think before you #include. Ask yourself, "Is my program going to call a lot of complex math functions that are prototyped in math.h, or is it only going to call one or two? Will the arguments I will be handing these functions be of the data type that can be directly used, or do they need to be cast to a different type?" By asking these questions, the powerful prototyping header file contained in Turbo C will be put to the best possible uses.

The remaining discussions and examples in this section are presented without inclusion of the math.h header file because more can be learned about these programs and functions by not counting on the programming advantages prototypes offer. In other words, it takes a little more thought to write a proper program without the math.h file. After you have grasped the workings of these functions, then you can better determine when prototypes are applicable and when they are not.

The next section of this text discusses a few of the Unix math functions and other mathematical functions available in Turbo C. Only a small sampling of these functions are actually presented, because most are called and used in a similar manner. Therefore, if you understand how the sample selection is called and used in C programs, then you should have no problem calling and using the rest.

Abs( )

In Turbo C, *abs( )* may be a function or a *macro-definition*. A macro-definition is a preprocessor command that tells the compiler to insert the definition every time it encounters the #defined name within the program. If the stdlib.h header file is included with a program that calls abs( ), then you get the macro; otherwise, you get the function. The macro-definition is the standard shown below:

```
#define abs((X))  ((X) < 0) ? -(X) : (X)
```

This means that if the argument is less than zero, then you remove the minus sign (multiply by −1). If the argument is zero or positive, then you leave it as it is. This is the same type of definition found in stdlib.h. Now, when you #include this header file in a program that calls abs( ), the definition line is compiled in place of abs( ). The following programs demonstrate this:

```
#include <stdlib.h>
main()
{

        int x, xx;
        double y, yy;

        x = 21;
        y = -3.56

        xx = abs(x);
        yy = abs(y);

        printf("%d  %lf\n", xx, yy);

}
```

Because stdlib.h is included, abs( ) is a macro. When this source file is passed through Turbo C, this is the program that is actually compiled:

```
main()
{

        int x, xx;
        double y, yy;

        x = 21;
        y = -3.56;

        xx = ((x) < 0) ? -(x) : (x);
        yy = ((y) < 0) ? -(y) : (y);

        printf("%d  %lf\n", xx, yy);

}
```

The macro is type insensitive, because it is not a function at all. Its sole purpose is to convert a negative value to its absolute value, which is always zero or positive. If the argument to abs( ) is double, then the return (as such) is double. Actually, there is no return from this macro. It is a conditional expression that evaluates to either the argument itself or to the argument multiplied by −1.

If the argument is an integer, then it will always evaluate to an integer. This is one of the advantages of a macro definition.

If stdlib.h had not been #included, then the abs() function would have been called. Like all functions, it is argument type sensitive, and abs( ), as a function, will return an integer value and expects an integer argument. Its source code probably looks something like the following:

```
abs(x)
int x;
{

    return((x < 0) ? -x : x);


}
```

This is very similar to the macro, except the conditional expression is used in standard function format.

There are advantages in using the function, in that the macro definition is substituted every time abs( ) is used in the program. This means that more code is required, because the conditional expression is rewritten each time. On the other hand, the function code is compiled only once. When abs( ) is called, control is temporarily transferred to the function. Therefore, the object code will be smaller. For this reason, use the function if you only require an integer return from abs( ), otherwise, use the macro.

Acos( )

The acos( ) function is a complex math function that returns the trigonometric arc cosine of a double precision value. This function is prototyped in math.h. The following program shows how it may be used:

```
main()
{

    double acos(), x;

    x = 2.3;

    printf("%lf\n", acos(x));


}
```

If the math.h header file is #included with the above program, then it is not necessary to declare the function a double. Also, all arguments to this function will be coerced to type double, regardless of their actual type.

Atof( ), Atoi( ), and Atol( )

The atof( ), atoi( ), and atol( ) functions perform conversions. Their sole purpose is to extract the numeric content in a string. Atof( ) returns a double precision value, while atoi( ) returns an integer. Atol( ) returns a long integer value. All three of these functions are prototyped in stdlib.h. Atof( ) is also prototyped in math.h. The following program shows how all three are used:

```
main()
{

        double atof(), d;
        int i;
        long atol(), l;
        char a[20], b[20], c[20];

        strcpy(a, "113.75ROP");
        strcpy(b, "257.226");
        strcpy(c, "1478923RR2");

        d = atof(a);
        i = atoi(b);
        l = atol(c);

        printf("%lf  %d  %ld\n", d, i, l);

}
```

This program will display the following:

113.75 257 1478923

The atof( ) function reads numeric characters in a string and recognizes the decimal point as a valid character, because it can be a legal part of a floating-point number. When an illegal character is encountered, the read stops and the double value is returned. The atoi( ) function recognizes all legal characters that make up an integer number. Although the string argument to atoi( ) in this example contains a decimal point and fractional value, the integer portion is all that is returned. Atoi( ) stops reading the string when it detects the decimal point, an illegal character in an integer value. The same process occurs with atol( ). Like atoi( ), only numeric quantities are legal. A decimal point, an alphabetic character, or any other character causes the string read to terminate and the present value to be returned.

All three functions, recognize the plus and minus signs (when used as prefixes) as optional legal characters. These functions also ignore leading spaces and tabs. No provision is made for overflow in these functions. So, if you use atoi( ) to extract a value from a string that is larger than 32767, an erroneous value will be reported. When no numeric information is contained in an argument string, these functions return a value of zero.

Ceil( ) and Floor( )

The ceil( ) function, which stands for ceiling, accepts a double argument and then finds the smallest integer value not less than that argument. It returns this integer as a double (i.e., 4 = 4.0). The floor( ) function rounds the double argument to the largest integer not greater than its argument. This, too, is returned as a double. This is an awkward way of saying that ceil( ) rounds up and floor( ) rounds down, but remember that this applies to negative values too. The following program demonstrates the use of ceil( ) and floor( ):

```
main()
{
```

```
double floor(), ceil(), d, e;

d = 5.3;
e = -5.3;

printf("%lf  %lf\n", ceil(d), floor(d));
printf("%lf  %lf\n", ceil(e), floor(e));
```

}

This program will display the following:

$$6.000000 \ 5.000000 \ -5.000000 \ -6.000000$$

In both instances, ceil( ) has rounded up and floor( ) has rounded down. When the argument values are positive, ceil( ) returns 6.0, the next highest integer above 5.3. Floor( ) returns 5.0, the next lowest integer value below 5.3. However, when the arguments are negative, one must remember that −5.0 is higher than −6.0, as the second line demonstrates. Again, both functions return double values that are really whole numbers (integers) that have been converted to double precision.

Rand( ) and Srand( )

The rand( ) function is one that returns a random number which is an unsigned integer with a range of 0 to 32767. The srand( ) function initializes the random number generator (*reseeds* it). This function accepts an unsigned integer seed value. The following program will generate a series of 100 random numbers:

```
main()
{

    int x, seed;

    seed = 1345;

    srand(seed);
    for (x = 1; x <= 100; ++x)
        printf("%d\n", rand());

}
```

The Turbo C function set offers no function that will return other than an integer random value, but this can quickly be amended by writing a function of your own. The following function returns a double precision value between zero and one:

```
double drand()
{

    double x, y;

    x = rand();
    y = rand();

    if (x == y)
        ++y;

    x = (x > y) ? y / x : x / y;

    return(x);

}
```

This function must be declared double by any program that calls it, or it may be defined in a prototype file. It is assumed that the generator will be reseeded with a call to srand( ) prior to making the call to drand( ). The reseeding should be done at least once, in order to jumble the pattern a bit.

Modf( )

The modf( ) function splits a double value into two parts, the integer and the fraction, or to be very scientific, the mantissa and the exponent. The fraction is returned by this function, while the integer portion is written to the memory location reserved for a double variable. The function requires a double value for its first argument and a double pointer for its second. The following program shows how modf() can be used:

```
main()
{

        double v, m, e, modf();

        v = 14.228;

        e = modf(v, &m);

        printf("%lf  %lf\n", m, e);

}
```

This program will display the following values:

14.000000 0.228000

The double precision value has been broken down into two double values, one the integer component of the original argument and the other is the fractional component.

The source code for this function is quite simple to imagine. The following is my interpretation of modf( ):

```
double modf(v, m)
double v, *m;
{

        long x;

        x = v;
        *m = v - x;

        return((double) x);

}
```

The function is declared a double and the arguments are also named double variable and double pointer. An internal variable, x, is declared a long integer.

Initially, x is assigned the value of y, but x can only hold the integer portion of y. The fractional component is not carried over. Next, *m is assigned the value of v − x. The integer value of v is subtracted from this value, leaving

52

only the fractional component. Because this value is written to a memory location, the variable in the calling program will now be equal to v − x. The return statement coerces the long value in x to a double value, and this is passed back to the calling program. This is a fair representation of the contents of the Turbo C function modf( ).

SUMMARY

Turbo C offers a wealth of math functions that can be invoked to perform operations that range from simple to complex. Equally as important, is the fact that these functions can serve as "primitives" for building even more complex math functions. There is nothing especially exotic about complex math functions in C. They are called in a similar manner to other functions. Some return values, some write values in memory. Some do both.

By using the powerful prototyping available in Turbo C, use of these and other functions can be simplified, especially when there is a need for argument type conversion. Most C programmers attempt to work with integers when at all possible. This results in the fastest execution time. However, when these integer values must be passed as arguments to functions that require other numeric data types, such as doubles, they must be coerced to type double. It is here that prototyping can play a very important role.

Chapter 4

Strings and
String Functions

Like most general-purpose programming languages, C offers methods by which strings of characters may be contained and manipulated as a group. Programmers who come from a BASIC-only background are often downright perplexed over the method by which strings are handled in C. There is also confusion over exactly what constitutes a string, what kind of variable is used to hold a string, and the difference between a char variable and a char pointer, char array, and string pointer.

Without a doubt, Turbo C will be used by a larger number of people who are attempting to learn C. Many of them will come from a BASIC programming background. Others will have some other language training. All of these people, and possibly even some programmers who have been using C for a year or less, will benefit from an in-depth discussion about C language strings and string functions. Also, Turbo C offers some new and useful string-handling functions that will prove to be of benefit in text operations. This chapter addresses these functions and provides an in-depth discussion on the standard C functions that are used to manipulate character strings, as well as the specialized string functions that have been made a part of the Turbo C language and are becoming standards in the newer C compilers and interpreters now being released.

The original C programming language offered only a few, basic string-handling functions. Programmers would use these and other more primitive operations to build string functions that suited their needs. Turbo C offers many of these formerly customized string functions as a regular part of the Turbo

C function set. Many of these functions have been designated a part of the relatively new ANSI-defined C language.

STRINGS

In BASIC, string constants may be composed of numerical and/or alphabetical characters that are contained between double quotes. Special variables are used in this language to represent string values. String variables in BASIC are identified by the trailing dollar sign.

There are similarities to some of these BASIC string attributes in C. That is, string constants can be represented by alphanumeric characters surrounded by double quotes. However, C tends to treat strings, also called character strings, on a more primitive level.

Char Variables

To start at the bottom, let's discuss the char variable. This type of variable is used to represent a single character, like A, B, C, W, Q, etc. More accurately, the char variable is used to hold an ASCII value of from 0 to 255, the total possible range of characters that may be generated by your computer. A char variable may not be used to represent a value that lies outside of this range, like −1 or 276.

With this restriction in mind, it can be safely said that char variables hold integer values, although the range of integer values is restricted to positive (unsigned) numbers ranging from 0 to 255. True integer variables (int) may be used to represent negative as well as positive values over a much broader range.

A char variable may be assigned just like an int variable, as the following program demonstrates:

```
main()
{

        char a;

        a = 65;

}
```

This program is relatively useless except from a tutorial standpoint. It simply assigns char variable a the value of 65. First of all, a is declared to be a char variable. It is then assigned the value of 65 using the assignment operator (=). The following program does exactly the same thing as the one above:

```
main()
{

        char a;

        a = 'A';

}
```

Both of these programs assign a value of 65 to the variable a. However, in the second example, there is no value of 65 . . . or is there? In the ASCII character set, a value of 65 is used to represent the uppercase letter A. Computers do not manipulate letters. They deal in numbers. Therefore, the processor makes no distinction between the char constant 'A' and the integer constant 65. They are both represented as 65. In both programs, a is equal to 65. To assign a value of 66 to a, the assignment operator would again be used, this time with an argument of 66 or 'B'. The latter is the character constant that is represented by ASCII 66. Note that the character constant is surrounded by single quotation marks, also known as apostrophes. These differentiate it from a variable name. The single quotes are a signal that this is a character constant.

Don't be mislead into thinking that only char variables may be assigned in this manner. All other variable types may be assigned in exactly the same manner when programming in C. If the variable a in the preceding programs were declared an int or a long or unsigned variable, the value of 65 or any other value between 0 and 255 could be assigned to it via the choice of the appropriate character constant.

As a matter of fact, a variable that is declared to be numeric may be used to display letters and even strings of letters, just as a char variable may be used to display numbers. All values stored in all variables in C may be assigned as character constants or as actual numbers. Admittedly, this becomes difficult when a numeric value is less than zero or more than 255, but this is only a representational problem from the programmer's point of view. The computer works in numbers only. From the standpoint of practicality, however, most C programmers will use character constants to build routines that display characters, and numbers for purely mathematical operations. This is the practical way to program most applications.

The following program will display the letter A on the monitor screen using the standard C function, printf( ):

```
main()
{

    char a;

    a = 'A';
    printf("%c\n", a);

}
```

The reason the character A is displayed, rather than its ASCII code or numeric value of 65, is because the %c conversion specifier is used in the control string to printf( ).

The following program will do exactly the same thing as the one above:

```
main()
{
```

```
int a;

a = 65;
printf("%c\n", a);

}
```

This program displays the letter A, even though the variable a is declared an int variable and is assigned 65 instead of the character constant 'A'.

Both of these programs are viewed identically by the C compiler and the computer, with one exception. Most C environments must set aside at least two bytes in memory to store int values. Typically, char values are stored in a single byte. The differences in storage set aside for each variable type has no bearing on the nature of this program, but it can be seen that the use of char variables to represent characters or values between 0 and 255 is more efficient from the standpoint of memory required than is int or another type when only character values are to be assigned.

Efficient memory management is an absolute essential in writing all programs. Some will maintain that the hobbyist programmer is generally unconcerned with memory management as long as he or she has a machine with enough RAM on board to run the desired applications. If this is true (and I'm not sure that it is), then it shouldn't be. When any program is written that does not utilize memory efficiently, this program is not as good as it could be and the programmer is perpetuating personal "sloppiness" in this area.

Newcomers to C often ask why there is a need for a char variable type at all, because int types may be used to represent exactly the same data. The reason was demonstrated above. Char type variables typically consume half the storage space as int types. In most MS-DOS implementations, one byte is reserved for char variables and two for int variables. The difference in size is due to the range of values each is designed to represent. With char variables, one byte is all that is necessary to represent values of from 0 to 255. The wider range of int type variables requires at least two bytes of storage.

Character Strings

To this point, it has been learned that the char variable may be used most efficiently to hold integer values that correspond to the characters that may be displayed by the computer. However, this discussion has centered around single characters, and not character strings. In a language like BASIC, single alphabetic characters and strings are treated as one and the same, i.e., the letter A in BASIC is represented as a string type, as in "A". The same applies to the word APPLE, which is represented by the string constant "APPLE". In MS-BASIC there are only two basic variable types, numeric and string.

In C, there is no such thing as a string variable. Instead, the char variable type, which is used to represent a single character, is used to name an array of characters. A *char array*, then, is a close equivalent of the string variable in BASIC. Think about it and it makes sense. If a single char variable can represent a single character, then an array of char variables may be used to represent a string of characters, one for each array element.

The following C program demonstrates the "difficult" method of using a char array to hold a character string:

```
main()
{

        char a[9];

        a[0] = 'C';
        a[1] = 'O';
        a[2] = 'M';
        a[3] = 'P';
        a[4] = 'U';
        a[5] = 'T';
        a[6] = 'E';
        a[7] = 'R';
        a[8] = '\0';

        printf("%s\n", a);

}
```

This program declares a char array with storage space set aside to hold nine characters (i.e., nine values from 0 to 255). Each character is assigned to each array element individually. Note that the ninth character at array element 8 (remember all arrays in C begin with an element base of zero) is '\0', also known as a *null character* or as ASCII zero. In C, this null character serves to make a series of characters a true string. A string, then, should be thought of as a series of characters that represent a single entity. The terminating null character transforms a series of individual characters into one combined string unit. Without the null character to terminate a string, the characters are simply individual units. With the null character, the various characters are one string unit.

This program could also have been written as follows:

```
main()
{

        char a[9];

        a[0] = 67;
        a[1] = 79;
        a[2] = 77;
        a[3] = 80;
        a[4] = 85;
        a[5] = 84;
        a[6] = 69;
        a[7] = 82;
        a[8] = 0;

        printf("%s\n", a);

}
```

This program does exactly the same thing as its predecessor. As a matter of fact, the compiler and the computer see no differences whatsoever between the two. Either program could also have declared the argument a as an int variable, and the same on-screen results would have been obtained. In this instance, however, a would have consumed 18 bytes of memory (two bytes per array element), while the char array would only consume nine (one byte per element).

The printf( ) function is given an argument of a and a conversion specification of %s. This means that a character string is to be displayed. The a argument is a pointer. This is sometimes difficult to grasp. Remember, a[0] is an array element, as are a[1], a[2], a[3], etc. But the argument a, when used by itself without brackets, is a pointer, a special data type that returns the memory location of the first element in the a array, or a[0]. Assuming that a[0] is located at memory location 20, then a, the pointer, returns the memory address of 20 to the printf( ) function. This function then begins writing the byte contents to the screen, starting at location 20, in the form of the ASCII characters these bytes represent. Printf( ) continues to read sequential memory locations (21, 22, 23, 24 . . . etc.) and writing the bytes as characters until a null byte (zero) is encountered. In C, this signals the end of the string. No further information is read or written by printf( ).

Again, a[0] is a member of the char array, as are all of the other elements in this array. The element a[0], then, is a variable, as are a[1], a[2], a[3], etc. On the other hand, a, when used without the brackets, is a *pointer* to the first element in the array. It gives the memory location of the start of the a array. Therefore, it is not really appropriate to say that printf( ) writes a on the screen, or that a is a string, or even that a is an array. Correctly stated, printf( ) writes the string that a points to, or a points to a string, or a points to the beginning of a char array. However, in popular usage, most of us would say that a is printed, or a is assigned, copied, etc. This terminology is used at points in this text.

Just remember that a pointer simply references a place in memory, and does nothing else. It is not the type of variable that can "hold" some quantity. Under certain circumstances, pointers can be redirected, that is, they can be made to point to specific areas of memory. This is discussed in a chapter devoted especially to the manipulation of pointers. For now, think of a pointer as a finger on a map. It's what that finger points to that is important, not the finger itself.

The operation of printf( ) when used to display a character string on the screen can be simplistically explained by writing a program that uses the standard C function, putchar( ). This function is used to display a single character on the screen. It won't display a string of characters, only the single character that serves as its argument. The program follows:

```
main()
{

    int x;
```

```
        char a[9];

        a[0] = 'C';
        a[1] = 'O';
        a[2] = 'M';
        a[3] = 'P';
        a[4] = 'U';
        a[5] = 'T';
        a[6] = 'E';
        a[7] = 'R';
        a[8] = '\0';

        for (x = 0; a[x] != '\0', ++x)
                putchar(a[x]);

    }
```

Here, putchar is used in a *for* loop that terminates when a[x] is equal to '\0'. This is similar to the way printf( ) works when displaying a string value, and even more like the way puts( ) operates. It can be seen that the displaying of string information in C is handled one character at a time. This applies to other computer languages like BASIC as well, although the character-by-character nature of string formulation and string display is often hidden.

Of course, it is very inconvenient to have to assign string quantities on a character-by-character basis. This is, however, the way it must be done in C. Don't be too discouraged, though, because a standard C function is already available that takes the trouble out of assigning string values to char arrays.

Strcpy( )

The strcpy( ) function is used to copy a string value to a char array or the contents of one char array to another. It is used in as follows:

```
        main()
        {

            char a[9];

            strcpy(a, "COMPUTER");

            printf("%s\n", a);

        }
```

This program does what previous examples have done, but the convenience of assigning a string as a single value makes the programming job far less tedious.

In this program, the standard C language strcpy( ) function takes the place of all of those laborious char assignment lines in previous examples. After strcpy( ) has been executed, however, the same condition exists, i.e., a[0] through a[8] are assigned 'C' 'O' 'M' 'P' 'U' 'T' 'E' 'R' and '\0'. In fact, strcpy( )

makes its assignments on a character-by-character basis, just as our previous examples did.

The source code for strcpy( ) is not usually included with most C programming environments, nor is the source code for all other standard C functions. This code has already been compiled and is included as a library file to be linked with source programs that you, the programmer, might write. However, if you could see the source code for strcpy( ), it might look like the following function listing:

```
strcpy(dest, source)
char dest[], source[];
{

    int x = 0;

    while ((dest[x] = source[x]) != '\0')
        ++x;

}
```

There are more efficient ways to write strcpy( ), but this example will allow for a clearer explanation. Newcomers to C should remember that this discussion is an exercise in understanding how C handles string values. The strcpy( ) function is already provided for you by the C environment, so it is not necessary to reprogram it as I have done here.

First of all, notice that strcpy( ) accepts two arguments. These are represented in the function by dest for destination and source for source. Both of these arguments are arrays of characters. This function assumes that, like all strings in C, the string information in the source array is terminated by the null character ('\0'). The destination argument names an array that is supposedly empty or is to be reassigned a string value. Any value already contained in it will be overwritten by strcpy( ).

Using the previous program as an example, the source string is the constant, "COMPUTER". Therefore, the source argument points to this constant. C will automatically store the constant with the '\0' as a terminator. In the strcpy( ) source code, int variable x is assigned an initial value of zero, which is the base, or starting element position, in C arrays. Next, the *while* loop begins to cycle. On the first pass, the first element position in dest is assigned the value of the first element in source. Assuming source is equal to "COMPUTER", the loop executes the assignment:

```
dest[0] = 'C'
```

This is the same type of assignment that was made in earlier program examples. After this assignment is made, x is incremented by one. Now, on the loop pass, dest[1] is assigned the value in source[1]. At this point, the letters C and M have been assigned at elements 0 and 1 of the destination loop.

This process continues up to the point where the null character (\0) is assigned to the last element position in dest. This signals the end of the *while* loop and the function is exited. The entire contents of source, which are equal to all of the characters in the constant "COMPUTER" plus the null character, has been copied to dest. However, no transfer of bytes has taken place. In other words, the bytes that make up "COMPUTER" in source have not been moved from one location to another. Rather, the character bytes in source have been copied to another place in memory. Therefore, "COMPUTER \ 0" exists at two places in memory. The first is the original location where the string constant was written, and the second is the starting memory location of dest.

In C, the strcpy( ) function allows for the easy assignment of string quantities to string arrays. Strcpy( ) makes these assignments very rapidly, because only a few lines of C code are required to effect this operation.

Beginners to C are often confused by pointers. These are special variables that actually point to a location in memory. They do not "store" quantities. They only provide the address of a quantity already placed in memory or, possibly, a memory address where a quantity may be written. In the previous example, source and dest are pointers. They point to the memory location where *source[0]* and *dest[0]*, the true variables or elements of a char array, are written. The variables have had space set aside so that they may store char quantities (ASCII 0 to 255). Source and dest are different from source[0] and dest[0]. The first two are pointers; the last two are variables.

When a string value is to be displayed by puts( ) or by printf( ), a pointer argument is required. The following program will demonstrate the difference between char pointers and char variables:

```
main()
{

        char a[9];

        strcpy(a, "COMPUTER");

        printf("%s  %c\n", a, a[0]);

}
```

This program will display the string "COMPUTER" followed by the letter 'C'. First of all, a is declared a char array with storage set aside for nine characters. The strcpy( ) function is used to copy the characters in COMPUTER to this array.

Next, printf( ) is used to display the array information on the screen. The first conversion specification in the printf( ) control string is %s. This causes printf( ) to substitute the first argument at this point. This argument is a, the pointer that points to the a[0] element in the char array. The next conversion specification in the control string is %c. This causes printf( ) to get the (usually) single byte stored in a[0] and display it as a character.

When printf( ) is executed, it first reads the memory address for the beginning of the string value. This is contained in pointer a. It begins to display each byte as a character, starting at this memory location and proceeding onward. When the null character is encountered, printf( ) terminates this portion of its screen write. Next, printf( ) is told to look for a char value in a[0], which is a variable and holds a single byte. This byte is displayed as a character, the letter 'C'. This is the same byte, at the same location, as the 'C' in the string just printed. The first portion of the write was directed by the pointer, a. The second write retrieved the value "contained" in a[0].

Now, let's examine another method by which strings may be assigned and displayed. The following program does exactly what the previous one does:

```
main()
{

    int a[9];

    strcpy(a, "COMPUTER");

    printf("%s  %c\n", a, a[0]);

}
```

This program is almost identical to the previous one, except that a has been declared an array of type int. From this point on, the two programs are the same.

In Turbo C, this program will compile and run without a hitch. Some other C environments might display warning messages regarding unusual pointer conversions, pointers not the same type, etc. However, most environments will run this program successfully, regardless of the warning messages.

As you might have guessed, this program is not as efficient as the previous one, at least from the standpoint of memory usage. The int array declaration usurps twice as many bytes of memory for storage as does an equivalent char array. However, this is no problem, because there is really more memory than is needed. The reverse situation (less than enough storage) would, indeed, be a very serious problem, and a potentially disastrous one. This will be discussed next. For now, remember that the declaration of a char data type really has nothing to do with the display of characters on the screen, only with the efficient storage of numeric quantities that are used to specify character values.

Strcpy( ) and other string manipulation functions have changed a bit since the inception of C language over a decade and a half ago. Originally, such functions were not designed to return any usable value, merely to copy the contents of one string to another. However, in recent years, most C environments have redesigned strcpy( ) to return a pointer to the destination string. Therefore, it is now perfectly legal to write a program that will copy the contents of one string to another using strcpy( ). The function itself supplies the pointer argument to another function, such as printf( ). The following program demonstrates this usage:

```
main()
{

    char a[20];
```

```
        printf("%s\n", strcpy(a, "COMPUTER");

    }
```

This program uses strcpy( ) to copy "COMPUTER" to char array a. Strcpy( ) makes the character transfer to the array and then returns a pointer to a. This pointer is used as the argument to printf( ). The result of this program is to assign the desired value to a and to write the contents of a to the monitor screen.

Many of the string functions found in the Turbo C compiler also return pointers after their respective operations. This feature can save several programming steps. However, there is certainly no requirement that these return values be put to any use. If your sole purpose in using strcpy( ), for instance, is to copy the contents of one string to another, then simply ignore the fact that the function will also return a pointer to the newly assigned string. On the other hand, if your use of strcpy( ) is to copy the contents of one string to another for the purpose of passing a pointer to this new string to some other function, then you can take advantage of the "two-fold" operation of strcpy( ) and use this function as the argument itself.

Memory Overwrites

One potentially serious drawback of C language is the fact that there is no *array bounds checking*. Put simply, this means that the executing environment has no way of telling when the memory set aside for a certain variable has been overrun. In the previous programs, arrays were declared with a subscript of nine. This means that the char array had nine element positions in which data might be written. The number nine was chosen because the constant, "COMPUTER", contained nine characters when you added the terminating null character ($\setminus 0$). This array, then, contained exactly enough elements to store the string "COMPUTER". However, suppose we used strcpy to copy the constant "MICROCOMPUTER" to array a? What would happen?

The answer is any number of things, many of them unpleasant!

The problem here is that the array is "sized" to hold a maximum of nine characters including the null character. When the program is executed, only enough memory to store these nine characters will be reserved for the array. If you write more than nine characters to this variable, then you will be "trespassing" in memory segments where you have no right to be.

The results of this will depend on many, many factors. These include the total system memory, the amount of memory required to initialize the executing environment, and the size of the program. The strcpy( ) function will copy "MICROCOMPUTER" to the specified array, starting at position zero. However, when it reaches the last allotted character position, it will continue writing the extra characters until the null character signals termination.

This condition is known as a *memory overwrite*, and, due to the many factors involved in memory management, you are involved in a computerized "crap shoot". Often, nothing unusual happens. This is especially true when the program is small. Other times, unusual characters may be written to the screen.

Sometimes, the program will terminate early or the computer will lock up and must be rebooted. Computer lock-ups are common when memory is overwritten. Usually, this is the worst thing that happens, and all that is necessary to recover from such an occurrence is to effect a soft or a hard reboot, whichever is successful.

When such a program runs successfully, you have been lucky. The memory overwrite occurred in a portion of memory that was not in use by the program currently being executed. You overwrote a "safe" area of memory by accident.

When weird characters appear on the screen, it usually means that the overwrite probably destroyed some data written into the program. This might change the contents of other variables or of the execution chain itself. When the machine locks up, it is a sign that you overwrote an integral element of the program, and the program flow is captured within an endless loop— basically, the computer has had a nervous breakdown.

In all of the above conditions, no program data have been permanently lost. You simply reboot, make the needed program corrections, and run it again. However, memory overwrites also offer the very real possibility of *serious data loss*.

Occasionally, the memory overwrite may affect that portion of your computer's memory that reads and writes to diskette or hard disk. Every C programmer's heart skips a beat when a program he or she is debugging suddenly causes the diskette or hard disk to be activated. With a diskette, excursions into possible memory overwrites can be rendered harmless by simply removing any valuable diskettes from their respective drives. With a hard disk, this is not possible. And, unless the entire hard disk data have been backed up on diskette or tape, very serious and financially disastrous losses can occur. Here, then, is the major concern of overwriting unassigned memory areas in your computer's RAM. If the area that controls your disk storage is "garbled" by stray bytes of data, your disk controller might receive an erroneous signal to erase an entire 40 megabyte hard disk, or to erase the portion of the magnetic disk that contains the file control block. Perhaps one of the many "disk repair" programs can be used to retrieve this lost information—perhaps not!

If you are a newcomer to C programming, you will end up overwriting memory many, many, many times during your training phase. If you are an experienced C programmer, you will *still* overwrite memory on occasion. This is one of the hazards of programming in C.

I don't want to alarm anyone unduly. In six years of programming daily in C, I have not (to my knowledge) lost a single byte of data from a diskette or hard disk drive due to a memory overwrite. And I have overwritten memory thousands of times. However, I am aware of the possible consequences of a memory overwrite, and such occurrences are relatively rare for me these days.

The severity of a memory overwrite can have a direct effect on the consequences. For instance, if you overwrite memory by a byte or so, or even ten or twenty, you don't stand much of a chance of doing any real damage. However, if you dump, say, the contents of the graphics screen on an IBM

PC (16384 bytes) to a memory location that has not been set aside to hold it, you stand a greater chance of doing some damage to disk files. In my years of programming, I have accidentally done this (and worse) on several occasions. Still, I didn't do any disk file damage. As a matter of fact, I can't ever remember accidentally triggering a disk drive via a memory overwrite. However, this doesn't mean that it won't happen tomorrow. I keep this in mind always!

How do you protect yourself from a memory overwrite? My best advice is to make certain that all arrays are declared with more than enough elements to contain anything that might possibly be written to them. You should always be aware of the general size of any character strings that may be copied or manipulated. I typically declare all char arrays with 250 elements if they are to be used for general purposes. Later, when the program has been completed and debugged, I will reevaluate the array size, calculating the longest possible string that might be contained, and then tacking on 10 or so extra bytes for safety. Naturally, if storage space is at a premium, I might cut the corners a bit closer.

Adhering to these safety principles will not guarantee that you won't overwrite memory. It will, however, make such overwrites rare, and when they do occur, they won't be severe in terms of the number of bytes that are overwritten. BASIC programmers who are making the switch to C should be aware that writing data to arrays that are not large enough to accept this information is exactly the same as POKEing random bytes of data into random memory locations. This is a form of Russian Roulette that can reach out to bite you!

Summarizing the discussion to this point, you have learned that:

• A string in C consists of a series of characters terminated by the null character, '\0'.
• A char array is an efficient device to hold a string.
• Char arrays are assigned string values one character at a time.
• To display the contents of a char array as a string, its name (without brackets) is a pointer that serves as the argument functions like printf( ) and puts( ).
• Char arrays must be declared with enough elements to hold the largest possible string plus the null character.

If you thoroughly understand the preceding discussion, then move on to the next section of this chapter. If you still have some doubts as to how strings are assigned and manipulated, reread the section(s) you don't understand.

COMPARING STRINGS

Now that you have learned just how strings are assigned and what the assignment function, strcpy( ), consists of, it's time to move on to another operation that computers are famous for. I am referring here to the comparison of two strings in C.

BASIC programmers use the same operator for assignment as they do for comparison. This is known as the equals sign (=). In C, one operator is used for general assignments and another for comparison. The assignment operator is the equals sign, and the comparison operator is the "double equals" sign (= =). The latter is called the *equality operator* in C language nomenclature.

Neither of these operators is used, however, when assigning or comparing strings. At least, they are not used outside of the functions that make string assignments or comparisons. The use of the equality and assignment operators should be rather basic to even beginning C language programmers, at least for comparing numeric quantities.

It has been shown through several examples in this chapter that strings are built a character at a time and, really, displayed a character at a time. For this reason, it is necessary to compare two string values on a character-by-character basis. The equality operator cannot be used as in:

if (a == b)

where a and b have been declared character arrays. Remember that, used in this manner, a and b are pointers to the first byte in each array. This equality comparison, then, simply compares the memory locations assigned to each pointer. Because array a[ ] is a separate entity from array b[ ], the two pointers will not be equal, even if their respective contents consist of exactly the same characters.

Strcmp( )

Just as the standard C language function set provides strcpy( ) to copy the contents of one string value to another on a character-by-character basis, it also provides a function to compare two strings. The strcmp( ) function (which stands for string compare) compares the elements of each of its two string arguments on a character-by-character basis.

Strcmp returns an integer value based upon the comparison of the two strings that serve as its arguments. When the strings are identical, a value of zero is returned. If the strings do not match, then a value of less than zero or more than zero is returned, depending on the conditions of the mismatch. When there is a character mismatch, a value of less than zero is returned if the character in the first string is smaller (of a lower ASCII value) than the character in the second string. A reverse condition causes a positive value return.

The following program provides a very graphic example of how strcmp( ) compares two string values:

```
main()
{

    char a[20], b[20];
    int x = 0;
```

```
strcpy(a, "COMPUTER");
strcpy(b, a);

while (a[x] == b[x]) {
    if (a[x] == '\0') {
        printf("Equal\n");
        exit(0);
    }
    ++x;
}

printf("Unequal\n");
```

In this program, the constant "COMPUTER" is copied to a and the contents of a are, in turn, copied to b. Both of these operations are accomplished using the strcpy( ) function discussed previously.

Next, a *while* loop is entered, which compares a[x] with b[x] using the equality operator (= =). As long as each character in a[x] is equal to its counterpart in b[x], the loop will continue to cycle. On each pass of the loop, an *if* statement tests for the end of the a string. This occurs when a[x] is equal to '\0'. This also means that b[x] is equal to '\0', otherwise, the loop would have terminated. When the end of the string is reached, it automatically means that all other characters in both strings match, and printf( ) is called on to display the "match" message on the screen.

When the if-statement test proves false, the end of the a string has not yet been reached, but the characters all match to this point in the test. Therefore, x, the variable used to count through the array element positions, is incremented by one. The loop goes through its next cycle and the next array characters are compared.

Should a mismatch occur at any point in the test, the loop is immediately exited (because a[x] no longer equals b[x], and this is the condition under which the loop continues to cycle) and the "no-match" message is printed.

The strcmp( ) function common to C language does basically the same thing as this program. In place of the match message, this function simply returns a value of zero. When a mismatch occurs, the same type of loop is exited, and the function returns a value that is equal to the mismatched element in the second array being subtracted from the element contained in the first array.

Summarizing the strcmp( ) function in C, it can be said that, like the strcpy( ) function, the character-by-character nature of handling string operations in C continues. With this function, the contents of two strings are compared, starting with the first character in each and proceeding to the last, or null, character. The argument to strcmp( ) consists of two string pointers, each of which provides the starting address of the first element in its respective array. The strcmp( ) function is normally used when it is necessary to compare two strings in order to determine whether their contents are identical, or to test the values of their mismatched states. The latter test might be necessary when writing an alphabetizing routine that would sort strings in ascending or descending order.

ADDING STRINGS

In many text-handling applications, it is desirable to add strings. The proper terminology for this sort of operation is *concatenation*. In BASIC, you can add one string to the end of the other with the addition operator (+). C, however, won't allow this, and neither will most other languages. From the previous conversations, you could assume that if one string is to be tacked onto the end of another, it will probably have to be done on a character-by-character basis. This is a correct assumption.

The C language function set contains *strcat( )*, which stands for string concatenate. This function accepts two string pointer arguments and adds the second argument onto the end of the first. The function accomplishes this by stepping through the first string one character at a time. When it comes to the null character, it replaces it with the first character of the second string. It continues to copy characters from the second string until it encounters the null character in the second string. It writes this character to the end of the first string and the operation is complete.

The following program demonstrates the operation of strcat( ):

```
main()
{

        char a[14], b[9];

        strcpy(a, "MICRO");
        strcpy(b, "COMPUTER");

        strcat(a, b);

        printf("%s\n", a);


}
```

This program will display the combined string "MICROCOMPUTER" on the monitor screen. This is the result of concatenating the contents of array b to those of array a.

Like the strcpy( ) function discussed earlier, most modern C compilers, of which Turbo C is at the forefront, now implement strcat( ) in a form that also returns a pointer to the destination string, which is represented by the first argument to this function. The above program example is very rudimentary, having been written for clarity. However, it would be prudent programming, indeed, to combine the strcat( ) and the printf( ) statements in the above program to read:

```
printf("%s\n", strcat(a, b));
```

This would accomplish exactly the same results as before, but the programmer's job would be a bit simpler.

If you should wish to add the contents of more than one string to the end of another, this will have to be done in more than one step, using strcat( ) again and again until all of the concatenations have been made.

This is an excellent point in the discussion in which to return to a statement that was made earlier. The C programmer must be constantly on guard to avoid memory overwrites. This is especially true when the length of a string (i.e., the number of characters in a string) is being increased or modified in other ways that have the potential of producing a longer string.

In the previous program, array a is declared with storage set aside for 14 elements, while array b is declared with nine elements. This is the barest minimum of storage required to assure a successful program run. Initially, a is assigned the value of "MICRO". This requires only six storage bytes. Array b is assigned the value of "COMPUTER", which uses up all nine of its elements. Why has array a been declared with 14 elements, and why is this the bare minimum?

The answer lies in the concatenation procedure. This expands the length of the string in a from six characters (including null) to 14. If a had been declared with only six elements, or just enough to safely be assigned the string "MICRO\0", then the strcat( ) operation would have overwritten memory, possibly causing the machine to lock up or worse. Remember, when you overwrite memory, you poke random bytes of information into random memory locations. Anything can and does happen when this occurs. Always "size" a char array so that it may adequately handle *any* string lengths that could possibly be written to it.

STRING LENGTH

Another operation that is common in all types of computer languages involves determining the number of characters in a string. In BASIC, this operation is accomplished with the LEN function. In C, the strlen( ) function does the same thing. The following program illustrates how the strlen( ) function measures a string:

```
main()
{

        char a[20];
        int x;

        strcpy(a, "MICROCOMPUTER");

        for (x = 0; a[x] != '\0'; ++x)
            ;

        printf("String length = %d\n", x);

}
```

This program assigns array a the value of "MICROCOMPUTER". This constant contains 13 characters, excluding the null character, and is not counted by the strlen( ) function. A *for* loop is entered. It counts x from zero in increments of one until the exit condition is reached. This exit condition is signified when a[x] is equal to the null character. This signals the end of the string being measured.

The loop variable x is used by the exit condition statement, which tests for a[x] being equal to null. If this is not the case, then the loop cycles again and the next character in a is tested.

Remember, this program is used to demonstrate the basic workings of strlen( ), which returns the total number of characters in its string argument. This means that the first character should be one, the second two, etc. The loop, on the other hand, must start counting at zero, the first element position in the array. Therefore, character number one is found at element zero, character two at element one, etc. In this loop, x will be incremented up to and including the reading of the null character. While the null character is not a part of the total element value returned by strlen( ), it does serve as a convenient means of ending the loop and of converting from element positions to actual number of characters. Because a value of one more than the element position must be returned to arrive at the total number of characters, the counting of the null character automatically causes the value of x to be the same as the total number of characters in the string. This value is displayed by the printf( ) function.

Some beginning programmers mistakenly think that strlen( ) can be used to determine the total number of elements that have been set aside for an array. This is absolutely incorrect. The only way to determine this is to see the declaration line in the source code that establishes the array.

When an array is initially declared, it is filled with garbage, that is, random bytes. There might be a null character in there somewhere, but the chances are just as great that there is not. If the null character should happen to be at the beginning of the array (i.e., a[0] = '\0') then strlen( ) would return a length value of zero. If the first null byte occurred 5000 characters from the memory location of a[0], then strlen( ) would return a value of 5000.

The maximum number of elements established for an array during the declaration part of a C program simply sets the beginning address for the array and makes certain that the required number of sequential elements specified in the array subscript are made available for use by this variable. The memory locations that lay beyond this allocated area are not taken into consideration by this declaration operation. Strlen( ) will return the number of characters that precede the null character. It does not in any way know how many bytes of memory have been set aside for the array pointed to by its argument. It simply counts characters until a null byte is found.

In fact, C language does no array bounds checking. This is a feature that is simply not available in C. The programmer must be certain that arrays are made adequately large to safely contain all possible string combinations.

This concludes the discussion of the string functions that are common to all C libraries. Those discussed are the string functions found in the original

C programming language. They are few in number, but they can accomplish most of the operations generally required on string data. Additional functions (by the thousands) can be written by combining these standard string functions with other types of C functions. Indeed, many such specialized functions have now become standards.

The next section of this chapter briefly discusses many of these, telling what they do and how they compare or differ from the standard functions already discussed. This set of extra string functions is a standard part of the Turbo C compiler. Chances are you will use them again and again when writing programs that manipulate strings to a high degree. The fact that they are a part of the Turbo C library means that you will save a lot of extra effort by having them on hand. Other C environments that do not contain these functions would require the programmer to construct them from the available function set, should such operations be desired.

ADDITIONAL STRING FUNCTIONS

The functions discussed in this section were not a part of the original C language. These, then, are string functions that, over the last decade or so, have come into popular usage, having been built by many C programmers from the contents of the original function set. Because these functions have not become fully standardized, every C programming environment might not contain them. Some might contain functions that perform the same operations, but go by different names. For instance, the Lattice C compiler from version 3.0 on contains a function named strcmpi( ). This compares two strings in a case-insensitive routine. In other words, "COMPUTER" and "computer" would register as a match by strcmpi( ), because the case of the characters is of no consequence. The Turbo C compiler offers the same operation in a function named stricmp( ). Other examples of duplicate functions with different names can be found across the broad spectrum of today's C environments.

Strncpy( )

The strcpy( ) function discussed earlier in this chapter copied the contents of one string an array. The copy begins with the first character in the source string and ends when the null character is copied. Strcpy( ) has no way of determining the number of bytes of storage originally allocated to the destination array, so memory can be overwritten if the source string is larger than the allocated size of this target array.

To partially overcome the possibility of a memory overwrite when copying the contents from one array to another, the strncopy( ) function is provided in the Turbo C function set. This function acts just like strcpy( ), but a third argument is required which is an int value that names the maximum number of characters that are to be copied. Strncpy( ) is used in a format of:

```
strncpy(a, b, byte)
```

where a is the target array, b is the source string and *byte* is an integer value that determines the maximum number of characters that are to be copied from b to a. If the value of byte is larger than strlen(b), then the entire contents of b are copied to a. If byte is smaller than the number of characters in b, then only *byte* number of characters will be copied. If the value of *byte* is equal to or less than the number of elements declared as a maximum for the target array, then strncpy( ) will assure that memory will not be overwritten. However, this function is not a cure-all. Problems can develop when programmers expect it to be a magical panacea for the bane of memory overwrites.

The strncpy( ) function works just like strcpy( ), except that when the function has copied the maximum number of characters dictated by its third argument, the copy procedure is terminated. If the null character in the source string is reached before this point, then it is copied to the target array as well. However, if the copy is terminated before the null is reached, then the null is not copied over to the target array. What you end up with is probably an unterminated string. In C, the null character must terminate a string or it is not a string at all, only a sequence of individual characters. Any functions that accept string pointers as arguments will access that string by reading characters until a null is reached. Printf( ), for instance, when printing a string on the monitor screen, will read individual characters and write them to the screen until the null is encountered. The null signals the end of the string write. If there is no null at the end of the intended string, then printf( ) would continue to read on past the intended end of the string until it finally encounters, at random, a null character.

The following program shows a method of circumventing this possibility:

```
main()
{

    char a[9];

    a[8] = '\0';

    strncpy(a, "MICROCOMPUTER", 8);

    printf("%s\n", a);

}
```

In this example, char array a is declared with a subscript of nine. This means that strings of up to eight characters may be assigned to this variable, with the ninth character being the required null. Then, strncpy( ) is used with a length argument of eight. This assures that no more than the maximum eight characters will be written to a. To avoid the possibility of an unterminated string, the last character position in the array, a[8] (Remember that the first character position is a[0], so a[8] is the ninth position.), is assigned a value of '\0', the null character. Now it is not possible to overwrite array memory because of strncpy( ), and the array will always be terminated because of the null assignment.

In this program, the string "MICROCOMPUTER" is longer than the alloted space for a. A memory overwrite would occur with strcpy( ), but strncpy( ) has a length argument of eight, one less character than the alloted length of a. Therefore, only the first eight characters in "MICROCOMPUTER" will be written to a. Because the last element position in a has been previously assigned a null value, these eight copied characters will be terminated by the null which makes the ninth, and final, character. This null character can never be overwritten, as long as strncpy is used for all assignments with a length argument of eight. This program will display the properly terminated string, "MICROCOM".

To my way of thinking, strncpy( ) is not a terribly useful function, but this might simply reflect my programming style. To others it might be highly valued. If all declared arrays in any program are specifically assigned a null character at the end of their allocated space, then a macro definition could be used to replace the strcpy( ) function with an appropriate strncopy( ) construct. The following program fragment demonstrates this:

```
#define strcpy((A), (B))  strncpy((A), (B), 8)
main()
{

    char a[9], b[9], c[9];

    a[8] = b[8] = c[8] = '\0';

    strcpy(a, "longstring");

    ......................etc. program continues from here
```

This, again, is a program fragment, not a complete C program. It represents what might be thought of as a "fix" for a C program that seems to be overwriting memory.

Assume that you have written a program that contains three char arrays. Assume also that strings have been copied to each of these arrays on several occasions using strcpy( ). When this fictional program is executed, the computer locks up or garbage is written to the screen, and you suspect a memory overwrite. To confirm that an overwrite somewhere in your char arrays is the problem, it is necessary to add only two lines to your source program: the macro-definition shown here, and the assignment line that nulls out the last character·position in each array.

The macro-definition simply causes all strcpy( ) functions to be defined as strncpy( ) functions with a length argument of one less than your array allocation. In this example, all arrays are declared with nine character positions, so the macro uses a value of eight.

When the program is recompiled, the arrays are protected from overwrites via any string copying procedures. This might solve the problem completely, or at least help identify its source. If the problem persists, then memory is probably being overwritten at another point along the execution chain.

C programmers, after a bit of experience, become very, very watchful of potential memory overwrites. We are always (or always should be) concerned with the allocated memory of any target variable and the size of any source object that might be assigned to that target. It is for this reason that strncpy( ) might seem unnecessary except, perhaps, as a quick debugging tool. Again, this is a personal opinion. If you like the idea of a function that works in this manner, by all means use it to best advantage.

Strncat( )

Just as strcpy( ) has a sister function that allows an argument that sets a maximum on the number of characters to copy, strcat( ) also offers an alternate function with similar properties. Strncat( ) is used to set a limit on the total number of characters in the source string that are concatenated to the destination string. It is used in a format of:

strncat(a, b, bytes)

where a is the target or destination string, b is the source string and bytes is an int value that specifies the maximum number of characters to be concatenated. As with strncpy( ), if bytes is smaller than the string length of b, then the entire string is concatenated to a. If not, only the maximum number of characters specified in bytes will be concatenated. In such instances, a will not be a properly terminated string, unless the precautions discussed with strncpy( ) are followed.

COMPARE FUNCTIONS

The string compare functions are those which return an integer value that rates the comparison of the first string with the second. Typically, a value of zero is returned for a match, indicating that there are zero differences between the two strings. If a negative value is returned, this indicates that a mismatch exists and that, of the mismatched characters first encountered, the one in the first string is smaller in ASCII value than the one in the second string. A positive value return signals that the first set of mismatched characters in the comparison are aligned so that the character in the first argument is of a higher ASCII value than the character at the same position in the second string.

Stricmp( )

The stricmp( ) function was mentioned earlier in this chapter and is the equivalent of strcmp( ), except that the compare operation is case-insensitive. This function treats the letters R and r as one and the same for the compare operation. Such a function should be especially helpful in writing text processing software such as word processors and data bases. For instance, if a routine was needed to detect the presence of the word "computer" in a large text file and act upon this word in some form or other, stricmp( ) might be ideal. This is true because the word could appear as "computer", or as "COMPUTER", or even as "Computer". To stricmp( ), all of these are a match with "computer".

Only the first would be a match if strcmp( ) had been used.

Like strcmp( ), the case insensitive version returns integer values that indicate a match (zero), or the value of the first mismatch. Stricmp( ) accomplishes the task of comparing without regard to whether the individual characters are uppercase or lowercase by simply temporarily treating all characters it encounters as lowercase . . . probably. Perhaps they are all changed to uppercase. It makes no difference, as long as all characters are one case or the other. This conversion is done within the function and does not affect the actual contents of the string arguments themselves.

Strncmp( )

Another function that is closely aligned with strcmp( ) is used to compare portions of two strings. This function is called strncmp( ), and accepts two string pointers as arguments and an int argument that indicates the maximum number of characters to be compared. The following program demonstrates the use of strncmp( ):

```
main()
{

    char a[34], b[20];
    int x;

    strcpy(a, "Console");
    strcpy(b, "Consort");

    x = strncmp(a, b, 5);

}
```

Note that the unsigned integer value is 5, which means that strncmp( ) is to compare the first five characters of each string. While the two strings are different, the first five characters of each match, therefore strncmp( ) will return a value of zero to x, meaning that the first five characters match. If there is a mismatch, this function will return a positive or negative value, depending on whether the first mismatched character in a is larger or smaller than the character that lies at the same position in b.

Strnicmp( )

The case-insensitive version of the previous function is called strnicmp( ). It works just like strncmp( ) except that uppercase and lowercase characters are treated as one and the same. The operation of this function should be completely understood from the previous discussions.

STRING ALTERING FUNCTIONS

The following functions are used to rewrite portions or all of a string argument, modifying it in some manner. Each is a highly specialized function that might be called on heavily in certain sophisticated text-handling programs. Again, these functions actually rewrite the contents of their string arguments, permanently altering their contents.

Strlwr( )

The strlwr( ) function simply changes all characters in its argument string to lowercase. The source code for this function might look similar to the following:

```
char *strlwr(a)
char a[];
{

    int x = 0;

    while (a[x] != '\0') {
        if (a[x] >= 65 && a[x] <= 89)
            a[x] = a[x] + 32;

        ++x;
    }

    return(a);

}
```

This function accepts a pointer to a string as its argument (a). It then begins accessing each character position in the *while* loop. The *if* statement determines if the character is uppercase (having an ASCII value of from 65 (A) to 90 (Z)), and adds 32 to its current value if this is true. The value of x is incremented by one and the loop cycles again. This process continues until the end of the string ($\setminus$ 0) is reached. The return statement returns a pointer to this string, which has now been changed to contain all lowercase characters. Any characters in the string that lie outside of the range from A to Z are unaltered.

It should be noted that this function will do just what strlwr( ) does, but it is written in a form that should be easy for the newcomer to grasp. C offers many shorthand methods of accomplishing computer operations. Some of the most compact source code is quite difficult to decipher. The true nature of the strlwr( ) source code might be more like the following:

```
char *strlwr(char a[])
{

    int x = 0;

    while ((a[x] += (a[x] >= 'A' && a[x] <= 'Z') ? ' ' : 0))
        ++x;

    return(a);

}
```

This might look like a completely different function, but it is really the same basic example shown before, with a bit of C shorthand thrown in. The compiled code for this function will be nearly the same as the compiled code for the previous one. This might seem incomprehensible if you are a beginning C programmer, but it won't be too long before such constructs begin to take on meaning. As a key to unravelling the shorthand in the function above, bear in mind an earlier discussion about assignments to char variables and the fact that the statement:

$$a[x] = 'A'$$

is exactly the same as:

$$a[x] = 65$$

This applies to other operations as well, therefore, the statement:

$$a[x] <= 'A'$$

in the above line is really part of an abbreviated *if* statement test. This portion of the test is checking to see if a[x] is less than or equal to 65, but 'A' is substituted for 65. They both equal 65, because this is the ASCII code for the letter A. The second portion of the test checks to see if a[x] is also less than 'Z'. This could also read less than 90, the ASCII code for Z. Because this function deals with changing uppercase characters to lower case, it makes better sense to make such tests using the character constants themselves, rather than their ASCII codes. It adds to the clarity, although this might not be immediately apparent to the novice C programmer. In the example above there is also a weird-looking arrangement of making something equal to ' '. What is this? It looks like two apostrophes with nothing in between. Well, the apostrophes (single quotes) signify a character constant just like they do for 'A', 'B', 'C', etc. There is, in fact, something between the two quotes. That is the *space* character, the one that is written to the screen when you press the space bar on your keyboard. This is a bona fide character, just like all those others that you can actually see. The ASCII code for the space character is 32. You should be able to reference this from the first listing of the strlwr( ) function.

Do not be alarmed if you cannot figure out the full meaning of this shorthand method of writing strlwr( ). It is simply a convenience written into the C language that can be used to speed programming time. This method means that less lines have to be typed, and once you get accustomed to the unusual appearance of such constructs, their meanings become quite clear upon a closer examination.

For the sake of clarity, this text will usually attempt to avoid shorthand methods. However, you will encounter them from time to time in program listings from other sources, so a chapter in this text is devoted to explaining some of these shorthand methods and allowing the reader to gradually ease into this aspect of the C programming language that is very pleasing once it is understood.

Strupr( )

One would expect that a Turbo C function like strlwr( ) would have a complementary function that would convert all letters in a string to uppercase. Indeed, there is such a function, and it's called strupr( ). It works in exactly the same manner as strlwr( ) regarding its argument and return, but the string will contain all uppercase characters once strupr( ) has been executed. The following program uses strlwr( ) and strupr( ) to convert an uppercase string to lowercase and then back to uppercase again:

```
main()
char a[100];
{

    strcpy(a, "MICROCOMPUTER");
    printf("%s\n", a);          /* Displays MICROCOMPUTER */

    strlwr(a);              /* Change a to lower case */
    printf("%s\n", a);          /* Displays microcomputer */

    strupr(a);              /* Change a back to upper case */
    printf("%s\n", a);          /* Displays MICROCOMPUTER */

}
```

In this program, a is originally assigned the string value of "MICROCOMPUTER". The first printf( ) function displays this on the screen. Then strlwr( ) is used to convert all uppercase characters in a to lowercase. When a is displayed again, all letters are now lowercase. Next, strupr( ) is called on to make all lowercase letters in a uppercase. When a is again displayed on the monitor screen, the string is back to where it started from. Note that both strlwr( ) and strupr( ) not only rewrite the string argument, but they also return a pointer to this string. Therefore, it is perfectly legal to use lines like:

```
printf("%s\n", strlwr(a)); .
```

This line contains two functions. First, strlwr( ) converts the characters in a to lowercase, then printf( ) displays a on the screen. This was not done in the previous program to avoid confusion. When looking at multipurpose lines like the one above, beginners sometimes are lead into thinking that strlwr( ) simply allowed a to be *displayed* in lowercase. The "drawn-out" first version makes it clear that these functions actually change the contents of the argument string.

Strrev( )

The string function strrev( ) is one that also changes a string by rewriting its characters in memory. As the name implies, strrev( ) reverses all of the characters in its string argument, with the exception of the terminating null character, which remains at the end of the string where it belongs. The following program uses strrev( ) and will display "RETUPMOC" on the screen:

```
main()
{

    char a[20];

    strcpy(a, "COMPUTER");

    printf("%s\n", strrev(a));

}
```

The array is first assigned the value "COMPUTER". Then, printf( ) is used with strrev( ) as an argument. In turn, a is the pointer argument to this second function. The string is reversed by strrev( ) and a pointer is returned to printf( ) which displays the reversed string on the screen. Remember, the value of a is no longer that which was assigned by strcpy( ). Printf( ) has displayed the true contents of the array, which are now reversed.

The following source code is a method by which the strrev( ) function may be duplicated:

```
char *strrev(a)        /* Reverse a */
char a[];
{

    int x, y, l;
    char temp[100];

    l = strlen(a) - 1;  /* l = last char position in a */
    y = 0;              /* Starting position for temp */

    for (x = l; x >= 0; --x) /*step from last to first of a*/
         temp[y++] = a[x];   /* put reverse chars in temp */

    temp[y] = '\0';          /* Terminate temp with null */
    strcpy(a, temp); /* Copy reverse string to arg string */

    return(a); /* Return original string, now reversed */

}
```

It is necessary to use another char array within the function so that there is something to which to write the reverse sequence of the argument string. The *for* loop counts backward from the last to the first character position in a and writes the results from first to last(reverse order) to temp[ ]. When this is complete, the loop is exited and a null character is placed at the end of the reverse string written to temp[ ]. As a final step before the return, strcpy( ) is used to copy the contents of temp[ ] to the original argument string. Thus, this original string is overwritten by the new reverse string. Finally, a pointer to this array string is returned to the calling program.

Sprintf( )

The last string function, sprintf( ), discussed in this chapter is a very useful one, and yet, it is seldom seen in most C programs. It is a standard function that has been with C language since its inception.

The sprint( ) function works exactly like printf( ), except that the output is written to a char array instead of to the monitor screen. This function, then, allows for complex formats to be easily and effectively written to a string array. For instance, suppose you wanted to write the floating-point value 149.075 to a string? The easiest way to accomplish this is demonstrated in the following C program:

```
main()
{

        char a[250];

        sprintf(a, "%f", 149.075);
        printf("%s\n", a);

}
```

This program will display 149.075000 and, in this example, works like the STR$ function in BASIC. However, sprintf( ) can be used to write *anything* to an array that could have been written to the screen.

Suppose you wish to emulate the BASIC language ability to add string values, as in:

```
10 A$="ADD"
20 B$="ING "
30 C$="STR"
40 D$="INGS"
50 X$=A$+B$+C$+D$
60 PRINT X$
```

This program will print "ADDING STRINGS" when it is run in BASIC. You could use repeated calls to strcat( ) in C to do the same thing, but a single call to sprintf( ) is more efficient, as the following C translation of this BASIC program demonstrates:

```
main()
{

        char a[20], b[20], c[20], d[20], x[100];
```

```
            strcpy(a, "ADD");
            strcpy(b, "ING ");
            strcpy(c, "STR");
            strcpy(d, "INGS");

            sprintf(x, "%s%s%s%s", a, b, c, d);
            printf("%s\n", x);

     }
```

Here, sprintf( ) uses the %s conversion specifiers in the control string to write
the four string values to x in concatenated form. This function is extremely
useful for many custom formatting operations involving strings, and for writing
other quantities to char arrays as string values. Be aware of its existence and
its many uses.

SUMMARY

The discussions and examples in this chapter are intended to clear up the
confusion that exists when dealing with strings in C language. Such confusion
is rampant among the BASIC-only crowd, because this language does not offer a separate char data type. In C, think of strings as separate characters that
can be referenced as a single entity or, just as easily, as the individual characters
themselves.

The manipulation of strings in C, the use of arrays of characters, and the
connection between char arrays and char pointers are all essential elements
of programming in C language. This chapter has provided the basics and a
foundation upon which more can be learned via experimentation with your
Turbo C compiler.

Chapter 5

C Language Pointers

When it comes to pointers, newcomers to C, especially those who have come from a BASIC programming environment, fall into two categories: those who don't understand what pointers are and those who fear them more than anything else. Yet, the pointer is one of the most powerful variables in all of C language, enabling the user to do many things in a straightforward and easy manner.

As one who went through the usual rigors of programming incorrectly in C due to ignorance about pointers, I can sympathize with the fear that some people have about learning C. However, a little knowledge in this area can go a long way toward erasing this fear. You can be assured that there is nothing especially gruesome about the idea of pointers. All languages use them, although pointer operations are often hidden from the user. C language allows pointers to be specifically programmed and used to great advantage. Pointer operations in C are responsible for a major part of the versatility associated with this programming language.

A pointer is a variable that is used to hold the address of a memory location. That is its sole purpose. It gets its name from the fact that it "points" to a place in memory. Maybe this is a location where something has been stored. Maybe it's a place where something is to be stored in the future. Either way, a pointer "holds" no information, other than the address of a memory location. Because a pointer contains the address of an object, the object can be accessed indirectly through its pointer. A pointer is not directly equal to any user-defined object, but rather the place in memory where such an object is or can be stored. The "thing" a pointer points to might be the memory location that has been previously assigned to a variable. Therefore, whenever the value of that variable is changed, the "thing" the pointer points to is also changed.

In C, pointers are expressly declared using the *unary operator* (represented by an asterisk). This is also known as the multiplicative operator when used in performing arithmetic operations, but it is the unary operator when declaring pointer names. In other words, though they are identical in appearance, the unary operator and the multiplicative operator are totally different and unrelated.

A pointer may be declared as type char, int, long, unsigned, etc. Because the only purpose of pointers is to contain the address of a place in memory, it might seem that it makes little difference what their declared type is. However, a pointer is a variable, a special variable, and it can seemingly take on the characteristics of nearly every data type in C. For instance, consider the following:

```
int *a;
```

This is a declaration using the unary operator that names a as a pointer that is equivalent to a variable of type int. That is, the pointer may be used in place of an integer argument in expressions where a true int variable might be used. Such a declaration also implies that this pointer points to an object of type int, although this is, again, an implication and not always true.

The previous chapter discussed C language strings and string functions in detail. Char arrays were dealt with and it was learned that the array name (without the subscript brackets) is a pointer to the first element (position zero) in the array. Pointers to these char arrays are used as arguments to many of the string functions available in Turbo C.

In C programs, one often sees declared char pointers, as in the following:

```
char *a;
```

This declaration expressly names a pointer of type char called a. Like all pointers, a points to a random place in memory immediately upon being declared. It is easy to direct it to point to an assigned memory location with little programming effort, however. The following program demonstrates this fact:

```
main()
{

    char *a;

    a = "COMPUTER";

    printf("%s\n", a);

}
```

This program displays the string "COMPUTER" on the monitor screen. Here, variable a is declared a char pointer. The unary operator names this a pointer rather than a standard char variable. This special variable is now available to point to a specific place in memory that will contain a string of values which represent printable characters (ASCII 0-255). The end of the string is signified by a null character ($\setminus$ 0) just as it is when setting up a char array.

Like all pointers, this one points to a random location in memory. To make proper use of this pointer, it is necessary to give it something to point to. In this case, the object is the string constant "COMPUTER". A constant must be written somewhere in memory. During the compilation stage, the Turbo C compiler leaves instructions within the object code to find a clear place in memory and fill the sequential bytes at this location with the ASCII values that spell "COMPUTER". Furthermore, the compiler issues instructions via its output code to terminate this constant with the null character ($\setminus$ 0), which would be placed in memory at the byte immediately following the letter 'R' in the constant. This becomes a properly terminated series of characters or a string.

Because a has been declared a pointer, the following assignment line:

```
a = "COMPUTER";
```

does not mean that the variable a is equal to the string "COMPUTER". Rather, it states that a contains the address of the memory location where this constant has been written. Therefore, if we read the sequential bytes in memory referenced by a, we can extract the string, "COMPUTER". Specifically, a points to the memory location of the byte that contains the 'C' in "COMPUTER". By reading these bytes sequentially until we hit the null character, the entire string is extracted. Pointer a does not say where the memory locations used to store "COMPUTER" begin and end, only where the constant begins. The null character signals termination of the string. Like a long fall in a dark pit, we don't know when the end is reached until we hit bottom. This null character may be thought of as the bottom of the string, while the pointer points to the byte which is the top of the string. This is how printf( ) retrieves the string contents from the location in memory that is contained within the pointer.

To further grasp the operation and significance of pointers in C language, assume that the constant "COMPUTER" is stored in memory at location 20,000. This means that the letter "C" resides at 20,000 while the remaining letters are found at 20,001, 20,002, 20,003, 20,004, 20005, 20006, and 20007 respectively. A final character is stored at 20,008 and is the null character ($\setminus$ 0), which marks the end of the character string in memory. Pointer a points to location 20,000, the starting point for the string.

This should point out the relationship between character pointers and character arrays. They are almost one and the same, and it is for this reason that character pointers and char arrays may be treated identically in most C operations. This is especially true of functions that accept character strings as arguments.

It is important, however, to realize that the difference between a char array and a char pointer lies in allocated storage space. An array has a byte of storage space set aside for each declared element. This allocation is handled automatically when the array is declared. On the other hand, a char pointer has no such storage space set aside. It can only store the address of an object. This same principle applies to all pointers and all arrays, regardless of whether they are declared char, int, long, double, float, etc.

The following program does exactly the same thing as the previous example, except that a char array is used instead of a char pointer:

```
main()
{

    char a[9];

    strcpy(a, "COMPUTER");

    printf("%s\n", a);

}
```

In this program, the strcpy( ) function is used to copy "COMPUTER" into the storage location allocated specifically for the char array.

Students who are in the first throes of learning C language usually try, at some point, to copy something to a pointer. The key to the mistake is the word "copy." All that a pointer may hold is the address of an object. You may not copy any information to it, because no space has been set aside for such a copy. A pointer is a 16-bit variable, i.e., one that has two bytes set aside for it to store an address. (Note: Far pointers are 32-bit, four-byte entities. The extra storage is needed for the 32-bit address.) Anytime a pointer is used within a function or in an operation that involves copying bytes from one location to another, trouble is bound to erupt. This is where memory overwrites can occur. The previous chapter explained that this is like POKEing random bytes into random areas of memory. Anything can and does happen when this occurs.

What's wrong with the following program?

```
main()
{

    char *p;

    strcpy(p, "COMPUTER");

    puts(p);

}
```

Hopefully, you saw immediately that an attempt has been made to "copy" something to a pointer. The strcpy( ) function is used to copy the constant to the memory location pointed to by p. Where does p point? Has it been told to point to anything? Has p been told to point to "COMPUTER"? These questions should crop up immediately.

The answers are: p points to some random memory location, assigned to it upon declaration. No, p has not been told to point to anything. Generally speaking, pointers must be assigned memory locations. This location is a numeric value, and assignments are made in much the same manner as a simple variable would be assigned a numeric quantity . . . with the assignment operator(=). And, no, p has not been told to point to "COMPUTER". Rather, the bytes that make up this constant have been copied from their memory location to the location pointed to by p. If the random memory location arbitrarily assigned to p upon declaration is a part of the "stack" for your C program, then a crash is imminent. If p has been arbitrarily directed at the memory location which handles file control blocks, then maybe half of your hard disk will be erased by POKEing in this random string of bytes. Who knows? There is a fair chance that the program will run just fine. Again, when you try to copy something to an uninitialized pointer, you become embroiled in a logical crap shoot. Anything could happen.

The following program is just as wrong as the one that has preceded it:

```
main()
{

    char *p;

    gets(p);

    puts(p);


}
```

This program is another attempt to commit binary hari kari by trying to "copy" something to storage that does not exist. The gets( ) function retrieves characters from the keyboard and must write them to memory. The argument to this function is p, a char pointer. The pointer has not been told to point to any specific place in memory by the programmer, so it points to the random memory location it was assigned upon declaration.

As each byte is input via the keyboard, it is written at the sequential memory locations accessed by p. Maybe the first location p points to is safe. Therefore, you can go right on typing other characters. Perhaps the memory location at $p+1$ is also safe. Again, the second character input has created no problems. Now, suppose the memory location at $p+3$ somehow controls the internal audio speaker within your PC. When you hit that third key, you might hear a squeal or a rasp from that speaker. Suppose the pointer was initially directed at screen memory. Then, each letter typed would be written directly on the screen. When memory is overwritten, especially by undirected pointers, all of RAM becomes a giant roulette wheel with hundreds of thousands of slots.

A further discussion will explain how pointers can be directed to point to memory areas that have been set aside for storage using memory allocation functions. The cautions outlined here apply only to pointers that have not been initialized to point to these specially allocated areas of memory.

Pointers are variables that are used specifically to point to certain areas of memory. They contain only a memory address. Actually, all variables, be they int, double, char, etc., also point to areas of memory where their assigned values are stored. When any variable is declared, space is set aside to store whatever quantity it is designed to represent. A pointer, however, is free to roam anywhere in memory.

A pointer is not tied to a single area of memory as is a common variable. It can be made to point anywhere, and a pointer carries no storage space with it, so it can be used to move all around RAM memory to allow retrieval of previously written data or to allow for data to be written at these locations.

Character pointers can be used to good advantage in many applications, especially where it is desirable to count through each character position. The following program demonstrates this principle:

```
main()
{

    char *p;

    a = "COMPUTER";

    printf("%c\n", *p);

}
```

In this example, a character pointer is declared and points to the beginning of "COMPUTER". The call to printf( ) function prints *p. Again, the unary operator is used, but this time it is not to make a pointer declaration. Notice also that printf( ) uses the %c conversion specification rather than %s.

When a pointer is used with the unary operator, it indicates that the memory content (an integer) of one element in the string is to be read. The quantity referenced by *p is an integer value or, more appropriately, a char value in the range of 0 to 255. Another way of stating this is to say that *p is the first character in the string "COMPUTER". This is the character 'C' which is represented by its ASCII code, 67. Because the %c conversion specification is used in the control string of printf( ), this value is printed as the character C.

You can take this a step further and actually count through each element of the string accessed by the pointer. This is done using the increment operator (represented by ++). If *p points to the first character in the string "COMPUTER", then *p++ counts the pointer to the second element. Another *p++ counts on to the third element, and so on until the end of the string is reached. The following program demonstrates this:

```
main()
{

    char *p;
```

```
                    p = "COMPUTER";

                    while (*p != '\0') {
                        printf("%c\n", *p)
                        *p++;
                    }


            }
```

The result of either program is to print the following:

```
                            C
                            O
                            M
                            P
                            U
                            T
                            E
                            R
```

on the monitor screen. Each character in the string is accessed individually, displayed and followed by a linefeed.

Please understand that *p++ initially points to the first character in the string, and then counts *p by one. Following this incrementation, *p will point to the second character in the string. With each incremental operation, *p is directed to the next character in the string. This is an exercise in changing the location in memory referenced by the pointer.

Now, let's have a little fun with pointers and learn something at the same time. The following program will start off this discussion:

```
            main()
            {

                char a[60], *p;

                strcpy(a, "COMPUTER");

                p = a;

                printf("%s\n", p);

            }
```

What will be displayed by this program? If you answered "COMPUTER", you are correct. This program declares a to be a char array with the capability of holding 60 characters. A char pointer, p, is also declared. What can p hold? The address of an object.

The strcpy( ) function is used to copy "COMPUTER" to the array. Next, the pointer is assigned the address of the array. Remember, when an array name is used without the brackets, it is a pointer to the first storage location allocated for that array. Where does p point? If you answered "to

COMPUTER", you are technically right and technically wrong. In fact, p points to the first element of the 60 bytes of memory allocated exclusively for storage to array a. At the present time, the bytes at this memory location have been filled with the string "COMPUTER".

When this program is executed, "COMPUTER" will be displayed on the screen, because this is the information written at the memory location pointed to by p. However, if the contents of a are changed, then the string pointed to by p also changes. This assignment has also initialized p. This pointer now points to an area of memory that has been allocated to hold 60 bytes of information.

The following program shows a slightly modified version of the former example:

```
main()
{

    char a[60], *p;

    strcpy(a, "COMPUTER");

    p = a;

    strcpy(p, "MODEM");

    printf("%s\n", a);

}
```

What will this program display. If your answer is "COMPUTER", then you are dead wrong! This program will display "MODEM". Notice also that something has been copied to p, a pointer. This is not incorrect programming in this specific example, because p has been made to point at the memory location reserved for a. We know that 60 bytes have been reserved at this location, so there is no chance of an unallocated memory overwrite. We are, however, overwriting the memory reserved for a, which is done intentionally in this exercise.

After the declaration line, the constant, "COMPUTER", is copied to the bytes reserved for a. Next, p is assigned the memory location of a. This means that p now points to the 60 bytes reserved for a. Finally, the strcpy( ) function is used to "copy" the string "MODEM" to the location pointed to by p. This overwrites "COMPUTER", the string that was initially copied to a. This operation has not changed the location that p points to, but it has changed the contents of the memory location referenced by p. The printf( ) function is used to display the contents of a, which are now equal to "MODEM", the information that was written over "COMPUTER". The assignment of the address of a to p means that p will always point to whatever a contains.

The following program shows another twist:

```
main()
{

    char *a, *p;

    a = "COMPUTER";
    p = a;
    a = "MODEM";

    printf("%s\n", b);

}
```

What will this program display? The answer is "COMPUTER". Some readers will be surprised by this, having guessed that "MODEM" would be displayed. However, this program is very different from the previous example, because two char pointers are involved, as opposed to a char array and a char pointer.

The program sequence first assigns pointer a the memory location where the constant, "COMPUTER", is stored. Next, p is assigned the memory location contained in a. Unlike an array, a pointer doesn't have a specific memory location assigned to it. A pointer is a free agent that can move about memory. Therefore, the following assignment line:

$$p = a$$

doesn't mean that p will always point to what a points to, only that p points to the memory location "presently" contained in a. Next, a is redirected to point to the memory location where the constant, "MODEM", is written. Obviously, this must be a different location from where the other constant was written, because they both couldn't coexist at the same memory location.

With this last assignment, a has been redirected to a new memory location, however, p still points to the memory location to which "COMPUTER" has been written. Remember, when a char array is assigned a new value, its fixed storage locations are overwritten with the new information. When a pointer is reassigned to a new string constant, the memory address within that pointer is changed to the memory address of the new constant. An array's allocated space travels with it, while a pointer can point to any place in memory.

This next example mixes a char array with three pointers:

```
main()
{

    char *a, *b, *c, d[40];

    strcpy(d, "COMPUTER");

    a = b = c = d;

    printf("%s %s %s %s\n", a, b, c, d);

    strcpy(d, "MODEM");
```

```
        printf("%s %s %s %s\n", a, b, c, d);

    }
```

This program declares three char pointers and a char array. The strcpy( ) function is used to copy "COMPUTER" to the array. Next, a multiple assignment line ties all of the variables in this program to one location. Pointers a, b, and c are made to point to d. This means that the three pointers will always point to the string contained in d. The first printf( ) function displays the memory contents of each variable. The string "COMPUTER" will appear four times. Next, strcpy( ) is again used, this time to change the contents of d[ ] to the "MODEM". Now, what do the three pointers point to? The same memory location they pointed to previously. However, this memory location has been overwritten since the last call to printf( ). These bytes now contain 'M', 'O', 'D', 'E', 'M', '\0'. Thus, MODEM will be displayed on the screen four times.

PEEKING AND POKEING MEMORY

It has been repeatedly emphasized that a pointer can point to any area of available memory. It has also been learned that when a pointer points to a character string, it is possible to retrieve each character in the string individually. Because individual characters are stored as integer values in the value range of 0 to 255, you could also display the memory contents of a string as integer values as shown below:

```
        main()
        {

            char *a;

            a = "COMPUTER");

            while (*a != '\0')
                printf("%d\n", *a++);

        }
```

This program will display the ASCII values of the eight characters that make up the word "COMPUTER". What has happened here? It might not be obvious, but the pointer has been used to PEEK into memory and return the values at the location where "COMPUTER" was stored. When the Medium, Large and Huge memory models of the Turbo C compiler are used, free access to all portions of memory (instead of just a 64K segment) may be had. The pointers may be used to PEEK into any area of memory and to POKE as well.

Turbo C, like most full function compilers, offers several memory models. The small models usually offer the fastest execution times, but are also usually limited to a 64K data segment. Memory outside of this segment cannot be accessed directly by standard pointers. When PEEK or POKE operations are needed to access memory outside of this restricted area, most compilers provide functions that allow for this. The Turbo C compiler, however, offers the best of both worlds. You can have the speed of the small memory models and the convenience of directing pointers to locations outside of the restricted data segment. This is done with far pointer declarations and is explained elsewhere in this chapter. Of course, Turbo C also offers peek( ) and poke( ) functions to do the same thing, although direct pointer access will be faster. The following discussions provide program examples that must be compiled under the Medium, Large, or Huge memory models to run successfully.

In order to PEEK or POKE certain areas of memory, it is first necessary to direct a pointer to the desired area. All past examples of pointer operations have directed pointers toward areas of memory that were set aside to store constants, or to areas where storage had been allocated for an array. The specific addresses of these storage areas are unknown to us, because the program simply allocates space where it happens to be available. In these operations, it's not necessary to know the specific locations of this storage space in memory. However, for PEEK and POKE operations, you must first "aim" the pointer at a specific location.

To direct a pointer to a specific memory location, simply assign it a value of that location. It's really quite simple, as the following program demonstrates:

```
main()
{

    char *p;

    p = (char *) 31000;

    printf("%d\n", *p);

}
```

This program displays the byte at absolute memory location 31000 and assumes use of the Medium, Large, or Huge memory models of the Turbo C compiler. The char pointer is first declared and then directed to point to absolute memory location 31000. The cast operator (char *) is mandatory so that the memory location takes on the same data type as the pointer.

This assignment causes a to point to memory location 31000. To read the value at this location, you simply display the byte at *p. From an earlier discussion, you learned that this will return the value of the first character that p points to. The conversion specification in the printf( ) control string is %d, which means that the value read at this location will be displayed as an integer.

Using a pointer directed to a specific location in memory, this program has been able to PEEK that memory location. Remember, the memory location must be provided in absolute form. MS-DOS machines divide memory into 64K segments. In BASIC, the DEF SEG statement is used to choose the segment within which you wish to operate. For example, consider this code:

```
10 DEF SEG = &HB000
20 PRINT PEEK(26)
```

DEF SEG specifies the 64K segment beginning at 45056 decimal, or &HB000, and PEEK reads the memory location at byte 26 in this segment. This might lead one to believe that the absolute memory location is 45056 + 26, or 45082. This is totally incorrect, however, because MS-BASIC segment specifications use a truncated form. BASIC adds a zero to the end of hexadecimal segment specifications to get the absolute address. This is the same as multiplying the assigned segment value by 16.

Using Turbo C in the Medium, Large or Huge memory models, this value must be specified differently. To get the true segment, the value must be multiplied by 65536. This is the same as shifting 45056 by 16 places to the left. In C terminology, the equivalent of BASIC's &HB000 would be 0xb000. Adjusting for the proper segment (shifting 16 positions to the left) yields 0xb0000000. This is the 32-bit segment value which would be handed to the pointers (far) in the memory models mentioned. More on this later.

The BASIC program shown above could be written in C as:

```
main()
{

    char *p;

    p = (char *) 0xb0000000 + 26;

    printf("%d\n", *p);

}
```

It could also have been written as:

```
main()
{

    char *p;

    p = (char *) 0xb0000000;

    printf("%d\n", *(p + 26));

}
```

The last program accesses the character at offset 26 from zero, which is located at 0xb0000000. (Note: If your computer does not use the monochrome screen and monochrome display adapter board, then the color board is in place, and the proper segment value is 0xb8000000. Simply substitute this value for all designations of 0xb0000000 and the sample programs will run on a configuration that uses the color board and color monitor.)

The following program will PEEK 100 sequential memory locations starting at 0xb0000000. This is the start of the monochrome screen for IBM personal computers and most compatibles:

```
main()
{

    char *p;
    long l;

    l = 0xb0000000;

    for (p = (char *) l; p <= (char *) l + 99; ++p)
        printf("%d\n", *p);

}
```

Here, the long integer, l, is assigned the starting value to PEEK. This value is assigned to pointer p in the *for* loop, after it has been cast to a char pointer. On each pass of the loop, p is incremented to point to the next sequential memory position. The byte value at each location is contained in *p.

A similar programming sequence can also POKE memory locations using pointers in C. This next example writes a single byte to the memory location specified:

```
main()
{

    char *p;

    p = (char *) 31000;

    *p = 65;

}
```

This program is similar to previous programs that PEEKed a single byte of memory, but instead of reading the value pointed to by *p, a value is assigned to *p. Earlier, you were cautioned that pointers contain no memory storage of their own, and that copying information to pointers can cause memory locations to be overwritten. In a POKE operation, memory is purposely being overwritten. One memory value is being overwritten by another.

The following program will fill the IBM PC monochrome screen with the letter A by POKEing every other memory location with character 65.

```
main()
{

    char *p;
    int i;

    p = (char *) 0xb0000000;
```

```
        for (i = 0; i <= 3999; i += 2)
            *(p + i) = 65;


    }
```

The start of the monochrome screen memory on the IBM PC line of machines is given as 0xb0000000. This serves as the segment address. The offsets into memory are handled within the body of the *for* loop. In other words, *(p + i) accesses the i byte into 0xb0000000. The monochrome screen uses each odd byte to set character attributes, with the normal attribute being seven. This program writes 65 to all even bytes and to byte 0. Thus, the screen is filled with the character for ASCII 65, or A.

While only char pointers have been discussed to this point, C allows pointers of any type to be declared. Therefore, pointers may be of type int, unsigned, long, double, long double, float, etc. The following program demonstrates the use of an *int* pointer:

```
main()
{

    int *i, h;

    h = 37;
    i = &h;

    printf("%d\n", *i);

}
```

This program declares i an integer pointer. An integer variable, h, is also declared and assigned a value of 37. Next, i is directed to point to the memory location set aside for h. The memory address of h is obtained by preceding this variable with an ampersand. After this assignment, i points to the same place in memory that was set aside to store the values in h. The next line prints the value in memory that i points to. This will be 37, because this was the value assigned to h. When the assigned value of h is changed, then the value that i points to also changes.

The following program demonstrates this principle:

```
main()
{

    int *i, h;

    h = 145;
    i = &h;

    printf("%d\n", *i);

    h = 79;

    printf("%d\n", *i);

}
```

After *i is displayed the first time, the value of h is reassigned. When *i is displayed again, it will be equal to the new value of h. The pointer assignment line i = &h means that *i will always be equal to the value of h. Pointer i points to that location in memory which is used to store all assignments made to h. We can do the same thing with other types of pointers, as in:

```
main()
{

    float *i, h;

    h = 56.884;
    i = &h;

    printf("%f\n", *i);

}
```

Both the variable and the pointer have been declared float, so a larger area of memory is set aside to store a floating-point value (32 bits on most MS-DOS implementations). The pointer, i, is assigned the memory location set aside for storage to variable h.

When a numeric variable is preceded by the ampersand, this is a direct reference to the memory location of that variable. The designation &h is a pointer in itself. It returns the memory location of h.

When C compilers for microcomputers first appeared on the market, they were limited to small memory models, and the idea of writing or reading memory outside of the 64K data segment on MS-DOS machines was not possible. Such operations were usually handled by assembly language routines that were called from C. Later C compiler versions offered peek( ) and poke( ) functions, or their equivalents, to access any area of memory. Still later versions offered these features plus various memory model sizes. The larger memory models used four-byte pointers and could access any memory location directly, as the previous programs have done. The peek( ) and poke( ) functions were retained, because the small memory models were still dependent on these functions to write to memory locations outside of the local data segment.

From a programming point of view, the small memory models are still best, providing that the program will fit the restrictions of this model. The two byte pointers are far more efficient from the standpoint of execution speed. Data from outside the local segment may be accessed (PEEKed and/or POKEd) using the peek( ) and poke( ) functions. However, when memory allocation requirements become very large, it is necessary to switch to a larger memory model.

The latest C compilers, of which Turbo C is the very newest, offer another option for small memory model programmers. Large memory models allow all of memory to be accessed by using four-byte pointers, also known as far pointers, because they access far areas of memory, those that lie outside of the local segment. Turbo C allows far pointers to be specifically declared within the small memory model compiler version. This means that all of the speed advantages of the small memory model compiler versions can be had, plus immediate access to all of the available memory. The following discussion concerns programs that may be compiled under the small memory version of the Turbo C compiler.

The ability to mix near and far pointers within the confines of a single memory model is a feature that will be appreciated by the professional programmer immediately. Although the beginning C programmer is striving to progress to the professional level as well, he or she might not see an immediate need for such a convenience. Nevertheless, the time will come when this type of operation might be highly desirable, if not necessary. Therefore, it is important to know how to make use of far pointers to access those portions of memory that lie outside of the 64K local (near) segment of the small memory model versions of the Turbo C compiler.

Throughout this chapter, the term "large memory model" really refers to the Medium, Large and Huge memory models available in Turbo C. The term, "small memory model" refers to the Tiny, Small, and Compact memory models. The former use four-byte (far) pointers as the default, while the latter use two-byte (near) pointers as their default.

The following program uses a far pointer declaration to allow access to the monochrome display screen:

```
main()
{

    char far *a;

    a = (char far *) 0xb0000000;
    *a = 65;

}
```

This program writes the letter A in the upper left-hand corner of the screen. First, a is declared a far pointer of type char. Notice how the declaration is made, char far *a. Next, a is assigned a memory address corresponding with the beginning memory of the monochrome screen. The cast operator (char far *) is used just as char * was used with the large memory model programs discussed earlier. Remember, the pointer size in large memory models compilers is four bytes, thus all pointers are far types. In the small memory model compilers, all pointers are of near types (usually two bytes), unless specifically declared as far types. This is the case with this program. The last program line simply changes the byte at location *a to ASCII 65, which is the same as the character 'A'.

The following program fills the monochrome screen with the same letter as did a previous, large memory, program example:

```
main()
{
```

```
int x;
char far *a;

a = (char far *) 0xb0000000;

for (x = 0; x <= 3999; ++x)
    *(a + x) = 65;


}
```

PEEKB AND POKEB

As was mentioned previously, the Turbo C compiler offers peek( ) and poke( ) functions for easy access to memory in the same manner as the PEEK and POKE statements in BASIC. In Turbo C, there are two sets of memory access functions designed to conveniently reach into any portion of the computer's memory. The two we are most interested in for now are *peekb( )* and *pokeb( )*. The 'b' designation here means "byte." These functions return, or write, a byte to memory. The alternate Turbo C functions, peek( ) and poke( ), work in a slightly different manner. They return, or write, a 16-bit "word." Don't be alarmed about this difference. The explanation is simple. Peekb( ) returns a char value. From an earlier discussion, it was learned that a char variable could contain any value from 0 to 255. A char variable requires one single byte of memory to store any of its possible values. However, int values in C may represent values from -32768 to $+32767$. These quantities require two bytes for storage on the IBM PC and compatibles. If you think of a char as a byte, then an int is two char long. These two chars may be thought of as a "word." Therefore, peekb( ) returns a single byte, while peek( ) returns two bytes, also known as a word and also known as an int.

So, if you POKE the monochrome screen memory starting at memory with 65 (the letter A) and peekb( ) that same location, you will get a return byte value of 65. However, if you peek( ) the location, you will get a two-byte combination in the form of integer value 1857. This breaks down to 65 being the first byte and 7 being the second. The integer 65 was the byte POKEd into memory at offset zero and 7 was the attribute byte resident at all odd memory location on the screen, assuming normal character presentation (i.e., no underlines, boldface, flashing, etc.).

The following program POKEs a single byte at offset zero in the monochrome screen memory using the pokeb( ) function. It then reads the byte using peekb( ) and displays this value on the screen.

```
main()
{

    pokeb(0xb000, 0, 65);
    printf("%d\n", peekb(0xb000, 0));

}
```

Pokeb( ) requires three arguments. The first is the segment value. For BA-SIC programmers, this is the DEF SEG value, and it is specified just as it is when using Microsoft BASIC. We don't have to deal directly with far pointers when using these functions. The second argument to pokeb( ) is the offset value. This is zero, because we wish to access the first byte in the segment. The next argument is the actual byte value to POKE into memory. This is ASCII 65, which is displayed as the letter "A" on the screen. This argument could also have been written as A within the pokeb( ) function, instead of using its ASCII value. Remember, A and 65 are one and the same value as far as C language and your computer are concerned.

The peekb( ) function returns a char value that may be displayed as a char or as an integer in the range of 0 to 255. The printf( ) function uses a conversion specification of %d, indicating an integer or numeric display. Therefore, the numeric value at the memory location specified in the arguments to peekb( ) will be displayed. The peekb( ) function requires the same memory position arguments as pokeb( ). The first argument is the segment, while the second is the offset. Notice that these sets of arguments match the first two found in pokeb( ). The final result is to display 65 on the screen, the value that was just POKEd into memory. All segment and offset values should be unsigned integer values.

With what has already been learned about using pointers for memory access, there is nothing especially mysterious about the peekb( ) and pokeb( ) functions. Because these are used within the small memory models of the Turbo C compiler, we can assume that each uses a far pointer to access the desired memory location.

The following function source code will emulate the operation of peekb( ) in Turbo C:

```
peekb(seg, off)
int seg, off;
{

        char far *a;

        a = (char far *) seg * 65536;

        return(*(a + off));

}
```

A far pointer is declared, just as it was in some other programs in this chapter. Then the segment value is changed from a two-byte (16-bit) value to a four-byte (32-bit) value. Remember, far pointers are four bytes long. Multiplying seg by 65536 does the job nicely, but in C, we can also use the left shift operator represented by (< <) to accomplish the same thing. Therefore, the assignment line in the above program could also be written as:

```
a = (char far *) seg << 16;
```

The two lines mean exactly the same thing, but this one looks more professional (or maybe the phrase is "high falootin").

Once the segment is correctly phrased, the byte is returned in the following line:

```
*(a + off)
```

This was used in some previous examples.

There is nothing especially mysterious about pokeb( ) either. It could be emulated by the following program:

```
pokeb(seg, off, byte)
unsigned seg, off;
char byte;
{

    char far *a;

    a = (char far *) seg << 16;

    *(a + off) = byte;

}
```

The same thing takes place as with peekb( ), but the last line assigns the variable byte to *(a + off) instead of returning the byte at this location. Nothing could be simpler.

Which should you use, peekb( ) and pokeb( ) or the direct method with far pointers and the like? This will depend on several factors. First of all, if you do not fully understand memory access and 32-bit addressing using far pointers, then by all means use peekb( ) and pokeb( ). These functions will certainly be more familiar to BASIC programmers making the switch to Turbo C, because they work quite similarly to their BASIC counterparts and the address phrasing is the same. However, if you want to squeeze the most speed and efficiency possible out of your program, then use the direct route. This method offers excellent practice and people who use pointer operations frequently know and understand pointers much better than those who do not.

The following two programs do exactly the same thing. They fill the monochrome screen with the letter "A." The first program does this using pokeb( ), while the second program makes use of a far pointer. Both were compiled under the Small memory model of the Turbo C compiler:

```
main()
{

    int seg, off, x;

    seg = 0xb000;
    off = 0;
```

```
            for (x = 0; x <= 3999; ++x)
                pokeb(seg, off, x);

    }


    main()
    {

            char far *c;
            int x;

            c = (char far *) 0xb0000000;

            for (x = 0; x <= 3999; ++x)
                *(c + x) = 65;

    }
```

Both of these programs were run on a standard IBM PC. The first example required 11 hundredths of a second to complete execution. The second program required only 5.5 hundredths of a second to complete its run. The direct addressing of system memory via the far pointer in the second program allowed execution time to be cut by exactly one half. In these small, fast programs, the difference in total execution times is very small, but the percentage figures are significant. The direct method using far pointers accesses memory 50% faster than does the pokeb( ) function. Therefore, large programs that do a lot of memory addressing will benefit greatly by direct methods of memory address. Bear this in mind!

MEMORY ALLOCATION FUNCTIONS

Closely tied with pointer operations are the memory allocation functions. To repeat, pointers can be made to point to any area of memory. Typically, pointers are "aimed" at portions of memory where data have already been written or where space has been allocated to a variable. In the latter case, the pointer uses space allocated to some other variable. But, suppose you want a pointer to point to an area of memory that can be set aside specifically for storage, and use the pointer to access this area? Here is where the memory allocation functions come into use. These are especially desirable when it is necessary to set aside a large portion of memory, supposedly to store a lot of data. This can be done by declaring a large char array, but array space is limited, because only a certain amount is set aside for this purpose. Once it has been used up, the space set aside must either be enlarged (if possible) or you must resort to another means of storage.

The UNIX memory allocation functions allow areas of memory to be set aside and accessed by a pointer. You don't specify what locations in memory are to be used for this storage, only that you want so many bytes of storage space. These functions attempt to locate such an area that is not currently allocated to some other purpose. When an area, or "block," is found, the function allocates the desired number of sequential bytes and returns a pointer to the first byte in this block.

The standard memory allocation functions include *malloc()* and *calloc()*, both of which are a part of the standard C language function set and should be supported by every compiler.

Malloc( ) allocates a block of memory in a way that is compatible with the UNIX operating system. Admittedly, malloc( ) can be quite inefficient when many small blocks of memory are allocated from a single program, but it provides a universal function upon which to base a discussion on memory allocation.

Calloc( ) does about the same thing, except it clears, or sets to zero, each byte in the allocated block. Calloc( ) might be used in place of malloc( ) if it is necessary to know the length of a series of data that is written to the allocated memory location, with the count stopping at the first cleared byte. Otherwise, the two are identical.

The following C program demonstrates the use of malloc( ):

```
main()
{

        char *a, *malloc();

        a = malloc(256);

        strcpy(a, "Microcomputer");

}
```

This example calls malloc( ) to set aside a block of 256 bytes. A char pointer, a, is assigned the return value from malloc( ) that gives the location of the first byte in the reserved block of memory.

Next, the strcpy( ) function copies the string argument to the memory location pointed to by a. Earlier in this chapter, there was a warning not to copy anything to pointers, because they do not necessarily point to an area of memory large enough to hold a value. This could cause a dangerous overwrite of memory currently in use. However, this new example is different. Pointer a now has size. It points to an area of memory that contains 256 bytes set aside for access by this pointer only. It is now perfectly safe to copy data to the pointer's location, just as would be done with a declared char array. The pointer has now been initialized, or *sized*, as it is sometimes called. The following assignment line:

```
a = malloc(256)
```

is the same as this declaration:

```
char a[256];
```

as far as storage space is concerned. Both of these examples set aside 256 bytes of storage to be accessed by a.

This example has shown how a pointer may be "aimed" at a block of programmer-determined size. This leads to the next exercise, which involves an array of pointers. The following program declares an array of up to five pointers. This would be the BASIC language equivalent of a string array, because each pointer may point to a string.

```
main()
{

        int x;
        char *a[5];

        a[0] = "Microcomputer";
        a[1] = "Modem";
        a[2] = "Client";
        a[3] = "Customer";
        a[4] = "Business";



    }
```

This is a simple program using an array of pointers. This declaration:

```
char *a[5];
```

says that a is an array of five char pointers. Following this declaration, the pointers are assigned the memory locations of the various constants contained in double quotes.

This type of array is easily programmed when you are dealing with constants. However, how would you accomplish the same thing if, for instance, the string values were input via the keyboard? When a pointer is first declared, it points to no where in particular. Therefore, you cannot simply write an unknown string to the memory location accessed by each of the five pointers. In the previous example, the array of pointers was made to point to the location of a constant. Therefore, the random memory locations accessed by each of the five pointers upon declaration were changed to the memory locations of the constants.

If you start copying variable values to a pointer, then you use the current pointer address initially assigned to it. This space might be too small and might lie in a "dangerous" area of memory. This is where the memory allocation functions come into immediate use, as the following program demonstrates:

```
main()
{

    char *a[5], *malloc();
    int x;
```

```
                  for (x = 0; x < 5; ++x) {
                      a[x] = malloc(256);
                      gets(a[x]);
                  }


      }
```

The declaration char *a[5] establishes an array of char pointers. Before constants are actually assigned, a[x] is assigned the return from malloc( ). Therefore, the location in memory to which a[x] now points is returned by malloc( ), and consists of a clear and safe 256 sequential bytes. This function sets aside a maximum storage area of 256 bytes per pointer. Each pointer is sized, or directed, to a place in memory with adequate storage to hold the input string at the keyboard.

Malloc( ) is declared within the program as well. This declaration simply lets the compiler know that malloc( ) will be returning a pointer of type char. In Turbo C, malloc( ) returns a void pointer, which means it can be coerced into any valid pointer type. The declaration caused malloc's pointer to be coerced into a char type. It could also be int, long, unsigned, etc., depending on the declaration.

This program could also have #included alloc.h, which contains a prototype of malloc( ). This would provide some additional error-checking during the compile stage, but this header file is not mandatory. In fact, the declaration of malloc( ) is not mandatory in Turbo C, as it is in some other compilers. However, if malloc( ) is not declared a char * type or alloc.h is not #included, then a "non-portable" warning will occur during the compilation stage. The program will run correctly, but it will not be portable; it will run under Turbo C and (probably) not under any other compiler.

If malloc( ) can't find the memory requested by its argument (i.e., all computer memory is in use and there is no more remaining for this allocation), this function will return a NULL pointer zero. It's always necessary to check the return from malloc( ) and all other such functions to make certain that the requested amount of memory was, indeed, allocated. The following program is the same as the one above, but provides this safety check:

```
#define NULL 0
main()
{

    char *a, *malloc();
    int x;

    for (x = 0; x < 5; ++x)
        if ((a[x] = malloc(256)) == NULL)
            exit(0);
        else
            gets[a[x]);

}
```

This program contains an emergency exit sequence if the return from malloc( ) is NULL. NULL is #defined in this example, although the stdio.h header file also makes this macro definition. If stdio.h is #included in any program that uses malloc( ), the separate definition is unnecessary.

The use of the gets( ) function in this program means that characters from the keyboard are actually copied into the memory location pointed to by a[x]. This is perfectly legal, because malloc( ) has allocated the needed space.

The following C program demonstrates another use for pointers and memory allocation functions in C. It sets aside a large block of memory, and then writes information to fill the screen. The screen is then saved in this allocated memory block, one byte at a time. Later, the screen is cleared, but the saved screen still resides in that block of memory. The last stage of the program restores the erased screen by reading bytes from that block back to the screen memory location:

```
/* For PC's without monochrome display card, change 0b0000000 */
/* to 0b8000000 */
main()
{

      char far *a, *b;
      int x;

      a = (char far *) 0xb0000000;  /* Beginning of video memory */
      b = malloc(4000);

      system("DIR");  /* Put file listings on screen */

      for (x = 0; x <= 3999; ++x)
           *(b + x) = *(a + x); /* Read screen bytes to *b bytes */

      system("CLS");      /* Clear Screen */
      sleep(5);           /* Pause for 5 seconds */


      for (x = 0; x <= 3999; ++x)
           *a++ = *b++;  /* Put bytes from block back on screen */


}
```

The two char pointers are declared and a is made to point to the beginning of video memory at 0xb0000000. Notice that a is a far pointer while b is a standard, or near, pointer. This assumes compilation under the Small memory model. Malloc( ) is called and returns a pointer to a block of 4000 bytes of memory to b.

Next, the screen is filled with the file listings from the default drive. This is accomplished using the system( ) function with an argument of DIR. This function simply returns control to DOS temporarily. The DIR command in DOS causes the disk file directory to be displayed.

Once the write is complete, a loop is entered which counts a through 4000 memory locations comprising the screen. The byte at the screen location is read into b, which is also stepped a byte at a time. When this loop is exited, each of the screen bytes has been copied to the memory block.

The screen is cleared using the system( ) function again, this time with an argument of CLS, the DOS command to clear the screen and set the cursor to the upper left-hand corner. Due to the speed of Turbo C, it is necessary to program a pause at this point so you actually have time to witness that the screen is, indeed, cleared of all previous information. This pause is accomplished with the *sleep( )* function. Without it, the screen would be cleared and rewritten so rapidly that you probably would not see what was taking place. Sleep( ) is called only to allow you to see that the screen is actually cleared of all data before being rewritten. The argument to this function is five, which brings about a five-second delay.

The next loop performs a reversal of the previous one. During this stage of the program, the contiguous bytes from the allocated block of memory are read back into screen memory. Put simply, the block contains a copy of the original screen, so the block contents are transferred back to screen memory. The result is the recreated screen display that was present before the CLS command was called.

The same thing would have taken place if calloc( ), the other UNIX-compatible memory allocation function, were used instead of malloc( ). Calloc( ) accepts a two part argument in the format of:

calloc(number of elements, element length)

The first argument is simply multiplied by the second to arrive at the total number of bytes to reserve, but this type of notation allows the second argument to be the *sizeof( )* function, which returns the bytes required for storing various data types. This allows for more portability, because one system or memory model might use two bytes to store integers and another might use four. A call such as:

calloc(4000, sizeof(int));

sets aside enough memory to store 4000 integer values. If a system requires two bytes for each integer, then a total of 8000 bytes are set aside. But, if a program using this line were transferred to a system that used four byte integers, then sizeof( ) would return a value of four, and a total of 16000 bytes would be reserved.

This function is more portable than is malloc( ), although the latter could be made more portable by expressing it as follows:

malloc(4000 * sizeof(int));

This brings about the same portability.

The portability mentioned here is important if you are developing software under Turbo C that might also be compiled under other versions of C compilers.

Regarding calloc( ), there are times when it is desirable to have a whole block of memory containing null bytes (those that have been set to zero). Calloc( ) allocates and clears memory in this fashion. A null block could be used to fill a video screen, thus erasing or clearing it. This might serve in lieu of calling system("CLS") which might not be portable beyond MS-DOS machines.

The previous C program that saved a screen in a memory block and then called it back after the original screen was cleared performed what is known as a "block move." A block of memory from the video screen location was transferred to another area reserved by malloc( ). Technically, the video memory was not moved but copied from the source location to the destination block. Another block move was performed when the memory from the destination block was copied back to the cleared screen.

OTHER MEMORY FUNCTIONS

Borland's Turbo C offers several other memory manipulation functions that are very useful for block moves of the sort just discussed.

The special function discussed in this section were not a part of the original C programming language. They are, however, more or less standard within modern C compilers designed for MS-DOS applications.

Movmem( )

The movmem( ) function moves a block of memory from a source address or buffer to a destination address. This move is based upon the 32-bit addresses of the source and destination and the number of bytes to move. The destination is an unsigned value.

The following program will copy the contents of the monochrome screen to the color monitor buffer:

```
/* Move the mono screen to the color monitor */
        main()
        {

                movmem(0xb00000000l, 0xb80000000l, 4000);

        }
```

This is a simple program that uses constants for arguments. The first argument is the 32-bit address of the monochrome screen buffer. The second address is that of the color screen buffer. The last argument specifies the number of bytes to move. Because the monochrome screen is comprised of 4000 bytes, the entire screen will be moved to the color monitor.

Actually, it is more accurate to say that the contents of the monochrome screen are copied to the color screen buffer, because the monochrome screen contents will remain intact. Using movmem( ) in the Medium, Large, and Huge memory model compiler versions contained in Turbo C is a very efficient way of moving large blocks of memory at a very rapid rate. The speed with which the block is moved to the color screen seems to produce an instantaneous write of the whole screen.

Of course, this function is limited to those Medium, Large, and Huge memory model compiler versions. Incidentally, the prototype for this function is contained in header file <mem.h>. It is purposely excluded from this program so that the 32-bit offsets may be specified directly. If <mem.h> is included with this program, you will get an error message. This can be cleared up by casting the source and destination values as void pointers, as in the following:

```
#include <mem.h>
main()
{

    movmem((void *) 0xb8000000, (void *) 0xb0000000, 4000);

}
```

Movedata( )

If you want the convenience of exceedingly quick block moves but don't want to go to the larger memory model compilers, Turbo C also offers the smaller memory model equivalent of movmem( ). This function is called movedata( ) and allows addresses to be specified in eight-bit quantities, giving the segment and the offset as two separate arguments. The following program does the same as the previous two. When executed, the contents of the monochrome screen will be written to the color screen. Naturally, all of these programs assume that you are equipped with two monitors. If this is not the case with your installation, another method will be shown that will give you the same effect. The first example of movedata( ) follows:

```
main()
{

    movedata(0xb000, 0, 0xb800, 0, 4000);

}
```

Again, constants are used as arguments to this function. The first argument is the eight-bit address of the monochrome screen segment. The second value is the offset into this segment where the read is to begin. The third argument is the address of the color monitor buffer segment. Its matching offset argument is also zero. This means that the read is to start at the beginning byte of the monochrome screen buffer, and the beginning write will be to the first byte in the color screen buffer. The last argument states that 4000 bytes are to be transferred.

There is nothing especially mysterious about any of these functions. Almost certainly, they are written in 8086 Assembler and called from Turbo C, because their operation is extremely quick, quicker than is possible via functions that could be built from C language primitives.

When speed is of the essence, Assembler routines called from a C program might be the only way to accomplish a complex operation or one that involves copying a lot of data. The following function, called bmove( ), is one I wrote to mimic the movedata( ) function just discussed. It uses peekb( ) and pokeb( ) from the Turbo C library to accomplish the block move:

```
bmove(sseg, soff, dseg, doff, nbytes)
int sseg, soff, dseg, doff;
unsigned nbytes;
{

    unsigned x;
    int y;

    for (x = 0; x < nbytes; ++x) {
        y = peekb(sseg, soff + x);
        pokeb(dseg, doff + x, y);
    }

}
```

As can be seen by examining the few lines in this function, it is nothing more than a *for* loop that substitutes the source segment(sseg) and source offset(soff) values in a call to peekb( ). When the byte is returned, it is POKEd into the address referenced by the destination segment(dseg) and the destination offset(doff). The loop cycles from zero to one less than the value of nbytes. Remember, this count begins at zero, so when x has reached a value of nbytes − 1, nbytes of data have already been transferred.

This function will not execute nearly so rapidly as does movmem( ) or movedata( ), which reflects the fact that this function is written and compiled in C, while the others are Assembler routines called from Turbo C.

For those readers who are equipped with only a single monitor screen and who are getting frustrated over all of these examples that require a monochrome and a color monitor and display boards, the following program is just for you. This one assumes that you have only the monochrome display, but if you have only the color display, take heart, the proper conversions will be spelled out for you. This program writes the contents of the monochrome screen to a local buffer. This is a fancy way of saying that the screen contents are stored in an integer array, i[ ]. Notice that this array has been allocated to store up to 4000 integer values, the exact size of the screen you are going to transfer. The movedata( ) function is used to move the block from the screen to the array.

In order to write to the local array using movedata( ), it is necessary to find out where this array has been placed in memory. You can get the pointer of this array via *&i*. However, this just provides the memory offset in the data segment used by the small memory model compiler. You also need the eight-bit address of this data segment. To get this, the segread( ) function is called. This function reads segments and stores them in the SREGS structure that is defined in the <dos.h> header file #included with this program. After segread( ) is executed, *r.ds* is equal to the current data segment. This value is used as the destination segment to movedata( ). The offset is a pointer to the integer array, &i, which provides the address of the array within the data segment. Movedata( ) does the block transfer in a "split second."

After the bytes have been copied to the array, a printf( ) function is called to write a series of new-line characters to the screen. This will scroll most of the contents off the screen. Then, the sleep( )function is called to produce a five second pause. Finally, movedata( ) is called again. This time, the contents of the array are read back into screen memory. Notice that the arguments to movedata( ) have been reversed from the previous call to this same function. The screen seems to "blip" back in place instantaneously.

If you do not have the monochrome display adapter in place and are operating from the color graphics card, simply change the value 0xb000 to 0xb800 and everything will work perfectly for this configuration.

Turbo C offers several more memory functions, all of which perform similar operations to those discussed to this point. Some of these might be more applicable to certain jobs than others. This is why there is a fairly large number to choose from.

CLEARING ALLOCATED MEMORY

After a block of memory is allocated and used, it is desirable (and often mandatory) to release that block, so that it may be reallocated to another pointer or used for some other purpose. It is not efficient to keep allocating block after block of memory when one or two blocks would be sufficient. This would apply when a block is used for a singular purpose and then no longer needed. The UNIX-compatible memory-release function, standard with most C compilers, is *free( )*. It is used in a format of:

```
x = free(p)
```

where x is an integer variable and p is a pointer to a previously allocated block of memory.

The above call will attempt to free the block, making it available for other allocation calls. When free( ) is called, it returns an integer value to x. The value of x after the call will be zero if the release was successful, and equal to some other value (usually −1) if there is a release problem.

If a problem exists, it is usually a sign of some turmoil within your computer's memory management segment, or a sign that the pointer used as an argument to free( ) does not point to an allocated block of memory.

SUMMARY

Pointer operations are a major strong point of the C programming language. You can never say that you really know how to program in C until you have a firm grasp of just what pointers are, and how they are declared, aimed, assigned, read, and manipulated in general.

This chapter has tried to demonstrate that pointers are not something to be afraid of. Rather, they are a very powerful programming tool that can make short work of some rather tedious tasks. Admittedly, there is a lot to learn about handling pointers, especially in how they differ from traditional variables. However, pointers offer a new dimension in programming for those who have expertise in languages where pointer operations are unavailable to the programmer. Practice pointer operations regularly, and your C programming abilities will increase.

Chapter 6

C Language Shortcuts

This chapter is designed especially for the relative newcomer to C who might have had only a few weeks or months of programming in this language, or possibly as much as a year or so.

It seems that whenever I become involved in a "heavy-duty" C programming assignment, one that might take several months or longer, I learn something new and important about this language. From this standpoint, all of us can be classified as newcomers, especially with the recent changes that have been incorporated into new C programming environments like the Turbo C compiler.

C is a language that is small, versatile, and offers an excellent variety in the way programming concepts may be expressed through C source code. As is the case with any programming language, there are several ways to accomplish the same results. This means that a small routine that, for instance, alphabetizes a list of words, might be written in several different ways, depending upon the style and approach of the programmer. C also offers several conveniences that allow for a "shorthand" form of programming. Most of these are just different vehicles for expressing the same programming routines.

The discussions, sample programs, and suggestions in this chapter are intended to alert the newcomer to C programming to the various conventions and alternate conventions programmers often use. There is nothing more disheartening than learning to program in a new language and coming upon conventions that make no sense whatsoever just when you feel that you are beginning, finally, to grasp this new language.

To begin this discussion, let's consider the conditional expression in C. The following program illustrates the standard method by which the values of two integers can be compared and assignments made based upon the results of this conditional test:

```
main()
{

    int x, y;

    scanf("%d", &x);

    if (x == 10)
        y = 12;
    else
        y = 0;

    printf("The value of y is %d\n", y);

}
```

This program uses scanf( ) to obtain an integer value from the keyboard and assign it to x. The actual value of x is the test line for the conditional expression which assigns the value of y based upon the actual value of x. The value of y is then displayed on the monitor screen using printf( ).

This is a simple program, but it can be reduced to fewer lines by using the *conditional expression* in C. The following program does exactly what the previous one did, but it is accomplished with fewer program lines:

```
main()
{

    int x, y;

    scanf("%d", &x);

    y = (x == 10) ? 12 : 0;

    printf("The value of y is %d\n", y);

}
```

The alternate conditional test is shorter, more quickly programmed, and just as or more expressive than the previous example. The only change to this program is found in the single conditional expression line which replaced four lines of code in the first program. The following expression:

```
y = (x == 10) ? 12 : 0;
```

means exactly the same thing as this:

```
if (x == 10)
        y = 12;
    else
        y = 0;
```

The conditional expression uses the two-part *ternary* operator (represented by ?:). In this expression, two evaluations are made. The first is x == 10. If this is true, then the expression evaluates to nonzero. On the other hand, if x does not equal ten, then the expression evaluates to zero.

If the first evaluation is nonzero (true), then the question mark portion of the ternary operator causes the 12 to be evaluated. If the first evaluation is zero, then the colon causes the next value to be evaluated. The result is to assign y the question mark value if x == 10 or to assign it the colon value if x does not equal ten.

It is not necessary to surround the first evaluation with parentheses. However, this is usually done for the sake of clarity. The conditional expression line could have been written as follows:

```
y = x == 10 ? 12 : 0
```

This is confusing. Even seasoned C programmers will have to look an extra time or two at this one and it could get worse, because the above example doesn't use any logical operators.

A line of code can even look like the following:

```
y = x == 10 && y != 13 || y == x ? 12 : 0
```

This is a "legal" line of code, in that it will compile without an error, but it is becoming more and more difficult to understand. If you surround the first expression with parentheses, however, a lot of the difficulty is removed.

Returning to the first program example, here is another way of shortening the total amount of source code:

```
main()
{

    int x, y;

    scanf("%d", &x);

    printf("The value of y is %d\n", (x == 10) ? 12 : 0);

}
```

In this example, the conditional expression is contained within the printf() function argument. The conversion specifier, %d receives the argument constant 12 or zero, depending on the true or false nature of the evaluation of x == 10.

In this example, the alternate conditional expression is being embedded in the printf() function, something you can't do directly with the other conditional expression methods. The argument to printf() evaluates to 12 or zero. Writing code in this manner tends to hide operations as the embeddedness becomes more complex, at least to people other than the authoring programmer who might view such source code. However, the programmer writing such constructs might find them to be quick, helpful, and very clear.

The following program excerpts illustrate other methods of using the conditional expression:

```
strcpy(a, (y == 10) ? "COMPUTER" : b);

while (y < (x == 10) ? 14 : 22)

for (x = 0; x <= (y == 15) ? 22 : 44; ++x)
```

In the first example, strcpy( ) is used to copy the contents of one of two source strings to a. Which string is copied will depend upon the value of y. If this variable is equal to 10, then COMPUTER is the string that is copied. If y is not equal to 10, then the contents of b are copied to a.

The second example uses a conditional test within a while loop. The loop is terminated when y is not less than 14 and x is equal to 10, or when y is not less than 22 and x is not equal to 10.

The last example uses the conditional expression in a *for* loop to determine the exiting value of variable x. When y is equal to 15, the loop will terminate when x is counted to a value that is higher than 22. If y is not equal to 15, then the loop will terminate when x is counted past a value of 44.

The many uses for the conditional expression should be apparent at this point in the discussion. It can be used in places where if-else constructs cannot. All of the above examples demonstrate this. The alternate conditional expression can be used as an argument. This is not true of if-else statement constructs.

Alright, the value of the conditional expression has been illustrated, but it is only usable when an if-else expression is necessary, right? Wrong! Though it might not be immediately obvious, this expression lends itself perfectly to if-else-if-if constructions as well.

The following program provides an example of a conditional expression using the if statement:

```
main()
{

        int x, y;

        scanf("%d", &x);

        if (x == 10)
                y = 5;
        else if (x == 20)
                y = 10;
        else
                y = 25;


}
```

This program assigns one of several values to variable y, depending on the value of x. This same program could be written as:

```
main()
{

    int x;

    scanf("%d", &x);

    y = (x == 10) ? 5 : (x == 20) ? 10 : 25;

}
```

The conditional expression is used to test for x being equal to 10. If it is, then the five is evaluated, and this is the value assigned to y. However, if x is not equal to 10, then the second expression is evaluated. The second expression is another conditional expression which tests for x being equal to 20. If it is, then this expression will evaluate the 10 which will, in turn, be evaluated by the first expression and assigned to y. If x is not equal to 20, then 25 is assigned to y.

If this is difficult to grasp, just think of the second conditional expression as being the "false" choice for the first. If the first evaluation is false, then the second conditional expression is evaluated. It is of similar nature to a *nested loop*, which is a loop within a loop. This example shows a conditional expression within a conditional expression.

The conditional expression can be used to replace any *if* statement constructs. However, as these conditional tests become more complex and the execution chain (based upon the results of these tests) more elaborate, most programmers will elect to use the statement rather than the conditional expression. This is not mandatory, and there might be times when it is preferable to use the expression rather than the statement.

The following program uses the *if* statement to perform several tests and to effect several operations based upon the results:

```
main()
{

    int x, y;

    scanf("%d", &x);

    if (x == 10) {
        y = 11;
        puts("TEN");
    }
    else {
        y = 1;
        puts("Other");
    }

}
```

When x is equal to 10, y is assigned a value of 11 and the word "TEN" is displayed on the monitor screen. When x is not equal to 10, y is assigned a value of one and "Other" is displayed. Here, we have a conditional test with two operations being performed based upon a true false condition.

Using the conditional expression, this program could be written as:

```
main()
{

    int x, y;

    scanf("%d", &x);

    (x == 10) ? y = 11, puts("TEN") : y = 1, puts("Other");

}
```

Notice that the assignment statement and puts( ) function that are to be executed as two program statements are separated by commas. These match the same elements in the earlier program that were contained with the braces of the conditional test using *if*.

It can be seen that the conditional expression is very useful in performing complex conditional tests and executing instructions based on these tests. It is a very powerful tool that can speed programming time and, when used properly, aid in comprehension and expression. It is another aspect of the versatility of the C programming language.

SWITCH

Just as the conditional expression can be used more efficiently than the *if* statement in certain C programming exercises, the *switch* statement also serves a special need for conditional tests. The *switch* statement is a multiple decision maker that can be equated with a long series of if-else-if-else constructs. Generally, it is easier to use the *if* statement when only one or two conditional tests are to be made, but when it is necessary to make many tests and execute various alternate program branches accordingly, the switch is a very powerful tool.

The following program uses *if* to accomplish a programming task:

```
main()
{

    int x;

    scanf("%d", &x);

    if (x == 1)
        printf("ONE\n");
    else if (x == 2)
        printf("TWO\n");
    else if (x == 3)
        printf("THREE\n");
    else if (x == 4)
```

```
                    printf("FOUR\n");
          else if (x == 5)
                    printf("FIVE\n");
          else
                    printf("MORE THAN FIVE\n");

     }
```

This is an example of a long series of tests that determines which word is written to the monitor screen. This series of tests can be more expressively programmed using the *switch* statement, as in:

```
main()
{

     int x;

     scanf("%d", &x);

     switch(x) {
     case 1:
          printf("ONE\n");
          break;
     case 2:
          printf("TWO\n");
          break;
     case 3:
          printf(THREE\n");
          break;
     case 4:
          printf("FOUR\n");
          break;
     case 5:
          printf("FIVE\n");
          break;
     default:
          printf("MORE THAN FIVE\n");
          break;
     }

}
```

Switch must evaluate an integer expression. It cannot be used for a direct evaluation of strings or floating-point numbers. The *case* portion of switch is a label, and must be followed by an integer or character constant or expression. The *default* is another label that contains program statements to be executed if none of the case labels apply. In the above program, switch evaluates x. When a case label matches the evaluation of x (i.e., is the same as the value of x), the statements contained within that case are executed—and so are all of the statements that are contained in cases below the accessed one in the chain. This is the reason for the *break* statements. These allow the switch to be exited at any given point. If all break statements were eliminated from the above program and the input value of x from the keyboard was one, then every printf( ) function in the program would be executed.

Remember, the case designations are labels, points in the execution chain to which to branch when a match is found. Execution resumes at this point and continues to the end of the switch unless the switch is exited. This can be done with a break statement. In the above example, the *exit( )* statement could have been used in place of break, because program termination occurs anyway after the appropriate printf( ) function is executed. However, the break allows the switch to be exited and the program to continue if further lines are available for execution.

The default label is like the *else* portion of the previous program. The program lines that fall beneath this label are executed when switch can find no match.

The following program also uses switch:

```
main()
{

    int x;

    scanf("%d", &x);

    switch(x) {
    case 1:
    case 2:
    case 3:
    case 4:
    case 5:
            printf("Value is 1 to 5\n");
            break;
    default:
            printf("Value is not between 1 and 5\n");
            break;

}
```

This program prints one screen message if the value of x is between one and five, and another if it is other than five. If the input value is one, then case one is the branch-to label. All statements from this point on down the switch are executed.

Because the other cases have no program statements associated with them, the execution chain falls on the first printf( ) function. When this is executed, the next statement is the break. This causes the switch to be exited. If the input value is not in the range of one to five, then the default label is branched to. The break statement associated with default is not necessary in this particular usage, but it is a good idea to get in the habit of placing specific breaks in a switch at the points where execution is to be suspended. This habit can avoid unpleasant debugging operations in the future.

The switch statement is simply a formatted *goto* routine, branching to the appropriate label when a true condition is found in the comparison of the switch value and the case constant or expression. Again, arguments to switch must evaluate to integers, and case must be supplied with an integer or character constant or constant expression.

Switch is a very powerful statement in C, especially when it is necessary to compare a long series of values and branch to various program segments accordingly. This statement has the capability of presenting very complex branches in a format that is easily understood.

INCREMENT/DECREMENT OPERATORS

C language offers two very useful operators that will increment or decrement an integer value by one. The increment operator (+ +) and the decrement operator (– –) may be used before or after a variable, depending on how you wish the change to occur. When it is necessary to increase the value of a variable by one, this can be accomplished in several ways in C.

In BASIC, an increment might be written as follows:

```
X = X + 1
```

This can be done in C as well, and it's perfectly legal. However, there is another way to accomplish the same thing that is easier and just as expressive. The increment operator (+ +) may be used to increase the value of a variable by one or decrease it by one. Further, the point at which the value is actually changed can be controlled, and depends on whether these operators precede or follow the variable.

These operators are quite easy to use, as in this statement:

```
++x;
```

which increases the value of x by one. This is exactly the same as the following:

```
x = x + 1;
```

However, this latter method takes longer to type, and can be more confusing than the first method when a lot of operators and other complex math constructs are involved.

This example of the incremental operator has used it preceding the variable, but this usage could just have easily have been x + +; which would do the same thing. However, when increment operators are used in assignments, the difference in the two placements is critical. The following program demonstrates this clearly:

```
main()
{

    int x, y;

    x = 0;
    y = ++x;

    printf("%d    %d\n", y, x);

    y = x++;
    printf("%d    %d\n", y, x);

}
```

This program will display:

```
1    1
1    2
```

This might come as a surprise, because some newcomers to C would expect y to be equal to two during the second screen write. This is not the case, however, because the increment operator trailed x in the second assignment to y. The assignment y = + +x; first increments x and then hands the value to y. However, y = x+ +; works differently. Here, y is assigned the value of x, and then x is incremented by one. In both types of assignments, x is incremented by one. However, when the increment operator precedes the variable, the value is incremented before any assignment takes place. When the operator follows the variable, its value is used and then the incrementation takes place. Therefore y = + +x; is exactly like y = x + 1;. However, y = x+ +; is the same as the following:

$$y = x;$$
$$x = x + 1;$$

The decrement operator works in the same manner, except the value in the variable is decreased by one. When the decrement operator precedes the variable, the decrease takes place before the value is used. If it follows the variable, the decrease takes place after the value is used.

The increment/decrement operators form a very powerful and useful set of tools in C. Often, these operators are used to count through the various character positions in a char array as many of the examples on text handling in this book illustrate.

COMPRESSED FORM ARITHMETIC

Just as the increment and decrement operators offer easy and expressive methods of accomplishing arithmetic increases and decreases in C, there is a compressed form of arithmetic that offers similar advantages. The expression x = x + 1; is best written as + +x;. However, when expressions run to

Table 6-1. The Compressed and Standard Forms of Arithmetic Notation in C.

Standard	Compressed
x = x − 16	x − = 16
x = x * y	x * = y
x = x / (y / z)	x /= y / z
x = x << 16	x << = 16

increments or decrements of more than one, a new form of notation becomes necessary.

The compressed form of writing x = x + 2; is x + = 2;. This means the same as the previous expression, and, although it might look quite strange at first, it is a commonly seen construct in C.

Table 6-1 shows some other compressed forms and their equivalencies. The compressed form of arithmetic notation in C is often seen. It is a highly convenient and expressive way to handle arithmetic assignments and expressions.

A common example of this form of notation is found in *for* loops that increment or decrement a loop variable by more or less than one:

```
main()
{

    int x;

    for (x = 0; x <= 24; x += 2)
        printf("%d\n", x);

}
```

This loop counts from zero to 24 in steps of two. The expression x + = 2 is exactly the same as x = x + 2.

THE METHODS OF EXPRESSION

C is a language of shortcuts, which is another way of saying that C is a highly expressive language. The methods of expression can be simple, or they can be complex, elaborate, and combinatorial. The following program will begin this discussion:

```
main()
{

    char a[200];

    gets(a);

    while (strcmp(a, "END") != 0) {
        printf("%s\n", a);
```

123

```
            gets(a);
    }

  }
```

This pleasant little program is short and simple. As the program opens, the *gets( )* function is used to retrieve character string a from the keyboard. A *while* loop is entered that writes the value of a to the screen and then calls gets( ) again. The loop continues to cycle, displaying the keyboard input until this input is equal to "END". The strcmp( ) function within the loop returns a value of zero when the contents of the string, a, match the second argument, "END". This is the condition under which the loop exit takes place.

This program can also be written in a slightly shorter form, as in the following:

```
main()
{

    char a[200];

    while (strcmp(gets(a), "END"))
        puts(a);

}
```

This program is shorter, but it might be harder to decipher, especially by beginning C programmers. The difficulty lies within the *while* loop. To begin with, this loop is testing for a condition of true or false. As long as a condition is true, the loop cycles. When it is false, the loop terminates.

Mathematically speaking, a true condition evaluates to nonzero. A false condition evaluates to zero. The strcmp( ) function returns a value of zero when a match occurs. This, to the *while* statement, evaluates to false, and the loop is exited. The same function evaluates to nonzero when no match occurs. This is evaluated by *while* as true. Therefore, it is redundant to write:

```
while (strcmp(gets(a), "END") != 0)
```

because *while* makes this evaluation anyway. If you want to exit a *while* loop based upon a loop variable or expression being equal to zero, then you don't have to express this directly. The loop is automatically testing for a zero evaluation and will exit upon this condition.

Another aspect of this program that might confuse the beginner is the argument arrangement within strcmp( ). This is simple. Strcmp( ) requires two string pointers for arguments so that it can compare, on a character-by-character basis, the contents at each memory location. This is exactly what this example of strcmp( ) has been handed in the way of arguments. The gets( ) function in C returns a pointer to the retrieved string. Therefore, gets(a) evaluates to the pointer to the string just typed from the keyboard.

When functions are embedded within other functions, as is the case here, the innermost function is executed first. Therefore, gets(a) is executed and returns a pointer to the retrieved string to strcmp( ). This function compares the pointer with "END", its second argument. This is a constant expression which is as legal as a string pointer.

This method of embedding functions within functions can be confusing at first, but after an understanding is gained as to the types of values that are returned by various functions, one begins to gain a good grasp of what is taking place.

FOR LOOPS

A looping mechanism that is frequently used in C is the *for* loop, although loops may also be created with the *while* and the *do-while* statements. *For* loops are usually written in the following format:

for (starting value; termination value; increment value)

The following programs show this usage of the *for* loop:

```
main()
{

    int x;

    for (x = 0; x <= 10; ++x)
        printf("%d\n", x);


}
```

This program will display the following on the monitor screen:

```
1
2
3
4
5
6
7
8
9
10
```

It is important to understand that the *for* statement offers a convenient format in which to place the contents of a sequence that is to be executed over and over again, until a certain exit value is reached. The *for* loop in the above program is simply a branching construct that is equivalent to this:

```
            x = 0;
    TOP:
            if (!(x <= 10))
                break;

            printf("%d\n", x);
            goto TOP;
```

This is about what the *for* loop equates to in C. Note that the NOT operator (represented by !) is used in the statement if (!(x < = 10)), which means the same as if (x != 10 ¦¦ x > 10).

Specifically, the NOT operator makes this conditional test mean: if x is NOT less than or equal to 10, then break. From an earlier discussion, it was learned that such a test can end in only two possible outcomes, true or false. A zero return is the same as false. Use of the NOT relational operator reverses true and false. In other words, while the expression x < = 10 is true, the NOT operator causes the *if* statement evaluation to be false. Therefore, the break statement is not executed. When x reaches a value of 11, the expression is false, but the NOT operator causes it to be evaluated as true. In other words, NOT true is false, and NOT false is true.

Because of the way the *for* statement is constructed, the original program that started this discussion could have been written as:

```
    main()
    {

        int x;

        for (x = 0; x <= 10; printf("%d\n", x), ++x)
            ;

    }
```

This sort of shortcut is not used very often, but sometimes it is, and you should be aware of just what is taking place. As was the case with the conditional expression, when a comma is used with more than one program statement in an evaluation, it separates program statements used within the *for* statement.

Here's another example of a program that can be written several different ways:

```
    main()
    {

        int x, y;

        y = 10;

        for (x = 0; x <= 10; ++x) {
            printf("%d  %d\n", x, y);
            --y;
        }

    }
```

126

This program will display:

```
 0 10
 1  9
 2  8
 3  7
 4  6
 5  5
 6  4
 7  3
 8  2
 9  1
10  0
```

As the value of x increases, the value of y decreases. This same program could also be written as:

```
main()
{

        int x, y;

        for (x = 0, y = 10; x <= 10; ++x, --y)
            printf("%d  %d\n", x, y);

}
```

or even as:

```
main()
{

    int x, y;

    for (x = 0, y = 10; x <= 10; printf("%d  %d\n", x, y), ++x, --y)
        ;

}
```

This last example is, in my opinion, stretching a good thing too far. The idea is to use the expressive powers of C to write programs that are compact, but not impossible to decipher. The example prior to this last one, though, is quite expressive and in good programming taste. It is the equivalent of:

```
        x = 0;
        y = 10;
TOP:
        if (!(x <= 10))
            break;
```

```
printf("%d  %d\n", x, y);
++x;
--y;
goto TOP;
```

You can supply as many starting values as you wish and insert as many statements in the body as well. The body is represented by the "slot" in the *for* loop arrangement where the increments or decrements take place. You can even have more than one termination expression as in:

```
for (x = 0, y = 10; x < 11, y > 5; ++x, --y)
```

and this is perfectly legal. When there is more than one termination expression, the loop will exit on the one which proves false first. In the above example, the loop will terminate when y is counted down to 5. This means that y is no longer more than 5 and the loop is exited.

SUMMARY

The C programming language is extremely versatile in the tools it provides programmers to accomplish any task. As you gain experience with this language, your source code will tend to get more succinct. This is a boon to the programmer/author, but it is this capability that tends to discourage many beginners, because such code is not simplistically clear. However, when an effort is made to understand these alternate coding methods, the beginner soon sees that these shortcuts are clearly decipherable, and that they are one of the finest features of the C programming language.

Chapter 7

Turbo C Programs

This chapter offers a myriad of C programs and functions that are designed to be instructional and, in many cases, useful for other programming applications. Many of these program listings have been taken from courses that I teach on programming in C and come highly recommended by the students who attend these courses. The beginning C programmer might find some of these examples beyond his or her immediate comprehension, but eventually these will become more decipherable as experience is gained.

Most program examples in this chapter are purposely devoid of comment lines. Although one or two comment lines in a program often aid comprehension, a listing that is literally inundated by comment lines tends to become a mass of confusion. This is due, simply, to the quantity of material included. Thus, the defined programming blocks that can be so expressive in C tend to be hidden in the confusion. However, the appendices of this text contain each of the programs discussed in this chapter with full comment line insertion.

To make the best use of this chapter, try looking first at the programs as presented and read the description that is included in the text. If you still have questions about the operation of a program, look it up in the appendices and note the comment line that is provided within the portion you are having difficulty with. This "double listing" method of referencing each program should be helpful both to those who are beginning to learn C and those who are already relatively experienced in this language.

Several of the functions discussed in this section were taken directly from the CBREEZE Tutorial Translator software, which is a copyrighted product of Robert J. Traister & Associates in Front Royal, VA. All such functions are identified and used with permission.

STRING FUNCTIONS

This discussion concerns four C language functions that emulate the substring functions LEFT$, RIGHT$, and MID$, and the MID$ statement, in MS-BASIC. Put simply, the BASIC functions return a portion of their string argument as another string. The portion returned depends upon the numeric arguments provided.

Left$

The LEFT$ function in BASIC returns the leftmost characters in a string argument. The number of characters are determined by its second argument. Therefore the following statement:

LEFT$("COMPUTER",4)

would return this substring:

COMP

which consists of the left four characters in the original string argument.

There is no standard function in C that will perform this operation. Therefore, the programmer who needs such a function must write one from those functions and statements already included in the language. The following C function is one way of performing this task:

```
left(a, b, x)
char *a, *b;
int x;
{
        int i = 0;
        x = (x <= strlen(b) ? x : strlen(b);

        while (i++ < x)
            *a++ = *b++;

            *a = '\0';

}
```

This simple function is more aligned with the C language method of performing string manipulations. Instead of returning a pointer to a new string, it writes the new string to the memory location pointed to by a, which is a char pointer. This means that the variable that will hold the substring will be the first argument to left( ), the string from which the substring is to be taken

130

will be the second argument, and the third argument will be an integer that specifies the number of characters that are to be in the substring.

Note that the conditional expression is used to make certain that variable x, which is the value of the total number of characters to be contained in the substring, is not larger than the total number of characters in the source string. In other words, if left( ) is told to return the first 14 characters in "COMPUTER", the value of 14 will be reduced to eight, which is the maximum number of characters in the source string. Just like the BASIC function, this C language version will write a substring which is identical to the source string if the character number argument is equal to or more than the total number of characters in the source string.

The left( ) function is quite simple. Only one internal variable is used, i. This is initially set to zero. Note that a and b have been declared char pointers in this function, although they could just as easily have been declared char arrays. The value of i is used in a *while* loop which continues to cycle until i is equal to x.

On the first pass of the loop, the first character in b is copied to the memory location pointed to by a. This is accomplished using the unary operator (represented by *). The trailing increment operator (represented by + +) is also used, so the pointer to the source string and the pointer to the substring is advanced by one character position on each loop pass. This method allows the first character in b to be copied to the first character position in a, then the second character in b is copied to the second character position in a. This process continues until the loop times out. The time out occurs when x characters have been written into a. Notice that the termination clause in the *while* loop also increments i. This variable starts out with a value of zero, but is immediately incremented to one in the *while* loop.

Another way of writing this function would involve the use of char arrays instead of char pointers. The following listing demonstrates this principle:

```
left(a, b, x)
char a[], b[];
int x;
{

    int i = 0;

    while ((a[i] = b[i++]) && i < x)
        ;

    a[i] = '\0';

}
```

This function is just as simple as the previous version. It isn't necessary to make certain that x is not larger than the total character count in b, because the assignment line a[i] = b[i ++] is a part of the termination clause in the *while* loop, as opposed to a program statement that is executed as a part of the loop.

When a[i] is equal to '\0', the terminating character in b, the loop will automatically terminate.

When the loop is exited, the next character position in a is assigned the null character (\0), and the function is exited.

This next example would be the one to use if you wanted a function that would actually return a pointer to a string (as LEFT$ does in BASIC). Such a function would be written as:

```
char *left(b, x)
char b[];
int x;
{

    char a[250];
    int i = 0;

    while ((a[i] = b[i++]) && i < x)
        ;

    a[i] = '\0';

    return(a);

}
```

This function is just like the previous example, except that a is an internal char array (declared within the function body and not a part of the argument list). The substring contents of b are written to a as before, but when the write is complete, the return( ) statement is used to pass a pointer to the contents of a back to the calling program.

While some C functions return char pointers, this is often not the preferred way of handling operations similar to the left( ) function under discussion. The reason for this lies in the fact that the internal declaration of char array a requires that a limit be placed on the size of the substring that can be handled. Here, a is declared with an arbitrary size of 250 characters.

Assuming that this function is to be written once and then used over and over in many different programs, a real problem could occur. Because the programmer no longer controls the size of a (as he or she would if it were a passed program variable), any substring larger than 249 printable characters would cause a memory overwrite. On the other hand, small substrings would be handled perfectly, but the function would then be setting aside far more memory than necessary. This is a waste that could unnecessarily use up all available memory (and more) in programs that are "knocking at the door" of exceeding the available RAM.

All of these problems are overcome when the function is written in the manner of the first two examples. In these, the programmer determines the size of the array that is to receive the substring. This permits direct control over memory usage.

Of course, this last function could always be edited by the programmer to allow larger substrings to be safely contained. However, this voids many of the advantages of a function. After all, the same function might be called several times in one program to handle strings of different sizes. Any changes to the function would be reflected in all calls. Again, the first two examples show the preferred way of handling these operations, and all other similar functions discussed in this chapter will follow this lead.

Right$

Emulating the operation of the LEFT$ function was quite simple for several reasons, the main one being that the substring always begins with the leftmost character in the source string. It is simply a matter of copying characters from the source string until the correct number have been written. Emulating the operation of the RIGHT$ function adds another element of complexity. In BA-SIC, this function is used to retrieve the rightmost characters from a source string. The integer argument supplied to this function indicates the rightmost characters to be written. The added complexity involves locating the proper starting character in the string so that when this and all characters to its right are written, the number specified in the argument is satisfied.

The following function shows a method by which this operation may be written in C:

```
right(a, b, x)
char *a, *b;
int x;
{

    int i, l;

    l = strlen(b);
    x = (x > l) ? l : x;
    i = l - x;

    while (*a++ = *(b + i++))
        ;


}
```

The added complexity here is in properly identifying the starting character position in b to read. This is done by subtracting the number of characters in b (strlen(b)) from x, which is the total number of characters to write to the substring. The conditional expression assures that x is not larger than the total length of the source string.

The *while* loop counts through character positions in a, starting at position zero. To these memory areas are assigned the characters in b, starting at offset i. On each pass of the loop, the value of i is incremented by one, therefore, the next character in b is assigned to the next character position in a. This continues up to and including the null character ($\setminus$0), which is also copied to a. This character causes the loop to terminate. Remember, the termination clause is a conditional expression of sorts. In C, the line while (*a = *b) means the same as while ((*a = *b) != '\0'). The loop will cycle as long as the value of the expression is not zero. When it is zero, termination is immediate. In the second line shown here, the null character in the conditional expression is redundant.

When the loop is exited, the rightmost x contents of b have been written to a. Because the null character at the end of b was also copied to a, it's not necessary to assign that character in a different operation. The string a is already properly terminated.

In the LEFT$ emulation, successive characters were read and copied from the beginning of the source string to a specified point within this string. The RIGHT$ emulation reads and copies characters from a specified point within the source string to the end of the string. Calculating the "entrance" point adds a little more complexity to the right( ) function, but the looping mechanism is simpler and the null character is automatically copied from the source string.

Mid$

In BASIC, the MID$ function extracts any substring from a source string. Given the proper arguments, MID$ will operate identically to either LEFT$ or RIGHT$. With MID$, the beginning point and the ending point of the substring within the source string are specified in this function's arguments. The C language emulation of this function is a bit more complex than either of the previous two examples:

```
mid(a, b, x, y)
char *a, *b;
int x, y;
{
        int l;

        --x;
        y += x;
        l = strlen(b);

        while (x < y && x <= l)
            *a++ = *(b + x++);

        *a = '\0';

}
```

This function requires four arguments. The first two are pointers to the target string and the source string. The next argument is an integer value that specifies the beginning substring character position. The last argument specifies the number of characters in the substring.

The beginning character argument(x) is given as the character position itself. In other words, if x was equal to four and the target string was equal to "COMPUTER", then the fourth character would be P. Again, the x argument specifies character position in relationship to the other characters in the string. It does not specify the array position or the offset of that character in memory. The offset of the P in COMPUTER would be three, because the first character is an offset zero.

For this reason, x is decremented by one in this function. An internal integer variable, l, is assigned the character length of the b, the source string. The value of y, which gives the total number of characters in the substring, is changed to its original value plus the current value of x. Can you see what has taken place with the two integer arguments? Each has been translated from a character count value to its equivalent array offset value. Each now specifies the starting position within the array to start reading and copying characters and to stop this process.

From here on the job is simple. A *while* loop is used to count x through the specified character positions. On each pass, one character from b is copied to a. Notice that the write to a begins at offset zero, while the read from b begins at offset $0 + x$. The loop exit mechanism also checks for the length of the source string being exceeded by some erroneous argument.

When the loop is exited, the null character is tacked on to the end of a, creating a true string. The function is exited and the substring now resides at the memory location pointed to by a.

Mid$ Statement

All of the emulations to this point have concerned BASIC functions. However, BASIC also offers the MID$ statement, which writes a substring into a source string instead of returning a substring from the source string. The C function that emulates this BASIC statement is quite similar to the mid( ) function just discussed:

```
mids(a, x, y, b)
int x, y;
char *a, *b;
{

        int l;

        l = strlen(a) - 1;
        y += x;
        --x;

        while (x <= y && x <= l && *b != '\0')
            *(a + x++) = *b++;

}
```

Note that l is made equal to one less than the string length of a. This is to avoid the possibility of making the source string longer due to an improper argument value. In this function, a is the source string that is to have a substring written into it, starting at character x. The substring will be y characters long and is contained in b.

As before, x and y are converted to offsets within the string. The *while* loop works as before, although there is an additional exit clause that causes immediate termination when *b is equal to the null character. This is a signal that the end of the substring has been reached. It also prevents overwrites when improper integer arguments are handed to this function.

It is not necessary to terminate a with the null character, because this was a properly terminated string to begin with, and it is no longer than it was originally. The same null character that was present when a was used as the argument to mids( ) is still present after the substring has been inserted.

Using the four functions discussed to this point is simply a matter of including their source code in programs that call them. You might even wish to combine all four of the string functions into one file called bstring.c, for instance. The following program uses each of the string functions:

```
#include <bstring.c>
main()
{

        char a[80], b[80], c[80], d[80];

        strcpy(a, "MICROCOMPUTER");
        left(b, a, 5);
        right(c, a, 8);
        mid(d, a, 6, 4);

        printf("%s %s %s %s\n", a, b, c, d);

        mids(a, 1, 5, "MINI-");

        printf("%s\n", a);

}
```

When compiled and run under Turbo C, this program will display:

```
MICROCOMPUTER MICRO COMPUTER COMP
MINI-COMPUTER
```

Functions such as these can be written in several other ways, but all of these should be very efficient and easy to understand. The Turbo C compiler contains a large assortment of string handling functions that are discussed elsewhere in this text. The functions outlined in this chapter are those that are not a part of the standard C language function set, nor are they included in most supersets. They are, however, quite useful in many programming applications.

The next two string handling functions are "fun" functions, designed to teach various methods of character manipulation within a string. Both of these functions have equivalents in the Turbo C function set, but the examples here allow the reader to see the source code and understand how these other functions are designed.

Reverse( )

The reverse( ) function manipulates the characters in a string so that they are in reverse order. This function is already available in Turbo C under the name of strrev( ), and source code for such a function has been discussed elsewhere in this text. The following function does the same as this other, but it provides an alternate method of accomplishing this reversal.

It makes an interesting study in that it uses a *for* loop instead of the *while* loops that have been used in most examples in this chapter. The source code for reverse( ) follows:

```
reverse(a)
char a[];
{

    char temp[250];
    int x, y;

    for (x = strlen(a) - 1, y = 0; x >= 0; --x, ++y)
        temp[y] = a[x];

    temp[y] = '\0';
    strcpy(a, temp);
}
```

This function accomplishes most of the work inside the body of the *for* loop, which is handed multiple arguments. Both x and y are assigned values at the loop opening. Variable x will be used to count backward through a (from right to left) and is assigned the value of strlen(b) − 1. This converts x to the character offset value in a (i.e., x is now equal to the offset of the last character in a). On the other hand, y will be used to count upward from zero in order to access the sequential character position in temp. The latter is an array that will temporarily hold the reversed characters of a. The loop terminating clause is x > = 0.

On each pass of the loop, x is decreased by one. When this value falls through zero to − 1, the loop terminates. Due to the multiple arguments to the "stepping" portion of the *for* loop, as x is decreased by one, y is increased by the same amount. This is exactly what we are looking for; a is being counted down from right to left while temp is being counted up from left to right.

On each loop pass, the character read from a is copied to temp. When the loop is exited, the reversal is complete, except for the null character that must be placed at the end of temp. This array now contains a string that is the reverse of a.

However, a is still equal to its original value, because its characters were simply read and copied. Their order in a has not been changed at all. The purpose of the reverse( ) function is to actually change the character order by rewriting its argument string. To accomplish this final task, the contents of temp are simply copied to a using strcpy( ). Now, a has been permanently changed to the reverse of what it was before being passed to this function. I have said that the change is permanent, but it is not too permanent. If you want to change the string back to the way it was, simply pass the reverse string through the function once more and you're back to square one.

Space( )

All of the string functions discussed to this point in this chapter have not altered the size of the argument string. The next function does increase the size of its string argument, therefore it is mandatory that the char array argument (or initialized char pointer) be of adequate size to hold the expanded string. The space( ) function simply inserts spaces after every letter in the original string:

```
space(b)
char b[];
{

        char a[250];
        int x, y;

        x = y = 0;

        while (a[x++] = b[y++])
             a[x++] = ' ';

        strcpy(b, a);

}
```

When the string, "COMPUTER", is passed through this function, it is changed to:

C O M P U T E R

The string, which was originally nine characters long (including the null), is now 18 characters long. A space has been inserted after each of the visible characters. There is even a space between the 'R' and the invisible null character. In all cases, the size of the string will be doubled. Therefore, the array that serves as the argument to this function must be declared to contain at least double the character count of the original argument.

A temporary storage array, a, is declared within the function. Integer variables x and y are initially set to zero. A *while* loop copies characters from b into a. After each character is copied, a space is inserted, and x is incremented again. Every time y is incremented by one, x is incremented by two. When the null character is copied, the expression evaluates to zero and the loop terminates. Because the null character is copied from b, no separate assignment is necessary. Char a now contains a null-terminated string. The last step involves copying a to b, the latter being the initial argument.

What practical value does this function have? Little, if any. It is just an exercise to demonstrate the various manipulations that are often conducted on strings in C.

This function could also have been written using a *for* loop, as in:

```
space(b)
char b[];
{

    char a[250];
    int x, y;

    for (x = 0, y = 0; a[x] = b[y]; ++x, ++y)
        a[++x] = ' ';

    strcpy(b, a);

}
```

Again, a *for* loop is used with multiple statements that initialize x and y to a value of zero, assign a[x] the character in b[y], and increment x and y by one on each pass. Another statement within the loop body adds the space character and increments x again.

Notice that the increment operator (+ +) precedes the variable name when the space is assigned to a. This means that the variable is incremented first, then the assignment is made. The loop mechanism will not increment x on its own until all loop statements have been executed. Therefore, x is incremented first by the loop statement, a[+ +x] = b[y], and then again when the loop recycles.

STRING/MATH FUNCTIONS

This next series of functions interfaces math and string operations. One function converts an integer quantity to its Roman numeral equivalent, while another converts a Roman numeral string to its decimal equivalent. The Turbo C compiler already offers a host of functions that will convert various numeric quantities to their string equivalencies and vice versa. The functions discussed in this section, however, are of a much more specialized nature, and provide an excellent tutorial.

Roman( )

The roman( ) function accepts an integer value of 0 to 3999 as its argument. This value is then converted to its Roman numeral equivalent, which is returned as a string. The argument value must be held to less than 4000, because at this value and above, the Roman numeral characters used for designating such values are unusual and not contained in the computer's character set.

The source code for this function looks a bit complex, but a close examination reveals that it is straightforward programming:

```
char *roman(d)
int d;
{

    int y;
    char temp[100], roman[100];

    static int dec[] = {1000, 900, 500, 400, 100 },
                       {90, 50, 40, 10, 9, 5, 4, 1 };
    static char *rom[] = { "M", "CM", "D", "CD", "C", "XC", "L" },
                         { "XL", "X", "IX", "V", "IV", "I" };

    y = 0;
    temp[0] = '\0';
    roman[0] = '\0';

    if (d > 3999 || d < 1)
        return("ERROR");

    while (y < 13) {
        while ((d - dec[y]) >= 0) {
            strcat(temp, rom[y]);
            d -= dec[y];
        }

        strcat(roman, temp);
        strcpy(temp, "\0");
        ++y;
    }

    return(roman);

}
```

Of immediate importance in understanding this function are the two *static char* arrays. The first one, dec, contains the 13 decimal number combinations that match the equivalent designations in Roman numerals. These latter characters are found in the second static char array, named rom. The two arrays form a perfect match of elements, with the first using decimal designations and the second using Roman numerals. For instance, 1000 decimal is the same as M in Roman numerals. Each element in one array is the conversion equivalent of the same element in the other array.

Below 1000, the next Roman numeral step would be 900, represented by the combination CM. Again, both values match in the arrays, which act as *conversion look-up tables*. This matching continues down to, and includes, the decimal value of 1. Again, at decimal 4000 and above, the Roman numeral character set is not contained within the computer's character set, although any decimal value can be handled if you are willing to substitute other characters contained within the computer's set for the true Roman numeral characters.

Two other arrays (called *auto arrays*) are found in this function. The first is temp, which provides temporary storage of discrete elements of the final Roman numeral value to be returned. (More about this later.) The other auto array is roman. The various elements of temp will be concatenated to this array, building the entire Roman numeral value that will be returned by this function as a string.

Initially, each of these arrays is assigned a value of '\ 0', the null character. In other words, the first element (offset zero) in each array is assigned the null character. This is absolutely mandatory, because this function will concatenate information to these arrays using strcat( ), which reads the target string until it detects the null character. This character is then replaced with the source string, which serves as the second argument to strcat( ).

Because both *temp* and *roman* start out as empty arrays, it is mandatory that their first elements be '\ 0'. This produces what is known as a *null string*. Strcat( ) will read this null character and use its position for placement of its source string. Therefore, when strcat( ) initially concatenates to either of these variables, it is really like a strcpy( ) operation. However, strcat( ) will be used many times to build the Roman numeral string. On each successive use, strcpy( ) adds its source strings to the end of the string already contained in each array.

Before the function executes further, a conditional test is made to check d, the decimal argument to roman( ), to make certain it is within the range of 0 to 3999. If not, this function is exited, returning the string "ERROR". If everything is alright to this point, the process of building the Roman numeral string begins.

A *while* loop is entered that allows all 13 values from each static char array to be accessed. It is in this loop that most of the work is done. Again, dec holds 13 decimal values, and rom holds the 13 matching Roman numeral equivalencies. On each pass of the outside *while* loop, a nested *while* loop subtracts the current element in dec from the decimal argument to the function in d. If the difference is more than or equal to zero, then it means that the value contained in dec is a part of the decimal argument. Therefore, the matching Roman numeral element in rom is concatenated to temp. The inner *while* loop continues to cycle until the referenced decimal element in dec can no longer be subtracted from the decimal argument without falling over into negative values.

To provide a more graphic explanation, assume that the decimal argument to this function is 3100. On the first pass of the inner *while* loop, dec[y] is equal to 1000. This value is subtracted from d, which is equal to 3100. The difference is greater than zero, so rom[y] is concatenated to temp. This is the Roman numeral M, which is 1000. Then the value of d is changed to 2100, and the inner loop cycles again. On this pass, 1000 is again subtracted, and again the result is more than or equal to zero. Again, rom[y] is concatenated to temp. The value in d is reduced to 1100, and the loop recycles. This time the difference is 100, which is still acceptable, and another M is concatenated to temp. But on the next loop cycle, the difference is less than zero (−900). This causes the inner loop to terminate, and the contents of temp are concatenated to the variable named roman.

At this point, we know that the Roman numeral equivalent of decimal 3100 will be composed of three "M" characters. However, there's more. The outer *while* loop hasn't been exited yet. On the next pass, y is incremented by one, so the decimal value in dec[y] is now 900. However, when this value is subtracted from the present value of d (100), a negative value results, so the inner loop terminates without doing anything more. This means there is no 900 element present in the decimal value.

On the next pass of the outer loop, the next element in dec is accessed with the same results. This process continues over and over until the value of dec[y] is 100. This causes a difference of zero or more, and the C, representing 100, is concatenated to temp. On the next pass of the inner loop, a negative difference results, so the inner loop is exited, and the C is concatenated to the end of "MMM," which was previously written to roman.

The *while* loops will test the remaining values in the static arrays, but will come up with nothing, because there is no longer any numeric content in d (other than zero, of course). When the outer loop finally terminates, the string contained in roman is returned to the calling program. This string equals MMMC, the Roman numeral designation for 3100.

This is a very interesting exercise in building a string via a step-by-step procedure, interfacing this process with a step-by-step mathematical procedure. This type of operation is quite prevalent where string and number interfacing is a requirement.

The above function can be contained in a file named roman.c and called in the following manner:

```
#include <roman.c>
main
{

        char *roman();
        int x;

        x = 3100;

        printf("%s\n", roman(x));

}
```

Notice that roman( ) is declared a *char pointer* within the calling program. This tells the program to expect roman( ) to return a pointer to a string. This is required in C language when functions return other than integer values. The function serves as an argument to printf( ), although a char array could also have been declared and the value returned by roman( ) copied to this array using strcpy( ). Note that the argument to roman( ) is the int variable x. This could also have been the constant 3100. When this program is executed, the string "MMMC" will appear on the monitor screen.

Rom2dec( )

While the previous function converted a decimal value to its Roman numeral string equivalent, this next exercise does just the opposite. It accepts as its argument a Roman numeral string value, and returns the decimal equivalent. Using this function, you could easily convert "MMMC" back to decimal 3100 again. The source code for rom2dec( ) follows:

```c
rom2dec(rn)
char rn[];
{

    int x, y, l, ret;
    char temp[3], roman[20];

    static int dec1[] = { 900, 400, 90, 40, 9, 4 };
    static int dec2[] = {1000, 500, 100, 50, 10, 5, 1 };
    static char *rom1[] = { "CM", "CD", "XC", "XL", "IX", "IV" };
    static int rom2[] = { 'M', 'D', 'C', 'L', 'X', 'V', 'I' };

    strcpy(roman, rn);
    l = strlen(roman);
    ret = 0;

    for (x = 0; x < l; x += 2) {
        sprintf(temp, "%c%c", roman[x], roman[x + 1]);
            for (y = 0; y <= 5; ++y)
                if (strcmp(temp, rom1[y]) == 0) {
                    roman[x] = ' ';
                    roman[x + 1] = ' ';
                    ret += dec1[y];
                }

    }

    for (x = 0; x < l; ++x) {
        if (roman[x] == ' ')
            continue;

        for (y = 0; y <= 6; ++y)
            if (roman[x] == rom2[y])
                ret += dec2[y];
    }

    return(ret);

}
```

This function involves a bit more complexity than the previous example, but again, a thorough study of the source code on a step-by-step basis should clear up any misunderstandings.

While the last function used two static arrays, this one uses four. Three are int arrays, and the fourth is an array of char pointers as was the case with rom in the previous function. It is necessary to use an array of char pointers when string quantities are represented. Therefore, rom1 in this function returns pointers to the constants contained within its braces. Note that each constant consists of more than one character. This is the reason why the array must be declared an array of pointers. The rom2 array also represents character information, but this is in terms of characters, not strings. For this reason, it has been declared an int array.

Each constant is expressed within single quotes. This array could also have been declared a char type with the same results. As a matter of fact, a char array would have conserved more memory space, but this example serves to stress once again that char values may be expressed as the character itself or as an integer between 0 and 255.

The two other static array, dec1 and dec2, contain the decimal equivalents of the Roman numeral values found in rom1 and rom2. As with the previous function, the decimal arrays match the Roman numeral arrays.

After the initialization process, the content of the function argument, rn, is copied to the internal array, roman. This function must alter the contents of the Roman numeral string, so the original argument is copied to this second array. In this manner, all changes are made to the copy, thus preserving the original argument. Next, the variable l is assigned a value which corresponds to the number of characters in the string argument to this function. A *for* then enters the picture, counting from zero to one less than the value in l. This means that x corresponds to the array offset position of each character in the function argument.

Within the *for* loop, the sprintf( ) function writes a string to temp that consists of the first two characters in the argument. The strcmp( ) function then compares the two character string in temp with all of the strings in rom1. This comparison takes place within the body of a nested *for* loop.

If a match is found, several things take place. First, the two characters in roman that matched a string in rom1 are replaced with space characters, ' '. (A space character is the character written to the screen when you press the space bar on your keyboard.) Remember, this character, although invisible as such, is a true character (ASCII 32) with just as much value as any other character. It is not "nothing."

Next, the value of variable ret, which was initially set at zero, is incremented by itself plus the value in dec[y]. The latter is the decimal value that corresponds to the Roman numeral value that was matched in rom1[y]. As with the previous function, the offsets into the Roman numeral array and the decimal array match in value. Therefore, rom1[y] is the same value as dec1[y], although each is expressed in a different number system.

The loops continue to cycle until all double-character values have been accessed. When loop termination occurs, any double-character Roman numeral matches in the copy of the argument string have been matched, ret has been incremented accordingly, and those matching numerals in the copy of the argument have been "erased" by replacing them with spaces.

The next sequence involves repeating of the above procedure, except in this mode, all remaining single-character Roman numeral designations are read. These characters are found in rom2, and their corresponding decimal values are in dec2. The value now found in roman is equal to the original argument string less the double character matches that were overwritten with space characters in the preceding operation.

The current *for* loop sequence consists of a nested loop. The characters in roman are accessed, and all spaces are passed over. When a character other than the space is encountered, the second *for* loop is entered. It counts from zero to six, thus accessing each of the seven characters in rom2. The *if* statement conditional test looks for a character match. When one occurs, ret is incremented by the decimal equivalent of that character, which is found in dec2. When this last loop is exited, the *return* statement is used to return the decimal value found in ret to the calling program. This value is now equal to the full decimal equivalent of the original Roman numeral string argument.

Both of the functions discussed here have dealt heavily with string/math operations. In one example, a string was built by dissecting a decimal number. In the second, a decimal number was built by dissecting a string. Operations of this type are quite common in C language. These sample functions go a long way toward teaching the differences between character counts (the number of characters in a string) and character offsets (the offset into memory that each character occupies). It is quite easy to confuse the two (i.e., thinking that the first character in a string is written at offset 1 instead of offset 0), but as you work more and more with strings, this becomes less of a problem, though one that is always guarded against.

Banner( )

This next function mimics the UNIX utility, *banner,* which is used to display a short message on the monitor screen in greatly enlarged letters. The function that follows might look quite complex, but it is broken down into three main bodies. The first is the function *banner( )* which accepts a string argument and, eventually, causes it to be displayed in larger letters. However, banner( ) calls two other functions, *bigprint( )* and *dec2bin( ).* The latter converts a decimal number into a binary string of ones and zeros. The other is used to read this data and actually perform the screen write. Thus, this function combines string and numeric operations, and throws in some memory access as well.

You are cautioned in advance to the fact that this function will work only with the IBM PC line of machines, and not with compatibles. However, another function, named banner2( ), will be presented after this one is described that will work on any MS-DOS machine. The source code for banner( ) follows:

```
banner(p)
char p[];
{

        int byte, seg, off, x, y;
        char b[10];

        seg = 0xf000;

        for (x = 0; x <= 7; ++ x) {
                for (y = 0; y <= strlen(p); ++y) {
```

```
                off = 0xfa6e + (p[y] * 8 + x);
                byte = peekb(seg, off);
                dec2bin(b, byte);
                bigprint(b);
                if (y == 8)
                        break;
        }

        printf("\n");

    }

}
dec2bin(c, x)
char c[];
int x;
{

    int a, ct;

    a = 128;
    ct = 0;

    while (a >= 1) {
        if ((x - a) >= 0) {
            c[ct++] = '1';
            x -= a;
        }
        else
            c[ct++] = '0';

        a /= 2;
    }

    c[ct] = '\0';

}
bigprint(a)
char a[];
{

    int x;
    for (x = 0; x <= 7; ++ x) {
        if (a[x] == 49)
            printf("%c", 219);
        else
            printf("%c", 0);
    }

}
```

It is best to study this function by first looking at the functions it calls. The first of these is dec2bin( ), which stands for "decimal to binary." This function converts a decimal integer to its eight-bit binary equivalent, returning this value in the array that makes up its first argument. This means that dec2bin(c, 255) would fill the c array with 11111111, the binary equivalent of 255.

The following source code is for dec2bin( ) only:

```
dec2bin(c, x)
char c[];
int x;
{

    int a, ct;

    a = 128;
    ct = 0;

    while (a >= 1) {
        if ((x - a) >= 0) {
            c[ct++] = '1';
            x -= a;
        }
        else
            c[ct++] = '0';

        a /= 2;
    }

    c[ct] = '\0';

}
```

To convert from a decimal value of zero to 255 to the eight-bit binary equivalent, you must subtract 128, 64, 32, 16, 8, 4, 2, and 1 from the number in eight different operations. If the difference is zero or greater, then this particular bit is said to be "ON". If the value is less than zero, then the bit is "OFF". This function uses one to represent an "ON" bit, and zero for "OFF". Notice that the descending succession of values listed above are arranged so that each is one half of the former.

This function initially assigns the internal variable a value of 128. When the loop is entered, a conditional test is performed to see if the difference of $x - a$ is zero and greater, or less than zero. If the former, then the first element of array c is assigned a value of one. This is the character, and not the number. Variable x is then actually decremented by the value in a. If the difference is less than zero, then '0' (the character) is assigned. Before the loop recycles, the value of a is divided by two. The new value of 64 is subtracted from the (possibly) new value of x. This process continues until x is no longer more than or equal to one. When the loop is exited, a null character is placed at the end of the string of characters in c, making this a properly terminated character string.

It is necessary to have a decimal-to-binary conversion for this function, because the information that makes up the characters in the ROM character set of the IBM PC, XT, AT, etc., is specified in decimal values of zero to 255, eight values to a single character. Each of the eight values indicates which of eight bits are to be turned on or off at the monitor screen. Therefore, each character is composed of eight decimal values that specify eight-bit positions.

This forms an eight-by-eight matrix controlling 64 total bits. Each of the decimal values forms a horizontal line of eight ON and OFF bits. When eight of these lines are stacked, one under the other, the entire character appears.

The banner( ) function serves to amplify the operation your computer uses to display standard characters. While each decimal value from the ROM character set represents only eight bits, or *screen pixels,* the banner( ) program displays each bit as a full character block. This is ASCII 219, a character that is composed of an eight-by-eight matrix of bits that are all ON. Each of the ASCII 219 characters represents a greatly enlarged ON pixel. If the pixel should be OFF, then the null character is displayed. This character is invisible. The end result is a magnified, but exact, duplication of your computer's character set.

The bigprint( ) function receives the binary string argument derived from dec2bin( ), and is listed below:

```
bigprint(a)
char a[];
{

    int x;
    for (x = 0; x <= 7; ++ x) {
        if (a[x] == 49)
            printf("%c", 219);
        else
            printf("%c", 0);
    }


}
```

It then reads each character in this string. When the character is '1', this function prints ASCII 219. If the value is '0' rather than '1', a null is printed. The *if* statement within the *for* loop actually tests for a value of 49, the ASCII value of '1'. Either designation is acceptable, because they are both the same thing.

Notice that the arguments to the printf( ) functions used in bigprint( ) do not contain newline characters (represented by \n). This means that all characters will be printed side-by-side. However, the banner( ) function will print its own newline character after bigprint( ) has completed one line of information. Each eight characters represents one row of pixels in the original character set. Once this row has been displayed, it's time for a new line, so the next row can be displayed.

Finally, we can return to banner( ) itself. The purpose of this function is to access the ROM character set in the IBM PC, XT, AT, etc. This program will not work with most compatibles, because they do not contain the character sets in ROM. Most of these compatibles get their character sets from software. In any event, the ROM character set on IBM machines is found in the eight-bit segment designated, 0xf000. The actual start of the first character in the

148

set is at an offset into this segment of 0xfa6e. This is the start of ASCII 0. ASCII 1 would begin at offset 0xfa6e + 8 into this segment.

A *for* loop is entered, which counts from zero to seven. This is the total number of lines in any ASCII character. The zero represents the top line of bit information, while the seven represents the bottom line. When all eight lines are stacked, a character appears. A nested loop is also entered. This is used to read each of the characters in p, the original string argument to banner( ). Here is where the confusing part comes in.

This function cannot simply read the eight values associated with one character before moving on to the next. It must read the top line of all characters in the string. Then bigprint( ) can print the entire top line of the string. Next, the second bit line of every character in the string is read, and bigprint( ) writes the second line of each to the screen. Assume a string argument to banner( ) contains three characters. Bigprint( ) receives the binary information for the top line of the first character and displays it as a series of blocks (ASCII 219) or nulls, printed side-by-side. Bigprint( ) is exited and the top line of the second character is retrieved within the *for* loop found in banner( ). The dec2bin( ) function converts this to another binary value and this is, again, passed to bigprint( ). This latter function prints another top line of information, this time for the second character. This process is repeated for the third character.

After this, banner( ) causes a newline character to be printed to the screen. Then the process starts over again with the second line of each character in the string being received, converted to binary, and displayed in magnified format by bigprint( ).

In the *for* loop in banner( ), the address in memory of the decimal character bit line information is determined by the following formula:

$$off = 0xfa6e + p[y] * 8 + x$$

This provides the offset into the ROM information. You have already learned that the first character in the set begins at offset 0xfa6e into the segment. Therefore, the offset of any character in the set is designated as:

$$0xfa6e + character * 8 + character\_line$$

In this example, *character* is the ASCII code of any character, and character_line is one of the eight lines that form the character, numbered zero to eight. Thus, the offset in memory for the first line of character 'A' would be:

$$0xfa6e + 65 * 8 + 0$$

Here, 65 is the ASCII code for 'A'. The mathematical operation indicated will equate to the offset in memory of the byte that specifies the first line of the character 'A'. The next successive seven bytes contain the ON/OFF information for the next seven lines in this character.

The result from this formula in the function is assigned to *off*. Then, this same variable is used as an argument to peekb( ), along with *seg*. This function returns the byte at the offset to the variable, *byte*. Then, dec2bin( ) is called to convert this decimal byte to its eight-bit binary equivalent. The binary string is written to b. This array serves as the argument to bigprint( ), which displays this value as a character line on the monitor screen.

An *if* statement is used to automatically break out of the loop when the looping variable, y, is equal to eight. This will occur when the string argument originally handed to banner( ) contains 10 characters or more. The maximum number of these enlarged characters that can be displayed on the screen at one time is nine. The tenth and all succeeding characters in the string are ignored by this function.

When the nested *for* loop is exited, a printf( ) function is executed. This simply prints a new line, which reverses the electronic carriage and moves down one line. The outside loop, however, is still in effect, and the process starts all over again for the next line of character information. This will occur until all eight lines of all characters in the string have been displayed in magnified format.

It was explained previously that this function is designed to work only on true IBM PCs, XTs, etc. Most compatibles can't use this program properly, because the ROM character set is nonexistent, this being derived from software instead. However, the following modification of the previous program should work fine on any MS-DOS PC, including true IBM machines. Instead of looking in ROM for the character set information, this program supplies its own:

```
#include <dec2din.c>
#include <bigprint.c>
banner(p) /* Enlarge letters from character set contained in array */
char p[];
{

    int off, x, y;
    char b[10];

    static int charset[1024] = {  /* Character set values */
                0, 0, 0, 0, 0, 0, 0, 0,
                126, 129, 165, 129, 189, 153, 129, 126,
                126, 255, 219, 255, 195, 231, 255, 126,
                108, 254, 254, 254, 124, 56, 16, 0,
                16, 56, 124, 254, 124, 56, 16, 0,
                56, 124, 56, 254, 254, 124, 56, 124,
                16, 16, 56, 124, 254, 124, 56, 124,
                0, 0, 24, 60, 60, 24, 0, 0,
                255, 255, 231, 195, 195, 231, 255, 255,
                0, 60, 102, 66, 66, 102, 60, 0,
                255, 195, 153, 189, 189, 153, 195, 255,
                15, 7, 15, 125, 204, 204, 204, 120,
                60, 102, 102, 102, 60, 24, 126, 24,
                63, 51, 63, 48, 48, 112, 240, 224,
                127, 99, 127, 99, 99, 103, 230, 192,
                153, 90, 60, 231, 231, 60, 90, 153,
                128, 224, 248, 254, 248, 224, 128, 0,
                2, 14, 62, 254, 62, 14, 2, 0,
                24, 60, 126, 24, 24, 126, 60, 24,
```

```
102, 102, 102, 102, 102, 0, 102, 0,
127, 219, 219, 123, 27, 27, 27, 0,
62, 99, 56, 108, 108, 56, 204, 120,


0, 0, 0, 0, 126, 126, 126, 0,
24, 60, 126, 24, 126, 60, 24, 255,
24, 60, 126, 24, 24, 24, 24, 0,
24, 24, 24, 24, 126, 60, 24, 0,
0, 24, 12, 254, 12, 24, 0, 0,
0, 48, 96, 254, 96, 48, 0, 0,
0, 0, 192, 192, 192, 254, 0, 0,
0, 36, 102, 255, 102, 36, 0, 0,
0, 24, 60, 126, 255, 255, 0, 0,
0, 255, 255, 126, 60, 24, 0, 0,
0, 0, 0, 0, 0, 0, 0, 0,
48, 120, 120, 48, 48, 0, 48, 0,
108, 108, 108, 0, 0, 0, 0, 0,
108, 108, 254, 108, 254, 108, 108, 0,
48, 124, 192, 120, 12, 248, 48, 0,
0, 198, 204, 24, 48, 102, 198, 0,
56, 108, 56, 118, 220, 204, 118, 0,
96, 96, 192, 0, 0, 0, 0, 0,
24, 48, 96, 96, 96, 48, 24, 0,
96, 48, 24, 24, 24, 48, 96, 0,
0, 102, 60, 255, 60, 102, 0, 0,
0, 48, 48, 252, 48, 48, 0, 0,
0, 0, 0, 0, 0, 48, 48, 96,
0, 0, 0, 252, 0, 0, 0, 0,
0, 0, 0, 0, 0, 48, 48, 0,
6, 12, 24, 48, 96, 192, 128, 0,
124, 198, 206, 222, 246, 230, 124, 0,
48, 112, 48, 48, 48, 48, 252, 0,
120, 204, 12, 56, 96, 204, 252, 0,
120, 204, 12, 56, 12, 204, 120, 0,


28, 60, 108, 204, 254, 12, 30, 0,
252, 192, 248, 12, 12, 204, 120, 0,
56, 96, 192, 248, 204, 204, 120, 0,
252, 204, 12, 24, 48, 48, 48, 0,
120, 204, 204, 120, 204, 204, 120, 0,
120, 204, 204, 124, 12, 24, 112, 0,
0, 48, 48, 0, 0, 48, 48, 0,
0, 48, 48, 0, 0, 48, 48, 96,
24, 48, 96, 192, 96, 48, 24, 0,
0, 0, 252, 0, 0, 252, 0, 0,
96, 48, 24, 12, 24, 48, 96, 0,
120, 204, 12, 24, 48, 0, 48, 0,
124, 198, 222, 222, 222, 192, 120, 0,
48, 120, 204, 204, 252, 204, 204, 0,
252, 102, 102, 124, 102, 102, 252, 0,
60, 102, 192, 192, 192, 102, 60, 0,
248, 108, 102, 102, 102, 108, 248, 0,
254, 98, 104, 120, 104, 98, 254, 0,
254, 98, 104, 120, 104, 96, 240, 0,
60, 102, 192, 192, 206, 102, 62, 0,
204, 204, 204, 252, 204, 204, 204, 0,
```

```
120, 48, 48, 48, 48, 48, 120, 0,
30, 12, 12, 12, 204, 204, 120, 0,
230, 102, 108, 120, 108, 102, 230, 0,
240, 96, 96, 96, 98, 102, 254, 0,
198, 238, 254, 254, 214, 198, 198, 0,
198, 230, 246, 222, 206, 198, 198, 0,
56, 108, 198, 198, 198, 108, 56, 0,
252, 102, 102, 124, 96, 96, 240, 0,
120, 204, 204, 204, 220, 120, 28, 0,
252, 102, 102, 124, 108, 102, 230, 0,


60, 102, 192, 192, 192, 102, 60, 0,
248, 108, 102, 102, 102, 108, 248, 0,
254, 98, 104, 120, 104, 98, 254, 0,
254, 98, 104, 120, 104, 96, 240, 0,
60, 102, 192, 192, 206, 102, 62, 0,
204, 204, 204, 252, 204, 204, 204, 0,
120, 48, 48, 48, 48, 48, 120, 0,
30, 12, 12, 12, 204, 204, 120, 0,
230, 102, 108, 120, 108, 102, 230, 0,
240, 96, 96, 96, 98, 102, 254, 0,
198, 238, 254, 254, 214, 198, 198, 0,
198, 230, 246, 222, 206, 198, 198, 0,
56, 108, 198, 198, 198, 108, 56, 0,
252, 102, 102, 124, 96, 96, 240, 0,
120, 204, 204, 204, 220, 120, 28, 0,
252, 102, 102, 124, 108, 102, 230, 0,
120, 204, 224, 112, 28, 204, 120, 0,
252, 180, 48, 48, 48, 48, 120, 0,
204, 204, 204, 204, 204, 204, 252, 0,
204, 204, 204, 204, 204, 120, 48, 0,
198, 198, 198, 214, 254, 238, 198, 0,
198, 198, 108, 56, 56, 108, 198, 0,
204, 204, 204, 120, 48, 48, 120, 0,
254, 198, 140, 24, 50, 102, 254, 0,
120, 96, 96, 96, 96, 96, 120, 0,
192, 96, 48, 24, 12, 6, 2, 0,
120, 24, 24, 24, 24, 24, 120, 0,
16, 56, 108, 198, 0, 0, 0, 0,
0, 0, 0, 0, 0, 0, 0, 255,
48, 48, 24, 0, 0, 0, 0, 0,
0, 0, 120, 12, 124, 204, 118, 0,
224, 96, 96, 124, 102, 102, 220, 0,
0, 0, 120, 204, 192, 204, 120, 0,
28, 12, 12, 124, 204, 204, 118, 0,
0, 0, 120, 204, 252, 192, 120, 0,
56, 108, 96, 240, 96, 96, 240, 0,
0, 0, 118, 204, 204, 124, 12, 248,
224, 96, 108, 118, 102, 102, 230, 0,
48, 0, 112, 48, 48, 48, 120, 0,
12, 0, 12, 12, 12, 204, 204, 120,
224, 96, 102, 108, 120, 108, 230, 0,
112, 48, 48, 48, 48, 48, 120, 0,
0, 0, 204, 254, 254, 214, 198, 0,
0, 0, 248, 204, 204, 204, 204, 0,
0, 0, 120, 204, 204, 204, 120, 0,
```

```
                    0,  0, 220, 102, 102, 124,  96, 240,
                    0,  0, 118, 204, 204, 124,  12,  30,
                    0,  0, 220, 118, 102,  96, 240,   0,
                    0,  0, 124, 192, 120,  12, 248,   0,
                   16, 48, 124,  48,  48,  52,  24,   0,
                    0,  0, 204, 204, 204, 204, 118,   0,
                    0,  0, 204, 204, 204, 120,  48,   0,
                    0,  0, 198, 214, 254, 254, 108,   0,
                    0,  0, 198, 108,  56, 108, 198,   0,
                    0,  0, 204, 204, 204, 124,  12, 248,
                    0,  0, 252, 152,  48, 100, 252,   0,
                   28, 48,  48, 224,  48,  48,  28,   0,
                   24, 24,  24,   0,  24,  24,  24,   0,
                  224, 48,  48,  28,  48,  48, 224,   0,
                  118, 220,  0,   0,   0,   0,   0,   0,
                    0, 16,  56, 108, 198, 198, 254,   0
                  };

for (x = 0; x <= 7; ++x) {
    for (y = 0; y <= strlen(p); ++y) {
        off = p[y] * 8 + x;
        dec2bin(b, charset[off]);
        bigprint(b);
        if (y == 8)
            break;
    }

    printf("\n");

}
```

Due to its length and the fact that it is very similar to the previous function, this function is not included in the commented list of programs and function found in the appendix of this book. The long series of values is the coding sequence for each of the characters in the character set. With these, the function carries its own character set, and doesn't need to access ROM for this information. All character set information is contained in array p. The equation that extracted the offset for the previous function is used again, however, this now becomes the offset in p. No seq value is necessary, because the function gets this information from a "local" array. All that is needed is the offset into that array. It is assumed that bigprint( ) and dec2bin( ) are contained in separate files which are #included at the beginning of this function.

In UNIX, banner( ) is often used by the System Manager to send a "high profile" message to all system users.

FILE ACCESS

The Borland Turbo C compiler offers a large number of specialized functions that allow access to the disk files. These functions are not portable, and are intended for use on MS-DOS machines. They are quite powerful and very useful in building programs that need to effect complex access to the disk drives.

Two such functions are findfirst( ) and findnext( ). These are often used in the same program. The first function finds the first occurrence of a file, based upon its pathname and attribute. When a file matching the pathname and attribute is available, this function returns a value of zero and writes the filename to a structure called ffblk that is contained in the header file, dir.h. This header file must be #included in any program that uses either of these two functions. If a file is not available or there is an error in a filename, a value of −1 is returned.

Once findfirst( ) has located a file, findnext( ) can be called to get the next one that matches the pathname and attribute arguments of findfirst( ). The following C program uses both of these functions to list the directory of the current disk drive:

```
#include <dir.h>
main()
{

    struct ffblk r;

    if (findfirst("*.*", &r, 0) != 0)
        exit(0);
    else
        printf("%s\n", r.ff_name);

    while (findnext(&r) == 0)
        printf("%s\n", r.ff_name);

}
```

This program first declares r to be a pointer to the structure, ffblk. This structure is declared in dir.h. Next, findfirst( ) is used within the *if* statement line. A "wildcard" pathname is used, *.*, which in MS-DOS means all filenames. The address of the structure is the second argument. Because r points to ffblk, then &r is the memory location of ffblk.

The third argument is zero. This attribute specifies all "normal" files on disk. Therefore, the combination of these arguments causes findfirst( ) to locate the first standard file written to the current disk drive. If there are any files at all on this drive, the first one is written to char array ff__name[ ] in the ffblk structure. If there is no file available, then findfirst( ) returns a −1 and the program is ended via the *exit* statement.

Assuming that a file is available, it is displayed on the screen using printf( ), and a *while* loop is entered. It calls findnext( ) repeatedly until a nonzero return is detected. Remember, findnext( ) will find the next available file with the pathname and attribute originally specified in findfirst( ). The filenames are read into ff__name[ ] again and again. On each loop pass, the content of this array is displayed on the screen. The result of this program is to display the entire contents of the current disk drive on the screen. The same general operation occurs when you issue the DIR command in MS-DOS.

This next program is a modification of the first that uses a simple sorting routine to put all disk files in alphabetical order before listing them to the screen:

```c
#include <dir.h>
main()
{

    struct ffblk r;
    int x, y;
    char *hold[250], *malloc();

    y = 0;

    if (findfirst("*.*", &r, 0) != 0)
        exit(0);
    else
        strcpy(hold[y++] = malloc(20), r.ff_name);

     while (!findnext(&r))
        strcpy(hold[y++] = malloc(20), r.ff_name);

    sort(hold, y);

    for (x = 0; x < y; ++x)
        puts(hold[x]);

}
sort(x, i)
char *x[];
int i;
{

    char *y;
    int a, b, z;

    for (z = i / 2; z > 0; z /= 2)
        for (b = z; b < i; b++)
            for (a = b - z; a >= 0; a -= z){
                if (strcmp(x[a], x[a + z]) <= 0)
                    break;
                y = x[a];
                x[a] = x[a + z];
                x[a + z] = y;
            }

}
```

This program is identical to the first example, up to a point. The difference lies in the fact that when each filename is read into ff_name[ ], it is then copied into hold[ ], which is an array of pointers. The declaration provides for an array that can hold up to 250 pointers, accessed via subscripts 0 through 249. This means that the array is adequate to hold a maximum of 250 filenames simultaneously. If you need more storage than this, then make your changes in the declaration line.

From an earlier discussion, you learned that writing anything to an uninitialized pointer invites disaster. The problem could be 250 times worse in this situation, but we have diligently remembered to initialize each pointer using malloc( ). This function allocates 20 bytes of storage for each pointer *as it is used.* In other words, if this program is called on to list the names of 100 files, then 100 pointers will be allocated 20 bytes each, for a total of 2000 bytes. The allocation occurs with the strcpy( ) function. The following program statement:

strcpy(hold[y] = malloc(20), r.ff__name);

is actually executed from the inside out. First, hold[y] is assigned the 20 bytes pointed to by malloc( ). Then, the contents of r.ff__name[ ] are copied into this safe area of memory. This assures that no uninitialized pointer is written to, and that no pointer is needlessly allocated space if no information is to be written to it.

When the loop is exited, all of the available filenames have been stored in hold[ ]. Now the sort( ) function is called. Its first argument is an array, hold, and the second is an integer, y, which is now equal to the total number of names stored in hold.

The sort( ) function has been around as long as the C programming language, having been discussed in Kernighan and Ritchie's *The C Programming Language.* All its function does is to read strings from an array and sort them in ascending order. This is the same as alphabetical order because the ASCII value of A is less than the ASCII value of B. The strcmp( ) function is used to determine the value of each string and to rearrange them in the array accordingly. When sort( ) is exited, hold will still contain all of the strings originally read into it, but they will be rearranged in alphabetical order.

The only job left for this function to perform is to display the contents of hold on the screen. This is done with the *for* loop as before. The screen write is performed with the puts( ) function, which is the same as printf( ) when the latter is used with one string argument followed by the newline character. In other words,

puts(hold[x]);

is the same as:

printf(%s \ n", hold[x]);

There is another difference in this program. I am referring to the *while* statement clause, while (!findnext(&r)). This means exactly the same thing as while (findnext(&r) = = 0).

This clause is often called an *exit clause* because it tells the looping mechanism when to exit. All such clauses are conditional expressions that return a value of true or false. Usually, a value of zero indicates false, while some other value, usually one, means true. The loop will continue to cycle until the expression evaluates to false, or zero. The findnext( ) function returns a zero when there is a file in its buffer. It returns one when there are no files. This works in the opposite way of most C functions and expressions. However, the expression in the following *while* line:

$$\text{while (findnext(\&r) } = = 0)$$

will evaluate to true or one as long as the function returns zero. Here we are not evaluating the return from the function, but the expression findnext(&r) = = 0. This expression returns one, while the function returns zero. The above program uses the logical NOT operator, which causes a zero return to evaluate to a one return, and vice versa. The expression in plain language means: continue to loop while findnext (&r) is NOT true.

The next program is a further modification of the previous two. This example will display the files from the current disk drive in alphabetical order and in four columns instead of just one. This allows more file information to be displayed on one screen. The source code for this program follows:

```
#include <dir.h>
#include <sort.c>
main()
{

    struct ffblk r;
    int c, x, y, z;
    char *hold[250], *malloc();

    y = 0;

    x = findfirst("*.*", &r, 0);

    while (!x) {
        strcpy(hold[y] = malloc(20), r.ff_name);
        x = findnext(&r);
        ++y;
    }

    sort(hold, y);
    x = z = 0;

    while (x < y) {
        for (x = z; x < y, x <= z + 20; ++x) {
            printf("%-15s%c", hold[x], ((y - (20 + z)) <= 0 ) ? '\n' : ' ');
```

```
            if ((x + 21) < y)
                printf("%-15s%c", hold[x + 21], ((y - (40 + z)) <= 0) ? '\n' : ' ');
            if ((x + 42) < y)
                printf("%-15s%c", hold[x + 42], ((y - (60 + z)) <= 0) ? '\n' : ' ');
            if ((x + 63) < y)
                printf("%-15s\n", hold[x + 63]);
            if (x >= y)
                break;
        }

        printf("\n\nPress Any Key For More");
        c = getch();
        printf("\n\n\n");
        z += 84;
    }


}
```

This program displays all disk files in a four-column format with 21 filenames
in each column. When a full screen of names is displayed, execution pauses
and you are prompted to press any key for more names. This prevents names
from scrolling off the screen before they can be viewed by the user.

The elaborate portion of this program, and the part that distinguishes it
from the previous examples, occurs within the *for* loop used for writing
information to the screen. This is nested with an outer *while* loop that signals
program termination after all filenames have been written.

The formatting of the filename information took a bit of forethought and
planning. It was necessary to calculate offsets into the array to get the
appropriate filenames. Due to the four-column format, filenames cannot be
accessed sequentially. While the display is columnar, the actual writing of the
screen is horizontal. Therefore, the first filename, hold[0], is accessed and
displayed, followed by hold[21], hold[42], and then hold[63]. This forms the
first printed line of the four-column directory listing. The next row will consist
of array elements 1, 22, 43, and 64, respectively.

This is fairly easy to calculate, but what happens when there are not enough
remaining filenames to warrant all four columns? This is where the complexity
begins. The printf( ) statements within this loop are activated when the *if*
statement determines that there are enough remaining filenames in hold[ ] to
warrant a printing in this column. Conditional expressions are contained within three of the four printf( ) function lines. These expressions determine if the
final character in the printf( ) argument is to be the newline character, signaling
that no further columns will be written, or the space character, which means
that another column will be written.

When 21 filenames have been printed in each column, the scrolling will
stop and a prompt will appear. A getch( ) function halts execution until any

key is pressed at the keyboard, whereupon the *for* loop is reentered and the next screen of filenames is written.

The final modification of these examples lists the files in a manner that columnizes the filenames and file extensions, and alphabetizes according to extension, rather than name:

```c
#include <dir.h>
main()
{

    struct ffblk r;
    int c, x, y, z;
    char *hold[250],n[80], e[8], *malloc();

    y = 0;
    x = findfirst("*.*", &r, 0);

    while (!x)
        {
        strcpy(hold[y] = malloc(20), r.ff_name);
        x = findnext(&r);
        ++y;
    }

    sort(hold, y);
    x = z = 0;

    while (x < y) {
    for (x = z; x < y, x <= z + 20; ++x) {
    fnsplit(hold[x], n, n, n, e);
    printf("%-10s%-8s%c", n, e, ((y - (20 + z)) < 0 ) ? '\n' : ' ');
    if ((x + 21) < y)
    {
      fnsplit(hold[x + 21], n, n, n, e);
      printf("%-10s%-8s%c", n, e, ((y - (40 + z)) < 0) ? '\n' : ' ');
    }
    if ((x + 42) < y)
    {
      fnsplit(hold[x + 42], n, n, n, e);
      printf("%-10s%-8s%c", n, e, ((y - (60 + z)) < 0) ? '\n' : ' ');
    }
    if ((x + 63) < y) {
      fnsplit(hold[x + 63], n, n, n, e);
      printf("%-10s%-8s\n", n, e);
    }
    if (x >= y)
      break;
    }

            printf("\n\nPress Any Key For More");
            c = getch();
            printf("\n\n\n");
            z += 84;
    }
```

159

```
}
sort(x, i)
char *x[];
int i;
{

    char *y, c[30], d[30], q[80];
    int a, b, z;

    for (z = i / 2; z > 0; z /= 2)
        for (b = z; b < i; b++)
            for (a = b - z; a >= 0; a -= z) {
                fnsplit(x[a], q, q, q, c);
                fnsplit(x[a + z], q, q, q, d);
                if (strcmp(c, d) <= 0)
                    break;
                y = x[a];
                x[a] = x[a + z];
                x[a + z] = y;
            }

}
```

This program is a close copy of the previous example, but a new function enters the picture. In Turbo C, fnsplit( ) is used to divide a filename argument into its various components, which include path, drive, directory, name and extension. This function is used in a format of:

```
fnsplit(path, drive, dir, name, ext)
```

Therefore, if path is equal to:

```
b:\newfil\test.c
```

then:

```
drive = b:
dir   = \newfil\
name  = test
ext   = .c
```

The program currently under discussion uses fnsplit( ) simply to obtain the extension from the filename written to r.ff__name[ ] by the fnfirst( )/findnext( ) functions. The first use occurs in sort( ), which has been altered to sort all filenames according to extension. Therefore, a file named xray.x will be placed before one named alpha.x.

Within the doubly nested *for* loop in sort( ), fnsplit( ) is used with only three separate arguments. Array x contains the full path, which in this case is simply the name and extension. However, this argument is broken down accordingly. Array q is used to satisfy the need for arrays for fnsplit( ) to write the separate drive, directory, and name to. The information is simply overwritten in the same array, because there is no need of this information within this program. Again, q is there only to satisfy the requirement of an array argument in these slots.

Arrays c and d are used, however. These serve as the last argument to the two fnsplit( ) functions in sort( ). Array c holds only the extension of one filename, while d holds the extension of another. The strcmp( ) function compares the two, and places the one of least value ahead of the one with a higher value. The sort( ) function works just as it did in previous versions, except that only the extension portions of filenames are used in the alphabetizing sequence. When sort( ) is exited, all of the filenames have been sorted according to extension value.

Back in the main calling program, fnsplit is used again in the sequence that displays the filenames on the screen. Here, fnsplit( ) is handed the full path, along with three successive arguments composed of array n. The last argument is array e. When fnsplit( ) is first entered, the path in hold[ ] will be broken down as follows. First, the drive identification will be copied to n. Next, the contents of n will be overwritten by the directory identification. This array (n) is overwritten again by the filename. This is what we are really after, the name of the file without the extension. Another array, e, is the last argument to fnsplit( ), and the extension is copied to this. Now, n holds the filename and e holds the extension.

The printf( ) function is used with −10 and −8 width specifications that reserve 10 and eight spaces to display the filename and file extension, respectively. This produces separate columns for the name and extension.

Admittedly, fnsplit( ) provides a greater capability than is needed in this program. It would have been a simple matter to have written a "custom" function that would have simply broken the filename down into the name and the extension. However, because fnsplit( ) could also do this (and a lot more), it was utilized.

For those who are interested in how such a separation is produced, the following C function will provide a partial explanation. This function will take a filename such as test.c and break it down into the name and the extension:

```
split(fn, n, e)
char *fn, *n, *e;
{

    *e = '\0';

    while (*n = *fn)
        if (*n == '.') {
            *n = '\0';
            while (*e++ = *fn++)
                ;
            break;
        }
```

```
        else {
            *n++;
            *fn++;
        }

    }
```

All this function does is step through the filename, one character at a time, copying characters from fn, which is the pointer to the full filename argument, to n, which is the pointer to the array that holds the discrete name. When the presence of the period is detected, this character is overwritten by the null character, thus terminating the string in n. Another *while* loop is entered which copies the period and the remainder of the full name, including the null character at the end of fn, to array e. This latter array holds the extension.

This function is complicated by the fact that it is necessary to guard against full filenames that do not have any extension at all. This is the reason that *e is assigned a value of '\0' at the opening of this function. Should the full filename not contain an extension, then no information will be written to e. The null character assures that the calling program is always passed by a string value in e, even if it is a null string. Without this precaution, the value of e could be any random string of characters.

If we could always be assured of a full filename having an extension, then the function could be made far simpler, as in the following:

```
split(fn, n, e)
char *fn, *n, *e;
{
    *e++ = '.';

    while ((*n++ = *fn++) != '.')
        ;

    *--n = '\0';

    while (*e++ = fn++)
        ;

}
```

In this function, *e is assigned the period (or decimal point). Then, a *while* loop assigns n all of the characters in fn up to and including the decimal point. However, the transfer of this character causes this loop to terminate. The next line moves the pointer back to the decimal point and overwrites it with the null character. Array n now contains the discrete name.

Another *while* loop is entered, which copies the remainder of fn to e. Remember that *e was assigned the decimal point and then stepped to the next character position. This allows the function to continue the copy after the name portion has been completed without having to "rewind" the fn pointer back to the decimal point that has already been transferred to n and then overwritten with the null character.

Again, this last version of split( ) can only be used when there will always be a file extension. If the extension is omitted, the function will hang up the machine while it goes on vainly searching for the decimal point character.

The Turbo C compiler is rich in special functions that can be used for very complex file and disk access. The few examples discussed here have only skimmed the surface of what is available. However, newcomers to C should be warned that such functions are a part of a "superset" within the C language, and are not yet commonplace in all or even many C programming environments. At present, you can be assured that programs which call these specialized functions will not be portable to other types of computers, nor to other C compilers. However, if you're writing a specialized program for MS-DOS computers, this bevy of specialized functions can save you many, many hours of hard labor writing your own. This especially applies if you are not terribly familiar with the internal architecture of your machines, DOS function calls, and interrupts.

GRAPHICS FUNCTIONS

C language is devoid of graphic functions, at least as far as the standard and portable function set is concerned. It is this way for good reason. C was designed to be a *portable* language, one that could be quickly brought up on different types of computers. Graphics operations, on the other hand, are notoriously machine-dependent. The originators of C were developing a language that would serve as a universal shell for all types of programming applications, programming environments (operating systems), and machines. It was probably assumed that machine-specific operations would be programmed in Assembler, although the capability is there to do the same thing in C. However, Assembler would offer faster execution times.

In any event, one sees relatively few graphics functions in most C compilers, and Turbo C is certainly no exception. However, graphics functions can and are written in this language, and this section will discuss several.

Screen( )

Before graphics operations can be performed, it is necessary to put the computer screen into graphics mode. The following function does this by interfacing with the machine itself through the ROM BIOS. These are the built-in assembly language routines contained in the read-only memory of your personal computer. The following source code is for the screen( ) function:

```
screen(mode, burst)
int mode, burst;
{


    union REGS r, *inregs, *outregs;

    inregs = &r;
    outregs = &r;
    burst = burst % 2;
    r.h.ah = 15;

    int86(0x10, inregs, outregs);
```

```
        if (mode == 0 && r.h.ah > 40)
            mode = 2 + burst;
        else if (mode == 0)
            mode = burst;
        else
            mode = (mode == 1) ? 4 + burst : 6;

        r.h.al = mode;
        r.h.ah = 0;

        int86(0x10, inregs, outregs);


    }
```

This function was taken directly from the CBREEZE translator discussed elsewhere in this text, and is used with permission. This is, in fact, not exactly a C operation. Rather, it is a C language function that calls a built-in routine via the software interrupt interface function, int86( ). When the proper information is fed to the various 8086 registers, the called routine does its job. All this specialized C function does is to load the registers with the correct information and then call for the interrupt.

This function works like the MS BASIC SCREEN statement in many ways. It may be used to designate any of the legal screens available with the standard IBM Color Card. For medium resolution graphics mode, an argument of screen(1,0) is used. For high resolution graphics mode, use screen(2,0).

The emulation of SCREEN in BASIC is very complete. This function actually makes two DOS interrupts. The first call to int86( ) gets the current screen mode. The current screen mode might determine how to interpret the new mode requested. For instance, a call for screen(0,0) is a request for the text mode in the current screen width. If the current screen is set to the high resolution graphics mode, screen(2,0), then screen(0,0) will result in the high resolution text mode. However, if the current mode is the medium resolution graphics mode, then screen(0,0) will result in the medium resolution text-only mode. To provide true emulation of the BASIC SCREEN statement, this CBREEZE function must first determine the current screen mode that is in effect. It can then base the new mode on what already exists.

Of course, people who already know how to program in C might not need this close emulation of the SCREEN statement in BASIC. This function can be made simpler and less emulative by simply removing the source code that addresses this area.

Once the current screen mode has been determined, the registers are reloaded according to the new mode of operation. The int86( ) function requires three arguments: the interrupt number, a pointer to the *inregs* structure contained with the REGS union, and a pointer to the *outregs* structure. These structures and union are found in the <dos.h> header file, which is included with any programs that call int86( ). Inregs and outregs are structures that contain the various 8086 register values. If you are not an Assembler programmer and/or do not understand how computer register operations are carried out, then you will need some separate tutoring in this area to fully understand the operation of the int86( ) interface function.

In any event, the current screen mode is returned in the ah register, and this value is used to determine the new mode of operation. The variable *mode* is assigned within an *if* statement construct, based upon the new screen argument value and the current screen mode of operation. This new value is placed in the ah register again for the new call from int86( ). Both calls use the HEX 10 for the first argument to int86( ). This is also known as the *video interrupt*. Refer to the IBM Technical Reference Manual for more information on ROM BIOS.

Pset( )

After a graphics screen mode has been set, it is necessary to accomplish two things to be able to even begin graphics operations. First, you must be able to write information to this screen via a set of coordinates. Second, you must be able to retrieve pixel information from the screen. With these two capabilities, all other graphic operations can be accomplished.

Writing a single point of light to a screen that is composed of over 64000 pixels is not an easy chore when it must be done by addressing memory locations. Add to the complexity of mathematically determining a set of coordinates for a specific write the fact that several color combinations are available, and the problem is multiplied at least fourfold.

The following function is presented only as an exercise to give an idea of what to expect if MS-DOS did not have a function interface that can be addressed by C. This function will place a pixel on the medium resolution graphics screen of the IBM PC genre in the color specified:

```
pset(x, y, c)
int x, y, c;
{

    int offset, seg, bit, d, f, g, col, valu;
    double pow();

    d = c;
    seg = 0xb800;

    offset = ((x / 4) + (y * 40));
    if (y % 2 > 0)
        offset = (x / 4) + (8192 + ((y - 1) * 40));

    bit = 2 * (x % 4);
    f = pow(2.0,  7.0 - bit);
    g = pow(2, 7.0 - bit - 1);

    valu = peekb(seg, offset);
    col = valu | f | g;
    pokeb(seg, offset, col);

    valu = peekb(seg, offset);
```

```
        if (d == 0){
            col = valu ^ f ^ g;
            pokeb(seg, offset, col);
        }
        if (d == 1){
            col = valu ^ f;
            pokeb(seg, offset, col);
        }
        if (d == 2){
            col = valu ^ g;
            pokeb(seg, offset, col);
        }

    }
```

I won't go into a full discussion of this function. It writes a pixel to the screen by POKEing the appropriate value into memory at the location determined by an offset formula. The segment is the graphics video buffer at 0xb800 (eight-bit). The graphics screen is divided into 16384 bytes, each of which contains four pixels. Pixel color is determined by the ON/OFF settings of two bits which each control one. Therefore, if you wish to write a pixel in color index 2 at coordinates 160,100 on the medium resolution screen, then you must first determine which byte in the screen memory contains the pixel position to be written. This is made more complex by the fact that the screen lines are interlaced. A pixel in one row may be at byte 400, while one in the next row down will be at byte $8182 + 400$.

Once the correct byte is found, then the offset of the pixel within that byte must be determined. When the two bits are found that actually control whether that one pixel in thousands is on, off, red, white, blue, etc., you must then determine the ON/OFF status of these two bytes to yield the correct color combination. This is a laborious task, and one that can result in slow execution because of the complexity involved. Of course, this discussion and function only address the medium resolution screen. If you switch to high resolution graphics, you have to switch to other formulas and bit combinations.

Now, consider the following source code:

```
pset(x, y, c)
int x, y, c;
{

    union REGS r, *inregs, *outregs;

    inregs = &r;
    outregs = &r;

    r.x.cx = x;
    r.x.dx = y;
    r.h.al = c;
    r.h.ah = 12;

    int86(0x10, inregs, outregs);

}
```

This function does everything the previous one does, and it also addresses whatever screen is currently in effect, medium or high resolution. The source code is a small fraction of what the previous function contained, because we let the routines in the ROM BIOS do all of the work. Routine 12 within the video interrupt (0x10) writes a dot to the screen. You will find the technical information needed to write a dot using the ROM BIOS in the IBM Technical Reference Manual under the BIOS listings.

The int86( ) function uses the structures and union contained in the <dos.h> header file to read and load registers and to make interrupts. The interrupt number is the first argument to int86( ). The next two arguments are pointers to the register structures referenced by the union call REGS. Now, the routine or function number is placed in the ah register. This is directly referenced by r.h.ah in the above function. The cx and dx registers contain the column and row information. These are referenced in the function by r.x.cx and r.x.dx. In this usage, the decimal point is not a decimal point at all but the "member of structure" operator. The color index value is placed in the al register via r.h.al. Again, these values, and where to place them, were derived directly from the ROM BIOS listings in the IBM Technical Reference Manual. If you've not attempted this type of programming before and are completely baffled by the BIOS listings, don't feel alone. All users have felt this way (and sometimes still do). Try comparing this function to the information contained in the manual (on page A-44). If your manual differs from mine, refer to the video section of the BIOS listings.

Now that the registers have all been loaded, it's a simple matter to perform the interrupt via int86( ). When this function is executed, the pixel will appear in the correct color on the graphics screen.

The reason this method seems so simple is because the difficult parts have already been programmed for you, and are contained within the ROM BIOS. All you do here is use a C function to call a ROM function. Incidentally, the pset( ) function was taken directly from the CBREEZE translator. This is the function the translator will output when processing any BASIC source code that uses pset( ). This function is used with permission.

Point( )

The previous function provides an easy, quick, and accurate way to write pixels to the graphic screen. We must now find some way to read individual pixels from this same screen. The following function shows the hard way to do it:

```
point(x, y)
int x, y;
{

    int offset, col, col1, seg, bit, f, g, valu;
    double pow();

    seg = 0xb800;
```

```
        offset = ((x / 4) + (y * 40));

        if (y % 2 > 0)
            offset = (x / 4) + (8192 + ((y - 1) * 40));

        bit = 2 * (x % 4);
        f = pow(2.0, 7.0 - bit);
        g = pow(2.0, 7.0 - bit - 1);

        valu = peekb(seg, offset);
        col = valu & f;
        col1 = valu & g;

        if (col == f && col1 == g)
            return(3);
        if (col == f && col1 == 0)
            return(2);
        if (col == 0 && col1 == g)
            return(1);
        if (col == 0 && col1 == 0)
            return(0);


    }
```

This function will read any pixel from the medium resolution graphics screen and return its color index as a value from zero to three. It accomplishes this task by going through a reverse procedure from the previous "difficult" function that wrote a pixel.

First, the coordinates that serve as arguments to point( ) are broken down into the correct video screen byte where the pixel is located. The pixel's offset into this byte is determined, and then the two bits controlling the pixel are read. This information yields the true color index after some ANDing and ORing.

The following point( ) function shows the easy way of accomplishing the same thing:

```
        point(x, y)
        int x, y;
        {

            union REGS r, *inregs, *outregs;

            inregs = &r;
            outregs = &r;

            r.x.cx = x;
            r.x.dx = y;
            r.h.ah = 13;

            int86(0x10, inregs, outregs);

            return((int) r.h.al);

        }
```

This is another CBREEZE translation. The point( ) function is able to return the color index of the pixel at coordinates specified by x,y by using routine 13 in the ROM BIOS video interrupt. This is the "read dot" routine. The routine number is assigned to the ah register, while the cx and dx registers get the coordinates of the pixel to be read. Next, the int86( ) function is used to effect the interrupt, and the value of the color index is returned in the al register. This is used as the argument to the *return* statement. This is an extremely simple function, but it calls a complex machine language routine buried in your system's ROM.

ADDING MORE GRAPHICS FUNCTIONS

Now you have three basic functions that can be used as "primitives" to write more complex graphics functions in C. The screen( ) function provides the capability of switching to the graphics screen, while pset( ) allows the graphics screen to be written one pixel at a time. The point( ) function allows the graphics screen to be read one pixel at a time. With this graphics tool set and the other, standard C language functions, any graphics program can be written.

Line( )

The following program uses the pset( ) function just discussed, contained in a filename "pset.c," to write another function called line( ). As its name implies, this function draws a line on the graphics screen based on a set of beginning and ending coordinates. A color index argument is also accepted. The source code for the function follows:

```
#include <pset.c>
line(x1, y1, x2, y2, c)
int x1, x2, y1, y2, c;
{

    int a, b;

    double m = (y1 - y2) / (double) (x1 - x2);

    for (a = x1; a <= x2; ++a) {
        b = m * a;
        pset(a, b, c);
    }

}
```

This function uses a simple formula that determines the slope of the line by dividing $y1 - y2$ by $x1 - x2$. Notice that the (double) cast operator is used in this divide operation. This lets the executing environment know that you are performing floating-point division, as opposed to integer division. The latter yields the integer remainder.

When integer variables or constants are divided in a C program, the default mode is integer division. The cast operator is a switch in this operation that specifies floating-point division. Double variable m is equal to the product of this division.

Next, a *for* loop is entered which counts from the value of x1 to a top value of x2. On each pass of the loop, variable b is assigned a value of the integer product of m, the line slope, and a. These two coordinate values are used by pset( ) along with the color index argument, c. A perfect line is drawn on the screen.

Note: Programmers who intend to use this line( ) function for serious work should be aware that it is limited to line coordinates that are in ascending order. In other words, x1 must always be less than x2, and y1 must be less than y2. Can you think of an easy way to modify this line( ) function to overcome this dependency? Perhaps the following rewrite will be more satisfactory:

```c
#include <pset.c>
line(x1, y1, x2, y2, c)
int x1, x2, y1, y2, c;
{

    int a, b, temp;

    double m = abs(y1 - y2) / (double) abs(x1 - x2);
    temp = x2;
    if (x1 > x2) {
        x2 = x1;
        x1 = temp;
    }

    for (a = x1; a <= x2; ++a) {
        b = m * a;
        pset(a, b, c);
    }

}
```

The abs( ) function will always return a positive value or zero. Therefore, if the difference of y1−y2 or x1−x2 is negative, the negative sign will be dropped. The abs( ) function does this by testing for a value of less than zero. If this is true, then the value is multiplied by −1, yielding a positive value. If the argument is already positive or zero, no action takes place. Incidentally, Turbo C offers abs( ) as a function and as a macro definition. If you #include the <stdlib.h> header file, then you get the macro. If not, you get the function. The function version will accept integer arguments only, while the macro will accept any numeric type.

The abs( ) function/macro solves one problem with the dependency mentioned, but there is still one more. The *for* loop counts from low to high. This means that x1, the starting value of a, must be lower than the value of x2 for any looping to take place. An *if* statement construct is used, which tests for the condition of x1 being more than x2. When this is the case, the values are simply swapped. A new variable, temp, has been added, and temporarily holds the value of x2. Variable x2 is then assigned the value of x1, and x1 is assigned the value of temp. The value in temp is no longer needed. The loop may now count from low to high.

Box( )

No graphics library would be complete without a function that will draw a box or rectangle on the screen. Actually, such a function is closely aligned with those that draw lines. In MS-BASIC, the two functions are combined. However, in C programming, it is probably more practical to make two separate functions for drawing lines and boxes.

As is typical with most box or rectangle functions, this one accepts the same sets of arguments as those for a line. However, these coordinates describe the upper left- and lower right-hand corner of the box. This function also allows for a color index value, so the box may be drawn in any available color. The source code for box( ) follows:

```
box(x1, y1, x2, y2, c)
int x1, x2, y1, y2, c;
{

    int a, b, temp;

    temp = x1;
    if (x1 > x2) {
        x1 = x2;
        x2 = temp;
    }

    temp = y1;
    if (y1 > y2) {
        y1 = y2;
        y2 = temp;
    }

    a = x1;
    while (a <= x2) {
        pset(a, y1, c);
        pset(a++, y2, c);
    }
    while (y1 < y2) {
        pset(x1, y1, c);
        pset(x2, y1++, c);
    }

}
```

The box( ) function is actually easier to write than the line( ) function, although box( ) contains more lines of source code. The reason for this is the "safety" net that is thrown in to make certain x1 and y1 are each smaller than x2 and y2. Variable temp serves double duty in this usage, first to store the value of x1 and then the value of y1. The values are swapped where necessary to assure that the first pair represent the upper left-hand corner coordinates and the second pair the lower right-hand corner coordinates.

From here, it's simply a matter of drawing horizontal or vertical lines. Within the loop, two pset( ) functions use the value of a to write dots forming two parallel lines that make up the top and bottom segments of the box. Note that the value of a, which starts at the value of x1, is incremented in the second pset( ) function. The *while* loop continues to cycle until a is more than x2. When this loop is exited, the top and bottom lines are complete. The next *while* loop draws the left and right sides of the box. This loop advances the value of y1 in the second pset( ) function line. Four loops could have been used, one for each of the four lines in the box. However, this would have added to the confusion and complexity. Furthermore, such a function would not be as fast as this one.

Circle( )

Another function that is always a part of any complete graphics tool set is one that will draw a circle on the screen. However, when you get into such geometric objects, more complex mathematical operations are required to plot the various points. This is where speed becomes crucial. For the most part, graphics functions like circle( ) are usually programmed in Assembler for the added speed necessary to make such functions practical.

The following function is written in C and will, indeed, draw a circle on the graphics screen, but it is hopelessly slow. This is true for several reasons. First, the sin( ) and cos( ) functions in Turbo C are called repeatedly. These are fast functions, but they process double-precision numbers. Double-precision floating-point values cannot be manipulated nearly as fast as integers. This is a major cause of the slowness. The function follows:

```
circle(a, b, r, c)
int a, b, r, c;
{

        int h, i, j, k, m, n, x, y;
        double sin(), cos(), t;

        h = a + r;
        i = a - r;
        j = b + r;
        k = b - r;

        for (t = 0; t <= 90; t += .025) {
            x =  r * sin(t) + a;
```

```
        y = r * cos(t) + b;
        pset(x, y, c);
        m = k + (j - y);
        pset(x, m, c);
        n = i + (h - x);
        pset(n, y, c);
        pset(n, m, c);
    }

}
```

Fortunately, this function takes advantage of several tricks to make it faster than it might be otherwise. A circle can be plotted based upon its radius (r) and sine and cosine values for only 90 degrees of its full 360 degree arc. This means that we only have to get the sine and cosine of the first quarter arc. Through interpolation, the other arcs can be plotted on these points.

Assignments to h, i, j, and k provide the conversions necessary to be used in the pset( ) arguments. A *for* loop is used to count from 0 to 90 in steps of .025. These small increments are wasteful but necessary to obtain a complete and full circle. The sin( ) and cos( ) functions return the floating-point sines and cosines of the various values of t, the loop variable. These are multiplied by the circle radius, r, and added to the a and b, respectively. The latter two values state the center coordinates of the circle.

The results of these mathematical operations are assigned to x and y, which are integers. All of this slow, floating-point math has to end up as an integer value again, but the floating-point portion is essential. Many values between 0 and 90 have to be worked through the formula to be certain that every integer point along the circumference of the circle is plotted. This means that many, many points in each arc are plotted, replotted, and re-replotted. This waste is necessary to ensure that the circle is fully enclosed. The loop increments used here are designed to fill in a circle with a radius maximum of 100 on the medium resolution screen.

Within the *for* loop, four pset( ) functions are used. Each draws a different quarter arc on each loop pass. These functions receive their coordinate arguments from the sine/cosine returns and from the conversion formulas discussed earlier.

I am not especially pleased with the algorithm used in this function, but again, C is not really the language for a graphics function such as this one with its complex and slow mathematics. However, the function can be speeded up enormously by making a "slight" adjustment.

In the above function, the real slowness is produced by thousands of calls to sin( ) and cos( ). Another slowing factor is the *for* loop, which counts in floating-point increments. If you could do away with most or all floating-point operations, this function would be far faster. Believe it or not, this is possible, maybe even practical.

What you have to do is get rid of sin( ) and cos( ). To do this requires what is known as a *look-up table*. This is a vast table of sine and cosine values contained in static arrays. The loop can then access each of the thousands of values in integer steps.

Let's assume a giant table is made consisting of, first, the sine of zero, followed by the cosine of zero. The next pair will be the sine of .025 and the cosine of .025, then the sine and cosine of .050, etc. Each of these floating-point values would be quickly accessed, because all of the values have already been calculated and placed in the array. The array would be accessed via integer offsets. Sine and cosine zero would be at offsets 0 and 1 in the array. Sine and cosine of .025 would be at offsets 2 and 3. This would speed up the function by a factor of several hundred.

But, how about programming such a table? Wouldn't it take hours, days, or maybe weeks even to look up all of these sine and cosine values and then type them into a program? The answer is no. It would only take a few seconds. We have computers for just such operations.

The trick is to write a program that will produce such a table for you. The following example will produce just the table we are looking for:

```c
#include <stdio.h>
main()
{

    FILE *fp, *fopen();
    double sin(), cos(), t;

    if ((fp = fopen("lookup", "w")) == NULL)
        exit(0);

    fprintf(fp, "static double sc[] = {\n");

    for (t = 0; t <= 89.975; t += .025)
        fprintf(fp, "{ %lf, %lf },\n", sin(t), cos(t));

    fprintf(fp, "{ %lf, %lf }\n };", sin(t), cos(t));

    fclose(fp);

}
```

This program will write the look-up table for you in less than a minute.

The truncated table is shown below:

```
static double sc[] = {
{ 0.000000, 1.000000 },
{ 0.024997, 0.999688 },
{ 0.049979, 0.998750 },
{ 0.074930, 0.997189 },
{ 0.099833, 0.995004 },
{ 0.124675, 0.992198 },
{ 0.149438, 0.988771 },
{ 0.174108, 0.984727 },
```

. . . .

```
{ 0.965195, -0.261532 },
{ 0.958356, -0.285578 },
{ 0.950917, -0.309445 },
{ 0.942885, -0.333119 },
{ 0.934263, -0.356584 },
{ 0.925058, -0.379827 },
{ 0.915274, -0.402832 },
{ 0.904918, -0.425586 }
};
```

This table represents just a few of the 7200 values that would be written to it in pairs. The previous function would remain basically the same, with two exceptions. First, there would be no calls to sin( ) and cos( ), and the *for* loop would count from zero to 7199 in integer increments of two. The loop portion of the program would be written as:

```
for (t = 0; t <= 7200; t += 2) {
    x = r * sc[t] + a;
    y = r * sc[t + 1] + b;
    etc.
    etc.
```

In this function, t would be declared an integer argument instead of a double and the vast static array would be placed at the opening of the function immediately following the declaration lines. This would be a very large function, due to the amount of data in the sc array, but it would be very, very fast, and the circle would be drawn quite quickly.

All of the graphics functions discussed in this text should only be used when the computer is operating from the color card. If you have two monitors, operating from the monochrome display and the color card, chances are the monochrome display is the default monitor. To use these graphics functions, use the MS-DOS MODE command in the format of mode co80. This will "normalize" the computer output to the color monitor. Then you may run any C program containing these graphics functions.

The screen( ) function must be called first. This sets up the graphics screen with arguments of one or two (medium and high resolution). Once your monitor is in graphics mode, the screen may be written and read using the functions outlined here.

SCREEN UTILITY FUNCTIONS

I can remember my first year learning to program in C, at a time when there were very few compilers and even fewer books on programming in this strange language with the weird syntax. One goal I tried to achieve took over a year. This goal was to clear the screen the way BASIC does with the CLS statement. One must remember that, during this time, C compilers for microcomputers were quite limited in regard to addressing purely machine-type operations—those that required access outside of the 64K work area provided by these first compilers. Later, peek( ) and poke( ) were offered, and then int86( ). Now, we were knocking at the door of some real control.

Knowing little or nothing about programming in Assembler, reading from and writing to ports, and setting and reading registers, it was a long, uphill climb. Armed with my IBM Technical Reference Manual and not enough sense to know my quest was hopeless, I set out to acquire cls( ). After months of study, thousands of failed programs, and threats of quitting C completely, I arrived at it accidentally. I was trying to manipulate the cursor and arrived at some combination that cleared the screen and set the cursor to the upper right-hand corner of the screen. This, I later discovered, occurred because I had not supplied some register arguments I should have. The program was an incorrect one, but luck, accident, and the fortunes of those that are as happy as if they had good sense prevailed.

Through this experimentation, I learned more about my computer than I ever would have otherwise. Today, I am grateful for these early experiences. However, I don't recommend them. Most people do not write about computer programming for a living, as I do. And these people cannot afford to spend hundreds, or even thousands, of hours just "playing" with their machines, as I have been forced to do over the past ten years.

Therefore, the first function in this discussion of screen utility functions is, indeed, cls( ). Today, with the advent of far more efficient and "user-friendly" C compilers, clearing the screen is no problem at all. This, however, is a machine-dependent operation, so this function is not a part of the C standard function set.

Clearly, the easiest way to clear the screen is via a system( ) function call from Turbo C. This is simply an interface to, or even a return to, DOS (temporarily). Therefore, the following line:

```
system("CLS");
```

when used within any C program running under MS-DOS will result in a temporary exit from the current program, the entrance to DOS control, and the execution of the CLS command. Then, this command clears the screen and repositions the cursor to the top left-hand corner of the screen. Control is returned to the C program, which is reentered at the point immediately following the system( ) call.

There are a few practical problems with this, however. The main fault lies in speed. This is a slow method, because several DOS functions must be called to retain the currently executing C program in limbo, to return control to DOS, to execute the argument to system, to find the program in limbo again, and to restart this program's execution chain.

However, a few years ago, DOS software became equipped with the famed ANSI driver. It's not important to know exactly what it does or how it does it. It's only important to know that when the driver is installed via the

CONFIG.SYS file, you have opened a whole new way of interfacing with your operating system. Today, most MS-DOS machines will install the ANSI driver on boot-up. This allows an easy access to cls( ) and other screen utilities that, generally, move the cursor, set colors, etc.

With the ANSI driver in place, a simple string printed directly to the console will clear the screen. This is best accomplished using the printf( ) function in Turbo C. Better yet, use cprintf( ), which is the same as printf( ) in this usage as long as the output stream is not redirected from the screen. Sometimes, via other utilities, a program that normally outputs information to the screen can have this output redirected to the printer or some other device like the COM port. However, cprintf( ) always writes directly to the screen.

Writing the proper character sequence to the screen can offer direct control of screen functions. The following C function uses printf( ) to clear the screen and to set the cursor at the upper left-hand corner of the screen. Remember, this will only work when the ANSI device driver has been installed when MS-DOS was booted. The function source code follows:

```
cls()
{

    printf("%c[2J", 27);

}
```

That's all there is to it. This sequence will cause the ANSI driver to invoke the routines that will clear the text screen. The sequence is simply a character code that begins with the "escape" character, which is ASCII 27. This alerts the driver that a code is coming in. The remaining characters in the string are the code for clearing the screen.

There is a problem, however. This sequence will clear the text screen, but it won't clear a graphics screen. When the text screen is cleared, every odd byte in the 4000 byte screen is set to zero. Every even byte is set to seven, the screen attribute. Using this form of cls( ) on a graphics screen (i.e., one set up using the previously discussed screen( ) function) will paint white lines down its center for every even byte. Of course, this cls( ) function is quite simple, and if you don't intend to do any graphics work, then this is the way to go. However, if you want to learn a little more about your machine's ROM BIOS, then the following function might be more to your liking. This cls( ) function is multipurpose. It will first detect which screen mode is currently in effect and then clear this machine in the proper manner.

Graphic screens are cleared in one way and text screens in another. Both operations, however, address the ROM BIOS, and do not require the ANSI driver to be in place. This function is the one output by the CBREEZE translator when translating a BASIC CLS statement. The source code for this function is used with permission:

```
cls()
{

        int attr;
        union REGS r, *inregs, *outregs;

        attr = 0;
        inregs = &r;
        outregs = &r;

        r.h.ah = 15;

        int86(0x10, inregs, outregs);

        if (r.h.al == 7 || r.h.al < 4)
            attr = 7;

        r.h.ah = 6;
        r.h.bh = attr;
        r.h.ch = 0;
        r.h.cl = 0;
        r.h.dh = 24;
        r.h.dl = 79;
        r.h.al = 0;

        int86(0x10, inregs, outregs);

        r.h.ah = 2;
        r.h.bh = 0;
        r.h.dh = 0;
        r.h.dl = 0;

        int86(0x10, inregs, outregs);

}
```

This function is much longer than the previous example, but it executes rapidly, and no difference in the two will be discernible. Also, this one may be used anytime and anywhere the screen is to be cleared, whether in text or graphic mode.

This function performs three discrete operations via the ROM BIOS. Using int86( ), the first video interrupt is called with ah equal to 15. This is a routine that returns the current video state to the al register. The *if* statement construct tests for the returned value in al after the call to int86( ). If the value is seven, or less than four, then this is text mode and attr is set to a value of seven, this being the correct attribute value for text screens. However, if the value is not in the range tested for by the *if* statement clause, then attr remains at its initial setting of zero, an assignment made earlier in the function. This latter value is the correct value for clearing the graphics screens.

This has described the first of the three discrete operations performed by the cls( ) function. Now that you know what type of screen you are working with and what attribute value to use, it is necessary to erase all information from the screen. This is done using routine number 6 within the video interrupt. This is known as the "scroll active page up" routine. It clears the screen by figuratively scrolling existing information up through the top of the screen.

To access this routine, ah is assigned the value of six. Registers ch and cl are assigned the upper left-hand corner coordinates of the screen portion to be scrolled. These coordinates are given in text form regardless of the type of screen being cleared. These specifications are actually the row and column of the left top of the screen. Registers dh and dl are assigned the bottom right-hand row/column coordinates, which are 24 and 79 respectively. Finally, al is assigned a value equal to the number of lines to scroll. A zero value means to scroll the entire screen.

With the registers properly loaded, int86( ) is called again to make the video interrupt. The current contents of the screen will disappear, seemingly, immediately.

This has described the second discrete operation of the cls( ) function. Some readers might think they are done at this point, but there is one last operation to be performed. The cursor has not been affected by any of these operations so far. You must now call a routine that will allow you to move the cursor to coordinates 0,0 on the cleared screen.

Routine number 2 within the video interrupt sets the cursor position. Registers dh and dl are handed the row/column coordinates of zero, and bh is also set to zero. The bh register contains the page number which is zero for all graphics modes and will also be at this same value for all calls to cls( ), regardless of the screen mode.

Again, int86( ) is called and these values are passed to the correct registers. The cursor is immediately positioned at the upper left-corner of the screen. The cls( ) function has completed its three separate functions, and its exit allows the calling program to regain control. Note that any program that calls this function must #include the <dos.h> header file.

The explanation of this function has been thorough, because its operation should suggest to you at least one more screen utility function, and possibly a specialty function for future consideration. The latter would be a special windowing function that would clear only a portion of the screen via the scrolling routine. Remember, it was necessary to supply the row/column coordinates of the upper left-hand portion and the lower right-hand portion of the screen to be cleared. The cls( ) function named the edges of the physical screen (i.e., 0,0 and 24,79). However, another function might clear only the bottom right quadrant by specifying coordinates of 12,39 and 24,79.

The new screen utility function that cls( ) should suggest is one that will allow the text cursor to be moved about the screen via row/column arguments. Such a function is absolutely mandatory for high-level text printing operations. It would operate in the manner of the LOCATE statement in BASIC. Borrowing from cls( ), it's an easy task to write locate( ):

```
locate(x, y)
{

    int attr;
    union REGS r, *inregs, *outregs;
```

```
        inregs = &r;
        outregs = &r;

        r.h.ah = 2;
        r.h.bh = 0;
        r.h.dh = x - 1;
        r.h.dl = y - 1;

        int86(0x10, inregs, outregs);

    }
```

This function is simply the segment from cls( ) that positioned the cursor at the top left of the screen. The only change is to rename this function, locate( ), and to assign the value in x and y to the dh and dl registers minus one to make the row/column arguments, which are usually specified as 1,1 for the upper left-hand corner, conform with this routine's coordinate requirements.

GENERAL PROGRAMS AND UTILITIES

I originally wrote this next program using another C compiler, years before Turbo C came along. It was inspired by a public domain program I downloaded from some bulletin board in executable form. This program allowed any area of memory to be "dumped" to the screen in the fashion of DEBUG in MS-DOS.

This C program has been modified to take advantage of the ability of Turbo C to mix near and far pointers. Most of the complexity of this program deals with formatting the on-screen display. It is necessary to constantly convert long hexadecimal values into string equivalents and to convert these strings back to numbers again. All of this work is not necessary, but it makes for a far more attractive display. This program is quite long and a bit complex:

```
#include <dos.h>
#include <ctype.h>
main()
{
    unsigned char far *l;
    long x, strtol();
    int y, z, zz, off;
    char a[10], val[10], val2[10], c[20], val3[15];

    printf("%c[2J", 27);  /* Clear Screen */

    strcpy(val, "0000:0000");
    locate(21, 35);      /* Position Cursor */
    printf("%s", val);
    locate(21, 35);

    z = 0;
    off = 1;

    while (off) {
        z = 0;
        strcpy(val3, "0x");
```

```
            while (zz = getch()) {
                if (zz == 27) {
                    printf("%c[2J", zz);
                    exit(0);
                }
                if (zz == 13)
                    break;
                zz = toupper(zz);
                if (zz < '0' || zz > 'F')
                    continue;
                if (zz < 'A' && zz > 57)
                    continue;
                printf("%c", val2[z++] = zz);
                if (z == 4)
                    locate(21,40);
                if (z == 8) {
                    val2[z] = '\0';
                    break;
                }
            }

            locate(1, 1);
            if (z < 7) {
                zz = z;
                if (zz == 4)
                    ++zz;
                while (val2[z++] = val[zz++])
                    if (val[zz] ==':')
                        ++zz;
            }
            strcpy(val, val2);
            format(val);
            strcat(val3, val2);
            x = strtol(val3, c, 0);
            l = (unsigned char far *) x;  /* Set pointer to address */

            for (z = 0; z < 256; z += 16) {    /* Display bytes */
                sprintf(a,"%lx", x);
                format(a);              /* Makes mem locations neater */
                printf("%s  ", a);
                x += 16;
                for (y = 0; y < 16; ++y) {
                    zz = *(l + y);
                    if (zz < 16)
                        sprintf(a, "0%x", zz);
                    else
                        sprintf(a,"%x", zz);

                    printf("%c%c " , toupper(a[0]), toupper(a[1]));
                }

                printf("  *");

                for (y = 0; y <= 16; ++y) {     /* Display characters */
                    zz = *l++;
                    printf("%c", (isprint(zz)) ? zz : '.');
                }

                printf("\n");
```

```
            }

            locate(21, 35);
        }
}
format(c)    /* Make Hex letters upper case and add colon */
char c[];
{

        int x, y;
        char a[40], b[40];

        x = strlen(c);
        switch(x) {
              case 1:
                    strcpy(b, "0000000");
                    break;
              case 2:
                    strcpy(b, "000000");
                    break;
              case 3:
                    strcpy(b, "00000");
                    break;
              case 4:
                    strcpy(b, "0000");
                    break;
              case 5:
                    strcpy(b, "000");
                    break;
              case 6:
                    strcpy(b, "00");
                    break;
              case 7:
                    strcpy(b, "0");
                    break;
              default:
                      strcpy(b, "\0");
                      break;
        };

        x = y = 0;
        strcat(b, c);
        while (a[x++] = toupper(b[y++]))
              if (x == 4)
                    a[x++] = ':';

        strcpy(c, a);

}
locate(x, y)    /* Position text cursor on screen */
int x, y;
{

        union REGS r, *inregs, *outregs;

        inregs = &r;
        outregs = &r;
```

182

```
r.h.ah = 2;
r.h.bh = 0;
r.h.dh = x - 1;
r.h.dl = y - 1;

int86(0x10, inregs, outregs);

}
```

This program is divided into fairly logical blocks, so it should not be too terribly difficult to decipher. Don't forget the commented programs in the Appendix that will also aid you in learning from the programs and functions in this chapter.

The following is a printout of a program run using this program, which I have named memlook.c. This shows the first 256 bytes of memory at the monochrome screen buffer location of HEX B0000000. Each row displays the HEX bytes from 16 successive locations. Then, the printable characters that these bytes represent are also displayed on the same line. Any characters that are not printable are replaced by a period.

The memory location mini-window is at the bottom center of the screen. When you input a memory value, the characters in this window change with each keypress. You do not have to input the entire address. For instance, the screen sample shows the results of a read at B0000000. Now, if the next read was to be at C1000000, all you would have to input would be C1. The memory window would replace the original B with the C. The next 0 would be replaced with the 1. By pressing <return>, the memory address seen on the screen is converted from a string value to a HEX value, and the bytes starting at this location are displayed.

B000:0000	42	07	30	07	30	07	30	07	3A	07	30	07	30	07	30	07	*B.0.0.0.:.0.0.0.0
B000:0010	07	20	07	20	07	34	07	32	07	20	07	30	07	37	07	20	*. . .4.2. .0.7. .
B000:0020	33	07	30	07	20	07	30	07	37	07	20	07	33	07	30	07	*3.0. .0.7. .3.0.
B000:0030	07	30	07	37	07	20	07	33	07	30	07	20	07	30	07	37	*.0.7. .3.0. .0.7.
B000:0040	20	07	33	07	41	07	20	07	30	07	37	07	20	07	33	07	* .3.A. .0.7. .3.0
B000:0050	07	20	07	30	07	37	07	20	07	33	07	30	07	20	07	30	*. .0.7. .3.0. .0.
B000:0060	37	07	20	07	33	07	30	07	20	07	30	07	37	07	20	07	*7. .3.0. .0.7. .
B000:0070	07	2A	07	42	07	2E	07	30	07	2E	07	30	07	2E	07	30	*.*.B...0...0...0.
B000:0080	2E	07	3A	07	2E	07	30	07	2E	07	30	07	2E	07	30	07	*..:...0...0...0..
B000:0090	07	30	07	20	07	20	07	42	07	30	07	30	07	30	07	3A	*.0. . .B.0.0.0.:.
B000:00A0	30	07	30	07	31	07	30	07	20	07	20	07	30	07	37	07	*0.0.1.0. . .0.7.
B000:00B0	07	32	07	30	07	20	07	30	07	37	07	20	07	32	07	30	*.2.0. .0.7. .2.0.
B000:00C0	20	07	30	07	37	07	20	07	33	07	34	07	20	07	30	07	* .0.7. .3.4. .0.7
B000:00D0	07	20	07	33	07	32	07	20	07	30	07	37	07	20	07	32	*. .3.2. .0.7. .2.
B000:00E0	30	07	20	07	30	07	37	07	20	07	33	07	30	07	20	07	*0. .0.7. .3.0. .0
B000:00F0	07	37	07	20	07	33	07	37	07	20	07	30	07	37	07	20	*.7. .3.7. .0.7. .

B000:0000

183

To repeat, most of the complexity of this program deals with the appearance of the on-screen display and the mechanisms converting a string to a hex number and a hex number to a string.

The screen is initially cleared with printf("*%c[2J*", 27); which was discussed in an earlier chapter. This is a code that will cause machines with the ANSI drive installed to clear the text screen. If your machine doesn't install the ANSI driver on boot-up, this code will not work. Consult your DOS manual for information on setting up a CONFIG file that includes the ANSI driver assignment.

Next, a string equal to "0000:0000" is copied to val[ ]. This array will serve as the beginning memory location window value. The locate( ) function discussed earlier positions the cursor at the bottom center of the screen and val[ ] is displayed. The locate( ) function is called again to reposition the cursor at the first zero in the screen window.

A *while* loop is entered. This is simply an endless loop that will continue to cycle, because *off*, an integer variable, has been permanently set to a value of one. Program exit occurs when the ESCape key is pressed. This causes a condition test within the loop to execute the exit( ) statement.

Upon entering the outside loop, variable z is set to zero and the string "0x" is copied to val3[ ]. This is the array that will receive the address that is input by the user to the memory window. This address originates as a string of characters, not a number. However, the characters in the string, if converted to the number that they, collectively, represent, name the desired memory address. In other words, when you input a value of B8000000, it is a string value derived via the keyboard. It is not a number, but rather the string of characters: 'B' '0' '0' '0' '0' '0' '0' '0' '\0'. Later, a function will be called that will convert this string to the HEX number B8000000. In order to do this, the string must have the 0x prefix. Val3[ ] contains the leading 0x. At another point, the input address string will be concatenated to val[3]. This will form a string consisting of the input address string preceded by 0x, the latter being the C code for a hex number.

A nested loop is entered, and this is where most of the work is done. Each time the loop cycles, a character is read from the keyboard into zz using getch( ). *If* statements abound at the opening of the loop to test for various values from the keyboard and execute other lines based upon this input. If zz is equal to 27, this means the ESCape key was pushed. This causes the screen to be cleared again and the program to be exited. If zz is equal to 13 (the ASCII code for the newline character), the inner loop is broken out of. This means the user has input all of the values needed to cause the address window to name the desired memory location. Remember, the keyboard input changes the address one character at a time. It is not necessary to input all eight values, because the window might reflect a large portion of the address desired already. Refer to the previous example of B0000000 and C1000000.

If the execution chain within this loop makes it this far, zz is converted to the uppercase equivalent of the character it presently holds. This is done with toupper( ). If the character is already uppercase, no conversion takes place.

184

The next two *if* statement constructs test whether characters other than A through F or 0 through 9 have been input. Characters a through f are also legal, because they are converted to uppercase by the time they reach these conditional tests. If a character is determined to be outside of the acceptable range of characters used to write hex quantities (the letter 'H' for instance), the *continue* statement is executed. This causes the execution path to immediately revert back to the top of the loop. The loop cycles again. This means that an illegal character will simply not be recognized as part of the address. The keyboard will continue to be read until a legal character is input, or ESCape or <Return> are pressed. Assuming a legal character, this is assigned to the current character position in val2, then it is displayed on the screen, overwriting the applicable character in the address window.

Another *if* statement test is performed to test for a value of four in z. This means that the next character-write to the window would occur at the position where the colon separator is positioned. In true hex numbers, there are no colons. This character is written in the window address for clarity and for the sake of convention. When z is equal to four, the locate( ) function is called again and simply repositions the cursor at the next column position. This means that the colon is fixed on the screen and can't be overwritten. The next screen write will be to the position immediately following the colon.

The last *if* test within this nested loop checks the value of z again. If it is equal to eight, then all eight characters have been input via the keyboard. This means the full memory address has been specified by the user, and no further characters are allowed. The characters in val2 are terminated with the null character when *if* detects a value of eight in z and the break statement exits from the inner loop.

Still in the outer *while* loop but outside of the inner loop, locate( ) is called again to position the cursor at the top left of the screen. This is where the listing of memory locations and bytes will begin. An *if* statement test for z being less than seven. If true, this means that the user changed less than eight characters in the address window. The remaining portion of the address must be obtained from the current value of val[ ]. Before going to this array, however, another test is made to see if zz is equal to four. This would be the offset of the colon in val[ ], and you don't want that. If zz is equal to four, it is incremented to five. Again, the colon has been skipped over. This test will prove true only when three characters were input by the user.

Next, a *while* loop is entered that copies the remaining contents of val[ ] (those that were not overwritten with user input) to the tail end of val2[ ]. The latter already contains the characters input by the user. Within this loop, an *if* statement checks for the return of the colon from val[ ]. This will occur if three or less characters were input by the user. If the colon is found, zz is incremented to the character beyond it. The transfer of characters continues until the null character terminating val[ ] is copied to val2[ ]. The loop terminates.

The next step uses strcpy( ) to copy the new memory address, still in string form, to val. The format( ) function is called with val as its argument. Format( )

is a function that is listed with this program. Its purpose is to "normalize" string arguments. It is called twice in this program. This particular call uses format( ) to simply insert the colon after the fourth character. A later call uses the abilities of format( ) to a higher degree. Again, you want val to contain the colon. You don't want val2 to have one, because this value will be converted to a true hex number and the conversion function doesn't allow for colons to be a part of the string argument.

This conversion process takes place by first concatenating the contents of val2 to val3 using strcat( ). This produces a string that consists of the 0x hex prefix followed by the memory address in string form. This string is now ready to be converted to a hex number.

The strtol( ) function is used for this purpose. An acronym for "string-to-long," this function assigns to x, a long integer, the long integer value contained in val3. If val3 had been equal to the string, "0xB1239875," then x would now equal the hex number, B1239875.

At the beginning of this long discussion, I stated that most of the complexity involved in this program dealt with display and string-to-hex or hex-to-string conversion. It is at this point in the program that the memory address has finally been determined and the memory locations are actually sought out.

A far pointer, l, was declared at the opening of this program. It is of type unsigned char, which means it may represent any value from 0 to 255. This is the total range of byte values in memory. This pointer is assigned the memory address contained in the value of x. This pointer now references the memory location input by the user.

A *for* loop is entered that counts variable z from zero to 255 in steps of 16. The full screen will display the 256 successive bytes from the user-supplied memory location in rows of 16 bytes. The sprintf( ) function is used to copy the numeric memory address in c to array a. This converts the address, which was so laboriously converted from a string to a number, back to a number again. Why?

The answer lies in how numbers are displayed. For instance, the string address 0100:0000 would be displayed as the number 100000. The string address 000:0001 would be displayed as the number one. This messes up our formatting. Now, it's easy to increment numbers, but it is not possible (in a practical sense) to increment strings that represent number unless they are converted to numbers, incremented, then converted back to strings. This is what is taking place here. We have converted the initial memory address to a number. This number was assigned to x and, in turn, to l, so that the far pointer could access the desired memory locations.

On the next loop pass, after the first 16 bytes at the beginning location have been displayed, the value of the number in x will be incremented by 16. This produces the next starting address for displaying the next 16 bytes. However, we want to print this new address on the screen. To do this in the format desired, it must be converted back to a string, one that reflects the incrementation. Then, this string can be formatted and displayed with a full eight characters and a colon.

186

After the value has been converted to a string, format( ) is called again. This time, the full features of this function are put to use. Format( ) counts the number of characters in the string, and "pads" it with zeros to arrive at a total character count of eight. It also inserts the colon at the right location. A switch is used that determines how many leading zeros are needed for the pad. When the loop is exited, array b contains a string of zeros that are to be the pad. The original content of the string argument is concatenated to b, then a *while* loop counts through the characters in this string, one at a time, and assigns them to array a, after converting each to uppercase. The colon is inserted at the fourth character position. Finally, the newly formatted string is copied over the contents of the original argument.

Returning to the main program, the formatted string is now displayed on the screen via printf( ). The value in x is incremented again, and a nested *for* loop is entered. This one displays the sixteen hex bytes at the memory offsets referenced by $*(l + y)$. However, even these bytes must be formatted based upon their content. Values of less than decimal 16 will contain only a one character number. Larger values will be represented by a two-character expression. Therefore, sprintf( ) is called again to write the string equivalent of the hex bytes to a. The *if* statement tests the value in zz. If it is less than 16, then the string pads with one zero. If it is more than 16, then the string is written as the original hex value. This is confusing, because the value of the byte in zz is tested in decimal form.

To C, a number is a number, regardless of the base. The number in **zz** is the byte at the memory offset. While it will be displayed in hex format, it can be referenced in any format. I conveniently chose to test for a decimal value of 16 (hex F), because I am more accustomed to thinking in decimal values. However, for the sake of clarity, the *if* construct could have been written as:

```
if (zz < 0xF)
     sprintf(a, "0%x", zz);
```

Next, the contents of a are displayed on the screen one character at a time by the printf( ) function. This allows toupper( ) to be used to convert any lowercase characters in the string to uppercase. This complex process of formatting bytes continues until a full row of 16 has been written.

But, you're not done yet. This program will also display the printable characters that these bytes represent. A printf( ) statement writes an asterisk to the end of the just-completed byte row. This character simply serves as a separator that is pleasing to the eye.

Another *for* loop is entered. This one also counts from zero to 16. Remember, in the former loop, the pointer to the base memory location was not incremented. Offsets were obtained from the expression $*(l + y)$. Therefore, when this last *for* loop is entered, $*l$ still points to the base memory location. However, $*l$ is now incremented by one after the byte to which it points is assigned to zz. Then, a printf( ) function is called to display the byte on the screen as a character. However, the conditional expression is used within the printf( ) function argument list.

Isprint( ) will return a value not equal to zero if the character is a printing type (as opposed to a control character). When the character is printable, it is displayed by printf( ). If, however, some other character is identified, the period is displayed instead.

When all 16 of the characters have been displayed, the first displayed line of the program is complete. The printf( ) function is called once more for a new line, and the next display line is begun. When all 256 bytes have filled the screen, the locate( ) function is called again to return the cursor to the memory window. The user may then input another location to "peek" at.

This is a rather intense program for relative newcomers to C, but as you attain a higher degree of understanding, aspects of this program will be more comprehensible and might even spark an idea for a new program or two.

Chapter 8

CBREEZE

Authors of books on microcomputer software generally tend to obtain research models of new software quite some time before the actual product is actually released to the general public, it should come as no surprise that as most of the words in this book are being written, the Turbo C compiler has not been released by Borland International. This chapter, however, is being written some two weeks after the official release of Turbo C, and to date only one company is offering a side product that specifically addresses Turbo C. When you read these words, there will probably be many adjuncts to Turbo C, including special libraries, diagnostic utilities, etc.

The single product that, at this writing, is packaged and released is called CBREEZE. This is a BASIC-to-C tutorial translator that is designed specifically for the BASIC programmer who wants to learn to program in C within the shortest time possible. CBREEZE has been on the market since the middle of 1986. Previously, this product was available for the Lattice C compiler, Microsoft C compiler (Version 4.0), and the RUN/C Interpreter. The latest addition to this repertoire is the version for Turbo C. Much of the following discussion uses sample programs and materials from the CBREEZE User's Manual that accompanies the software.

The CBREEZE BASIC-to-C tutorial translator was written to "think" like an experienced C language programmer whose duty is to translate Microsoft BASIC programs into C source code. Its output code is very close to that which would be rendered by a human programmer. The source code that CBREEZE outputs adheres strictly to the format and style presented in *The C Program-*

ming Language by Brian Kernighan and Dennis Ritchie. CBREEZE doesn't just display C source code equivalents of BASIC programs but displays this code in blocks (the way a programmer would), with special attention to providing correct indentations, spacing, etc.

For instance, the following BASIC code:

```
10 FOR I%=1 TO 1000
20 PRINT I%
30 NEXT I%
```

is translated into C as:

```
main()
{

    int i;

    for (i = 1; i <= 1000; ++i)
        printf(" %d \n", i);


}
```

This is exactly the way it would be expressed according to Kernighan and Ritchie, including indentations, line spacing, and white spaces on the line.

CBREEZE adheres to this style regardless of BASIC program complexity. The translator was designed specifically for tutorial purposes, but this doesn't mean that the code can't be compiled or used by the Turbo C compiler. All output code is fully compilable.

USING CBREEZE

To run CBREEZE, all that is necessary is to write a BASIC program, make sure it runs correctly under BASIC, and then save it as an ASCII file. Note that it is preferable to write the BASIC program using BASIC's editor as opposed to another line editor. CBREEZE expects all BASIC statements and variables to be in uppercase. The BASIC editor will do this for you automatically. If you use another editor, make sure that uppercase is used for all but quoted phrases. The following format is used for invoking CBREEZE:

TCB FILENAME.BAS FILENAME.C OPTION

FILENAME.BAS is the name of the BASIC file to be translated, FILENAME.C is the name of the new file to hold the translated C source code, and OPTION is equal to either zero or one. The zero option value is specified when the source code is not going to be executed. In this mode, the source code for special functions that emulate BASIC functions such as MID$, RIGHT$, and LEFT$ is not included as a part of the C file. If you intend to run your translated program under a C compiler or interpreter, then use an option value of one. This will trigger the translator to include the source code for any specialized functions, and the program should be fully executable.

When you press <Return>, the CBREEZE logo will appear on the screen and a prompt will tell you which BASIC program is being translated and what the name of the holding file is. If you would prefer to have the translated code displayed on the monitor, simply specify SCREEN for FILENAME.C. This file may also be directed to the parallel printer by specifying PRINTER. If you name a nonexistent or inappropriate file, or if you do not include enough arguments when invoking CBREEZE, an error message will appear and execution will be halted.

CBREEZE gives the BASIC programmer a great deal of flexibility in the types of programs that may be translated into C source code. However, its purpose is to teach C language, and not to reinforce bad habits by correcting obvious mistakes automatically. The user must be aware of the types of arguments certain C functions expect to receive, as well as the types of values they return. The documentation with CBREEZE informs the user of this fact and suggests methods for staying within the scope of what CBREEZE will accept and translate into executable C source code. For instance, arguments to functions such as LOG, SQR, and SIN must always be double-precision floating-point values. This means that all variables must be of double-precision type, or cast to double-precision using the BASIC CDBL( ) function. If a constant is used for an argument, then it must contain a decimal point, as in 23.7 or 3.0. CBREEZE won't balk if you provide an inappropriate argument. It will translate it without a single complaint. However, the C source code will not execute properly because the equivalent functions in C require double-precision arguments. CBREEZE will simply carry your error into the C program. Error messages generated by the Turbo C compiler will target such errors.

Of course, Turbo C offers some built-in protections. The above situation can be overcome by #including the math.h header file with any program calling a complex math function. CBREEZE, for the most part, simply makes a literal translation of the BASIC program. The use of integer quantities as arguments to functions that are supposed to be supplied floating-point values is considered improper programming, even if the program can be made to run correctly by the inclusion of a header file. CBREEZE makes you do a lot of the work, and won't make such corrections for you.

This is not a criticism of CBREEZE. As a matter of fact, the transference of errors provides a very strong tutorial advantage. It is not an error to provide a function such as LOG in BASIC with an argument that is not a double-precision value. This is, however, an error in C and log( ) will not return a correct value. Assuming that the math.h header file has not been #included in a program that calls one of these math functions, then an improper argument value will be picked up by Turbo C when you execute the compiled program. This will be a Domain Error and is a sure indication that an improper argument type has been handed to a function.

CBREEZE could easily have been modified to include the (double) cast operator within every function that requires a double argument. This way, any numeric argument to such functions would be acceptable, because it would be cast (coerced) to double-precision type. But this would have reenforced a practice that causes BASIC programmers tremendous headaches when making the switch to C. The purpose of CBREEZE is to teach C language, and not to simply translate any BASIC program to C source code. The actual beginning of this tutorial starts in the BASIC environment by instructing users as to the types of arguments that should be used with functions that have direct C equivalencies.

To further explain CBREEZE it is necessary to go through several program translations. The following pages will show actual BASIC programs and their C source code as translated by CBREEZE. In all cases, the BASIC source code is shown exactly as it was input to CBREEZE and the C source code is exactly as it was output by the Turbo C (Version 4.0) of CBREEZE.

The first translation involves a simple FOR-NEXT loop that counts from 0 to 1000 in steps of one (which is the default). On each pass of the loop, the value of the loop variable is displayed on the monitor screen using the following code:

```
10   FOR I%=0 TO 1000
20   PRINT I%
30   NEXT I%
```

This program requires no explanation other than to note that integer variable I% is used as a loop variable as opposed to the floating-point variable I. The reasons for this lie in the fact that the loop variable need only represent integer values, so this is the most efficient way of writing the program.

Assuming that this program was saved to a disk file as TST.BAS, the following CBREEZE invocation will translate it, storing the C version in a disk file named TST.C:

```
TCB   TST.BAS   TST.C   1
```

The option value of one is used in this example, although a zero would have sufficed, because there are no special functions such as MID$ or RIGHT$.

The following listing is the exact translation of the previous BASIC program as produced by CBREEZE:

```
main()
{

    int i;

    for (i = 0; i <= 1000; ++i)
        printf(" %d \n", i);

}
```

If this looks like standard, "textbook" C source code, that's because it is. Seasoned C programmers might have noticed a peculiarity in the printf( ) line. Most C programmers would have omitted the spaces before and after the %d conversion specification. However, CBREEZE translates quite literally, and in BASIC, the instruction PRINT I% will cause the value of I% to be displayed

192

with a preceding and trailing space. Therefore, this translated C source version is anactual equivalent of the BASIC program.

Now, suppose the BASIC source code had used a single-precision floating-point loop variable as in the following:

```
10  FOR I=0 TO 1000
20  PRINT I
30  NEXT I
```

This program would be translated by CBREEZE as:

```
main()
{

    float i;

    for (i = 0; i <= 1000; ++i)
        printf(" %f \n", i);


}
```

This program is perfectly correct, but the displayed results when run under C will not be the same as those of the BASIC program. The BASIC program example will display the values of 0 through 1000 as integers (i.e., no decimal portion). In BASIC, floating-point values that have no fractional portion (other than zero) are displayed as integers. Therefore, both BASIC program examples will display the same thing, although the integer version will run faster.

In C, the situation is different. The C translation of the first BASIC example will output the same information to the screen as the BASIC program did. The translation of the second BASIC example, however, will result in a screen display of:

```
1.000000
2.000000
3.000000
4.000000
5.000000
etc.
```

Notice that the printf( ) function in the second C translation uses a conversion specifier of %f. This tells the function to expect a floating-point argument, and to display it in standard floating format. Both the BASIC program and the C translation do exactly the same thing. They count a floating-point variable I(i) from 0.000000 to 1000.000. The differences lie only in the way the values of this variable are displayed. BASIC does it one way and C, another.

While these program examples have been quite simple, they do address the user-friendliness of CBREEZE. The FOR-NEXT statement in the BASIC programs did not contain a STEP specification. In BASIC, the omission of STEP simply brings about a default which tells BASIC that STEP is equal to one. CBREEZE makes the same assumption and outputs a *for* loop with a step value of one. In other words, CBREEZE defaults in the same manner as BASIC. The following BASIC program is a modification of the first two examples, and uses a STEP value of two. Also, a mathematical operation is performed on the loop variable before its value is written to the monitor:

```
10  FOR I%=0 TO 1000 STEP 2
20  PRINT I%*2
30  NEXT I%
```

This loop counts in increments of two for a sequence of 1, 3, 5, 7, etc. On each pass of the loop, the value of X% is multiplied by the value of four before it is written to the screen.

When run through CBREEZE, the above program is translated as:

```
main()
{

    int i;

    for (i = 0; i <= 1000; i += 2)
        printf(" %d \n", i * 2);


}
```

Again, this is a literal translation, and this C conversion will run exactly like the BASIC program it translated. The step value is represented in compressed form as $x + = 2$, which is the exact equivalent of $x = x + 2$. The mathematical operation is carried out within the printf( ) function and, again, is presented in standard textbook C format.

The following BASIC program uses nested loops:

```
10  FOR H%=1 TO 100
20  FOR I%=0 TO 1000 STEP 2
30  PRINT I%*2
40  NEXT
50  NEXT
```

This example takes the previous BASIC program and nests it within another FOR-NEXT loop. Each time the outer loop cycles, the inner loop is run in its entirety. The outer loop cycles 100 times, so the inner loop counts from 0 to 1000 one hundred times.

CBREEZE translated this BASIC program as:

```
main()
{

    int h, i;

    for (h = 1; h <= 100; ++h)
        for (i = 0; i <= 1000; x += 2)
            printf(" %d \n", x * 2);


}
```

This example relates directly to the formatting of the source code. Notice that CBREEZE observes the "whitespaces" C source code convention. Each line of code is indented the proper five spaces within each individual block. This is the way Kernighan and Ritchie would have written it.

Many textbooks devoted to teaching C language do not adhere as closely to these source code formatting conventions as does CBREEZE. You will also notice that mathematical and conditional operators are separated from their left and right values by a space. None of this is necessary to arrive at an executable or compilable C program. These formatting conventions are designed specifically to aid the programmer in quickly understanding what has already been written. Notice also that the BASIC program ended each loop with a NEXT statement followed by the name of the loop variable. In Microsoft BASIC, it is not necessary to include the loop variable with NEXT. MS-BASIC can figure out which loop is controlled by untitled NEXT statements. From the C translation, it can be seen that CBREEZE can do likewise.

The following program demonstrates how CBREEZE is able to handle the inclusion and/or exclusion of braces to contain multiple loop statements:

```
10  FOR H%=1 TO 100
20  PRINT"Start of run #";H%;"in nested loop"
30  FOR I%=0 TO 1000 STEP 2
40  PRINT I%*2
50  NEXT
60  NEXT
```

This program is not significantly different from the previous example. An extra PRINT statement has been added at line 20 and displays a prompt at the beginning of each entry into the nested loop, displaying the outer loop cycle count.

The CBREEZE translation of this program is:

```
main()
{

    int h, i;

    for (h = 1; h <= 100; ++h) {
        printf("%s %d %s\n","Start of run #", h, "in nested loop");

        for (i = 0; i <= 1000; i += 2)
            printf(" %d \n", i * 2);
    }

}
```

This is a correct translation, showing that CBREEZE knows when and where to include braces as well as when and where not to. The outer loop contains two program statements, *printf( )* and *for*. The latter is the nested loop.

When multiple statements are used within a loop, these must be enclosed by braces. However, when only one statement is found within a loop, braces are not necessary. In this example, the outer loop has multiple statements and these are enclosed by braces. However, the inner loop contains only a single statement so braces are not included. This program closely follows the unwritten rules of C source code formatting, although some programmers would not have included an empty line between printf( ) and for. CBREEZE will precede any loop with an empty line. This applies whether a loop is nested or not. The program invokes quite an elaborate routine in order to display the C source code in a textbook style. This occurs near the end of the translation and prior to this point, the C code lines effectively begin at the left hand margin. The formatting routine looks for indications of programming blocks, assignment operators, and a host of other C code factors. It then decides how much whitespace is required at each line to present a properly formatted display.

Moving on to other types of programs, we can see how CBREEZE translates other aspects of the BASIC language into C source code counterparts. The following BASIC program uses the MID$ function to extract a portion of a string value:

```
10   A$="Microcomputer"
20   B$=MID$(A$,6,7)
30   PRINT B$
```

This program extracts a seven-character substring from A$ and assigns this value to B$. The value of B$ is then displayed on the monitor screen. C language contains no equivalent of the MID$ function, so this is a situation where CBREEZE must supply its own function to cover the mechanics of MID$. Fortunately, any special functions such as this one causes CBREEZE to access certain built-in source files which are displayed as part of the translated C source code. This is demonstrated by the following translation:

```
main()
{

        char a_[80], b_[80];

        strcpy(a_, "Microcomputer");
        mid_(b_, a_, 6, 7);

        printf("%s\n", b_);

}
mid_(a, b, x, y)
char *a, *b;
int x, y;
{

        --x;
```

196

```
    y += x;

    while (x < y && x <= strlen(b))
        *a++ = *(b + x++);

    *a = '\0';

}
```

This is the first translated example involving string variables. All BASIC string variables are converted to lowercase, and the "$" symbol, illegal as a part of a variable name in C, is changed to the underline character, "_". Incidentally, this underline character in no way modifies a C variable as "$" does to BASIC variables. The underline character is just like any other character, and may be used as the part of a C variable's name, regardless of the type of data the variable is to represent.

All string functions in CBREEZE that emulate BASIC string functions are given similar names, but again, the customary "$" is BASIC functions like RIGHT$ and MID$, are replaced by the underline, as in right_( ) and mid_( ).

Notice that the original BASIC string variables have been translated as char arrays at the beginning of the program. Each array can hold up to 80 characters, which breaks down to a maximum of 79 standard characters plus the terminating null character. This is not an exact translation of the BASIC program example, although one would never know it by viewing the results of running the program. In MS-BASIC, each string variable can hold up to 255 characters. In C, this would mean char arrays dimensioned to 256 characters (255 standard and one null character). The author of CBREEZE chose to dimension the translated arrays to 80 characters because this represents more storage space than most programmers will ever need for a single string variable. If each array were sized to 256 bytes, there could be a problem with storage space when a program that contained many string variables was run.

When programming in C, character arrays are dimensioned with a knowledge of the size of the strings they will be used to hold. CBREEZE has no knowledge of what the programmer intends in this area, so a value of 80 was chosen, which should be large enough (or even overly large) for most applications and still small enough to at least attempt to conserve stack space. If there is a problem, you can always edit the translated program and increase the size of the arrays.

The strcpy( ) function is used to copy the string constant to array a_. Then, mid_( ) is called. This is a built-in CBREEZE function that is displayed properly at the bottom of the executable portion of the C program. In other words, CBREEZE has generated the code to emulate BASIC's MID$ function in C. This is a portable function that should work with any C compiler.

The CBREEZE generated function accepts four arguments. The first is the char array that will contain the extracted portion of the second argument, which is also a char array. The next two arguments are integers specifying the starting character position and the number of characters to be extracted.

The source code of the function is fairly straightforward and uses char pointers to assign the desired contents of b to a. Notice that at the end of the function the null character ($\setminus 0$) is tacked on to the end of a. This signals the end of the character string.

The next BASIC example dimensions a string array and fills it within the body of a FOR-NEXT loop with the constant "Microcomputer". Another loop is entered and the assigned contents of the array are written to the screen in sequential order:

```
10   DIM A$(10)
20   FOR X%=0 TO 10
30   A$(X%)="Microcomputer"
40   NEXT X%
50   FOR X%=0 TO 10
60   PRINT A$(X%)
70   NEXT
```

CBREEZE translates BASIC string arrays as arrays of character pointers in C. Multidimensional character arrays can also be used to represent the equivalent of BASIC string arrays, arrays of pointers were used to provide the user with some experience in handling them. The translation follows:

```
main()
{

        char *malloc();
        int x;
        char *a$[11];

        for (x = 0; x <= 10; ++x)
                strcpy(a_[x] = malloc(80), "Microcomputer");

        for (x = 0; x <= 10; ++x)
                printf("%s\n", a_[x]);

}
```

The malloc function is a standard UNIX memory allocation function that causes a__[x] to point to an allocated area of memory which is of adequate size to hold an 80 character string. The argument to malloc is 80. This sets aside 80 sequential bytes in memory to hold any assignments to this pointer, ensuring that a free area of memory is provided for storage and that important areas of memory are not overwritten.

On each pass of the loop, the strcpy function is called. It copies the string "Microcomputer" into the memory location pointed to by a__[x]. Notice that x has been declared an int. If the BASIC program had used a loop variable of X instead of X%, then the translated C code would have declared this variable a float. A floating-point variable should not be used to name an array position in C. The Turbo C compiler internally coerces all array subscripts to int values, so the use of floats, doubles, etc. for these subscripts will not generate an error message, and the program should run without any problem. However, this won't fly with most other C environments, and programs written without regard to the type of array subscripts used might not be portable.

When the first *for* loop is exited, another one is entered and the contents of the array of pointers is displayed in sequential order. The program then terminates normally, after displaying each array value on the screen.

Memory allocated by malloc( ) or other memory functions should be freed when those locations are no longer needed. This can present problems with CBREEZE translations that are actually executed if a great deal of memory allocation take place. CBREEZE does not provide the code for freeing allocated memory, because it has no way of knowing when a particular pointer is no longer required. There is no problem in the sample program, because allocated memory is freed upon program exit. However, if the program were expanded to include other arrays of pointers, it is conceivable that you could run out of memory storage space if you did not free up allocations to pointers that were no longer to be used. Also of note is the fact that this program does not check malloc( ) for a null return, indicating the unavailability of the requested memory. Most small programs translated by CBREEZE won't have a problem here, so this might be an area where a bad habit is reenforced. All uses of memory allocation functions should also include a check to see if the memory requested is indeed available. Fortunately, malloc( ) is only used in this manner when translating string arrays.

The next program example puts CBREEZE through some paces in translating BASIC mathematical operations and functions into C source code. This program uses double-precision, single-precision and integer variables along with the BASIC LOG and raise-to functions:

```
10   REM TEST OF MATH FUNCTIONS
20   X#=13.23
30   Y#=1.25
40   D%=LOG(X#)
50   A=X#^Y#
60   S#=LOG(X#^2.1^A.5^Y#)
70   PRINT D%;A;S#
```

In line 40, integer variable D% is assigned the value of LOG(X#). Because LOG returns a double-precision value, only the integer portion of this return will be represented by D%. In line 50, single-precision variable A is assigned the double-precision value of X# raised to the Y# power. Finally, in line 60, double-precision variable S# is assigned the return of the LOG of X# raised to various powers. Here, two functions are involved, with raise-to returning a value to LOG, which returns a value to S#.

CBREEZE translated the above program in the following manner:

```
/* TEST OF MATH FUNCTIONS */

main()
{

        double x, y, log(), s, pow();
        float a;
        int d;

        x = 13.23;
        y = 1.25;
        d = log(x);
        a = pow(x, y);
        s = log(pow(pow(pow(x, 2.1), 1.5), y));

        printf(" %d  %f  %lf \n", d, a, s);

}
```

This is an excellent translation. Notice that the various blocks of the program are separated by a full line of whitespace. The declaration block is separated from the assignment block, which in turn is separated from the screen display block. Block definition will not always be so well defined, but in every case the CBREEZE translations should be easy to read and understand.

C language treats individual characters as separate data types, different from strings and numbers. In BASIC, there are only two general data types, string and numerical. There is no direct equivalent to the C language char data type in BASIC. If you wish to represent alphabetic characters, then you must use a string variable. However, CBREEZE has the ability, in some translations, to make use of C's ability to display individual characters. The following BASIC program demonstrates this capability when translated into C:

```
10  PRINT CHR$(67);CHR$(68)
```

Here, the CHR$ function is used to return a string composed of the character represented by ASCII 67 and another composed of the character represented by ASCII 68. In C, single characters do not need to be displayed as a string. They stand on their own and can be represented as the character itself (contained in single quotes), or as the ASCII character code. The CBREEZE translation treats these ASCII values as char data types:

```
main()
{

        printf("%c%c\n", 67, 68);

}
```

The printf( ) function is provided with two %c conversion specifications to display the character equivalent of the integers that serve as arguments. All references to CHR$ have been deleted. Only the arguments to CHR$ have been retained and these values displayed as characters by printf( ). This can carry over to other BASIC functions as well, as the following program demonstrates:

```
10  PRINT CHR$(66),HEX$(48),OCT$(127)
```

This program displays the character represented by ASCII 66, the hexadecimal value of decimal 48 and the octal equivalent of decimal 127. The functions are separated from each other by commas instead of semicolons.

In BASIC, comma separators bring about a special formatting of arguments to PRINT; a field of fourteen spaces is set aside for each argument. This program will display:

```
B               30              177
```

CBREEZE translates the above example in C (as opposed to literal) form, as in:

```
main()
{

    printf("%-14c%-14x%o\n", 66, 48, 127);

}
```

As before, the special BASIC functions that display numbers in the range of 0 to 255 in other than decimal formats have been done away with. These functions are deleted because they are not necessary in C, at least not for displaying these various types of information.

Notice that the first two conversion specifications are preceded by − 14. This value indicates that 14 spaces are to be set aside for the display of the argument represented by this specification. This allows the literal translation of a PRINT statement line that uses comma separators. In addition to the %c conversion specification, you will also see %x and %o. The latter two convert integer values to hexadecimal and octal format, respectively. These are still integer values, but are displayed in a form that uses a base other than 10. They are not string values as they would be in BASIC.

The above example is not a literal translation, but an *interpretation* of a BASIC program, much like one that would be made by an experienced C language programmer. Either way, the C language version creates the same screen display as the BASIC program does.

BASIC allows string values to be added in a mathematical way. This is not the way it would be accomplished in C or, for that matter, in nearly any other language. The following BASIC program assigns two string variables the constants "MICRO" and "COMPUTER." Next, C$ is assigned the value of these two strings, added together. The result is then displayed on the monitor screen:

```
10 A$="MICRO"
20 B$="COMPUTER"
30 C$=A$+B$
40 PRINT C$
```

This program will display the word, "MICROCOMPUTER."

CBREEZE removes all mathematical references in the C translation:

```
main()
{

    char a_[80], b_[80], c_[80];

    strcpy(a_, "MICRO");
    strcpy(b_, "COMPUTER");
    sprintf(c_, "%s%s", a_, b_);
    printf("%s\n", c_);


}
```

An obvious C language method to add string values is via the sprintf( ) function, which works in the same manner as printf( ), except that the output is not written to the screen but to a char array. This function was discussed in an earlier chapter of this text. One must make certain that the array size (80) is adequate to contain the concatenated string values. For instance, if a__ contained 60 characters and b__ contained 25, then the total length would be 85 characters. This would be larger than the declared size of c__, because CBREEZE dimensions all char arrays to 80 elements. When two or more very large strings are added, it might be necessary to edit the C source code in order to enlarge the size of the array that receives these strings to a value capable of containing the new length.

The following BASIC program increases the complexity of a string-add operation:

```
10 A$="HEX VALUE OF DECIMAL 100 IS"
20 B$="OCTAL VALUE OF DECIMAL 100 IS"
30 C$="A$+" "+HEX$(100)+"  "+B$+" "+OCT$(100)
40 PRINT C$
```

When this program is executed, the screen will display:

```
HEX VALUE OF DECIMAL 100 IS 64  OCTAL VALUE OF DECIMAL 100 IS 144
```

This program adds seven separate string values (including string constants). C$ is equal to the entire phrase which is finally displayed. Notice that HEX$ and OCT$ are called to supply the proper values to match the quoted strings. The CBREEZE translation does the same thing, but in a style that is more suited to C language:

```
main()
{

    char a_[80], b_[80], c_[80];

    strcpy(a_, "HEX VALUE OF DECIMAL 100 IS");
    strcpy(b_, "OCTAL VALUE OF DECIMAL 100 IS");
```

202

```
        sprintf(c_, "%s%s%x%s%s%s%o", a_, " ", 100, " ", b_, " ", 100);
        printf("%s\n", c_);

}
```

This is a correct and literal translation of the BASIC program, except for the deletion of HEX$ and OCT$. However, it is a nonsense program, designed to test CBREEZE. The desired results of such a program can be better obtained without resorting to string-add operations.

Although CBREEZE is capable of making many complex translations, don't try to be overly complex with your BASIC programs. Highly complex constructs or combinations of functions and statements can sharply detract from the strong tutorial advantage that CBREEZE offers. C is a simple language that can be used to construct highly complex routines, but such construction involves the combination of many simple routines.

The following BASIC program is an exercise in the ridiculous:

```
10 DIM K$(1)
20 K$(0)="3"
30 K$(1)="1"
40 A$="1234567"
50 C#=2.23
60 X#=C#^(LOG(VAL(MID$(A$,FIX(VAL(K$(0))),FIX(VAL(K$(1)))))))
70 PRINT X#
```

This is the hard way of writing:

```
10  PRINT 2.23^LOG(3.0)
```

The ridiculous construct in line 60 is necessary to extract the numeric values from the string variable and string array which result in a value of 3.000000. The final result is the display of:

```
2.413526058197022
```

CBREEZE is fully capable of handling such a translation, as the following source code demonstrates:

```
main()
{

        char *malloc(), *pmid_();
        double c, x, log(), atof(), pow();
        char a_[80], *k_[2];

        strcpy(k_[0] = malloc(80), "3");
        strcpy(k_[1] = malloc(80), "1");

        strcpy(a_, "1234567");

        c = 2.23;
        x = pow(c, (log(atof(pmid_(a_, (int) (atof(k_[0])), (int) (atof
(k_[1])))))));
```

203

```
        printf(" %lf \n", x);

}
mid_(a, b, x, y)
char *a, *b;
int x, y;
{

    --x;
    y += x;

    while (x < y && x <= strlen(b))
        *a++ = *(b + x++);

    *a = '\0';

}
char *pmid_(a, x, y)
char *a;
int x, y;
{

    char *ptr, *malloc();

    if ((ptr = malloc(y + 1)) == 0) {
        puts("Insufficient Memory");
        printf("%c", 7);
        exit(0);
    }

    mid_(ptr, a, x, y);

    return(ptr);

}
```

This is an example of total programming chaos, and it confirms the fact that a ridiculous program in BASIC is even more ridiculous when translated into C. This program will compile and run without a problem, but it is of little practical use.

If you just want to play around with programs that will cause CBREEZE to spit out all kinds of outlandish code constructs, then this example will serve the purpose. But, if you are serious about learning to program efficiently and knowledgably in C within a short period of time, a simpler and more serious approach is necessary.

Don't think of CBREEZE as some sort of "MIRACLE" program that will take all of the hard work out of learning C. It won't do this. When used as a learning tool and as an element in a comprehensive study program, CBREEZE can allow its users to progress very rapidly. CBREEZE was never designed to be an all-purpose program converter. It is a *tutorial* translator that forces the user to think in terms of C, even while writing a BASIC program for translation. The CBREEZE documentation urges all users to write BASIC programs to be translated in a step-by-step, simplistic manner. In other words, program lines like:

```
10  PRINT MID$(LEFT$(A$,8),2,5)
```

should not be attempted. This is not to say that CBREEZE can't translate such a line, only that the structure and functions it must utilize to emulate this operation might not offer a good tutorial advantage. The above line is best written as:

```
40 C$=LEFT$(A$,8)
50 D$=MID$(C$,2,5)
60 PRINT D$
```

This program sequence performs the same operations as the single program line, but it is certainly easier to understand. Its CBREEZE translation also provides a very clear explanation of how this construct would be programmed in C. This is the way you should learn C, in a clear-cut, step-by-step manner.

It is important to remember that CBREEZE is intended for one purpose and one purpose only: to teach BASIC programmers C language in the shortest time possible. Naturally, the C language output from CBREEZE can be compiled and run under Turbo C, but it is not designed to be a program "converter." Therefore, BASIC programs should be fairly small, although several long programs were successfully translated during my tests.

The examples of CBREEZE translations could go on indefinitely, but the following BASIC program and its CBREEZE translation should serve as a measure of the capabilities of this software.

```
10 REM SAMPLE PROGRAM TO TEST CBREEZE
20 CLS
100 DIM A$(20),D%(15)
110 FOR X%=0 TO 15
120 D%(X%)=X%*550
130 A$(X%)=STR$(X%*22)
140 PRINT D%(X%),A$(X%)
150 NEXT
160 IF D%(10) MOD 2 = 0 THEN PRINT"This is a test":D%(10)=15:ELSE PRINT"test failed":D%(10)=0
170 W#=SQR(CDBL(D%(5)))
180 WHILE W# => 1.1
190 PRINT W#^3.3
200 W#=LOG(W#)
210 WEND
220 FOR X%=0 TO 10 STEP 2
230 FOR Y%=10 TO 0 STEP -2
240 PRINT X%;Y%
250 NEXT:NEXT
```

```
260 E$="CBREEZE"
270 EE$=MID$(E$,3,3)
280 F$=RIGHT$(E$,4)
290 G$=LEFT$(E$,5)
300 PRINT EE$;F$;G$
```

This is a BASIC program that was designed to allow CBREEZE to show off
some of its capabilities. This program was input to CBREEZE, resulting in
the following C language output code:

```
/* SAMPLE PROGRAM TO TEST CBREEZE */

#include <dos.h>
main()
{

     char *malloc();
     double w, sqrt(), log(), pow();
     int x, y, d[16];
     char e_[80], ee_[80], f_[80], g_[80], *a_[21];

     cls();

     for (x = 0; x <= 15; ++x) {
          d[x] = x * 550;
          str_(a_[x] = malloc(80), (double) x * 22);
          printf(" %-14d %s\n", d[x], a_[x]);
     }

     if (d[10] % 2 == 0) {
          printf("This is a test\n");
          d[10] = 15;
     }
     else {

          printf("test failed\n");
          d[10] = 0;
     }

     w = sqrt(((double) d[5]));
     while (w >= 1.1) {
          printf(" %lf \n", pow(w, 3.3));
          w = log(w);
     }

     for (x = 0; x <= 10; x += 2)
          for (y = 10; y >= 0; y -= 2)
               printf(" %d   %d \n", x, y);
```

```c
        strcpy(e_, "CBREEZE");
        mid_(ee_, e_, 3, 3);
        right_(f_, e_, 4);
        left_(g_, e_, 5);

        printf("%s%s%s\n", ee_, f_, g_);

}
mid_(a, b, x, y)
char *a, *b;
int x, y;
{

        --x;
        y += x;

        while (x < y && x <= strlen(b))
            *a++ = *(b + x++);

        *a = '\0';

}
right_(a, b, x)
char *a, *b;
int x;
{

        int i;

        x = (x > strlen(b)) ? strlen(b) : x;
        i = strlen(b) - x;

        while (i < strlen(b))
            *a++ = *(b + i++);

        *a = '\0';

}
left_(a, b, x)
char *a, *b;
int x;
{

        int i;

        i = 0;

        while (i++ < x)
            *a++ = *b++;

        *a = '\0';
}
cls()
{

        int attr;
        union REGS r, *inregs, *outregs;
```

```
        attr = 0;
        inregs = &r;
        outregs = &r;

        r.h.ah = 15;

        int86(0x10, inregs, outregs);

        if (r.h.al == 7 || r.h.al < 4)
                attr = 7;

        r.h.ah = 6;
        r.h.bh = attr;
        r.h.ch = 0;
        r.h.cl = 0;
        r.h.dh = 24;
        r.h.dl = 79;
        r.h.al = 0;

        int86(0x10, inregs, outregs);

        r.h.ah = 2;
        r.h.bh = 0;
        r.h.dh = 0;
        r.h.dl = 0;

        int86(0x10, inregs, outregs);
}
str_(a, b)
char *a;
double b;
{

        if ((b - (int) b) == 0)
                sprintf(a, " %d", (int) b);
        else
                sprintf(a, " %lf", b);

}
```

The translated program is quite long, only because the source code for such
functions as cls( ), right__( ), and left__( ), are included. This program compiled
without even a warning message on the Turbo C compiler, and ran just like
the BASIC version. Total translation time was 34 seconds on an IBM PC
operating at 4.77 MHz. The time would be about half this amount on a PC
AT or similar machine.

SUMMARY

For BASIC programmers who want to delve seriously into C programming,
CBREEZE is a valuable tool. It can reduce frustration by a very large factor.
With CBREEZE, there should be far less confusion on the part of BASIC
programmers, and their journey to a working, practical knowledge of C
language should be a speedy one.

CBREEZE can be ordered using the coupon in the back of this book.

Chapter 9

HALO Graphics and Turbo C

HALO is a very sophisticated graphics package that is written in Assembler and may be called from a number of languages, including C. HALO has set a graphics standard for the MS-DOS computer and offers a professional graphics language that far outshines anything most programmers have used previously. HALO may be called by other Assembler programs, from COBOL, Fortran, Pascal, or compiled BASIC. There is even a version for the BASIC interpreter. However, the HALO version for this discussion is called from C language.

HALO is a product of Media Cybernetics in Takoma Park, Maryland. It was originally authored by Jan Gombert of SOFTWRITERS, Inc. in Baltimore, Maryland. The original version was written to be called from BASIC. The copyright to this program was purchased by Media Cybernetics and later versions were written to be called from Pascal. HALO Graphics expanded based on demand. As Media Cybernetics, a custom software and systems company, took on more clients with varied needs, the HALO Graphics interface was expanded.

As of this writing, there is no official release of a Turbo C version of HALO Graphics, but I was fortunate to obtain a Beta test model for use with Turbo C. And, for programmers who need a professional quality graphics capability from within C language, I can personally recommend HALO Graphics, because I have been using it since the early 1980s.

HALO, AN OVERVIEW

HALO is a collection of high-performance subroutines that allow the applications programmer to implement highly sophisticated computer-generated graphics. The current library consists of over 170 graphics functions written in Assembler and supplied to the programmer in object (library) module form, ready to be linked to high-level language applications.

HALO offers many device drivers that allow programmers to interface with a wide variety of graphics display, input, and hardcopy devices. It has been my experience with HALO and Media Cybernetics that if a graphics board, printer, mouse, digitizer, etc., has reached a state of even mild popularity, there is a HALO a graphics driver available for such a device. Media Cybernetics seems to accurately take the pulse of the new product market, offering drivers for these new devices and language versions almost as soon as they are officially released.

HALO Graphics offers the capability of dynamic configuration at runtime to address a large variety of system configurations. This means the programmer can write a program that can sense the environment to some degree and adjust accordingly. Alternatively, the programmer can write routines that get user input about the configuration and make adjustments based on this input.

HALO has facilities for both bit-mapped and stroke text, lines, circles, polygons, area fills, linestyles, crosshair cursors, and many other attributes. Additionally, HALO provides device, world, and normalized device coordinate systems. You will also find a complete window management system through the use of viewports.

In addition to this wide range of graphics functions, HALO provides support for palette control and image digitizing on boards that support these functions. HALO has a display list facility that can be used to generate files of vector information for use as input to vector-based devices.

Of great importance to every programmer is the fact that HALO is very easy to learn. Included with every HALO package is a program called LEARNHALO that can be used interactively to test and use the functions contained in the HALO library.

CALLING HALO GRAPHICS FROM C

Using all of the HALO Graphics functions in the Turbo C environment involves a simple calling procedure. For the most part, all HALO Graphics functions require int values. There are a few that require floats. When dealing in world coordinates, most of the former integer values must now be floats. In all cases, however, arguments to HALO functions must be *pointers*. You cannot supply a numeric constant, nor can you pass a value to a HALO function. You must always hand a HALO function the memory location of the value you are trying to pass. A few HALO functions require string values. In such cases, constants (in double quotes) may serve as arguments to these functions.

If you remember the above rules, you should have very little difficulty calling all of the HALO Graphics functions from Turbo C. The trick to learning the functions, then, is to treat HALO as an entirely new language. Using the LEARNHALO utility that comes with each HALO Graphics package, you can quickly get an idea of the basics of using this excellent graphics interface.

When a basic understanding is achieved, you can then start calling these functions from C.

The advantage of the interactive LEARNHALO environment lies in the fact that you use numeric constants with each function and write graphics to the screen one command at a time. LEARNHALO is really a HALO interpreter. For instance, you can issue the statement movabs(160,100) and the graphic cursor will be moved to the center of the medium-resolution screen. Next, you can use cir(60) and a circle will be drawn with its center at the current graphics cursor position (160,100) and with a radius of 60 pixels. A third call to fill(2) will fill the circle with the color referenced by color index #2. Each statement is executed before the next one is written. In this manner, HALO Graphics can be learned, as a graphics language, outside of the influence of any programming language.

HALO functions are written in assembler and are *called* from C programs. While these functions will not be portable outside of the MS-DOS machine environment, the vast array of drivers available for HALO should allow such programs to address any popular MS-DOS configuration, regarding color boards, graphic printers, screens, mouse devices, digitizers, etc.

A FIRST PROGRAM

The following C program will draw a circle at the center of the medium-resolution graphics screen. However, it does far more than this, as will be learned from the discussion that follows:

```
main()
{

        int x, y;

        setdev("haloibm.dev");

        x = 0;
        initgraphics(&x);

        x = 160;
        y = 100;
        movabs(&x, &y);

        x = 60;
        cir(&x);

        x = 2;
        fill(&x);

}
```

This C program declares x and y to be int variables. These variables will be assigned various values throughout the program and their memory locations will then be passed to several HALO functions.

The first HALO call in this program is to setdev( ). This function tells the environment the type of color graphics board your system is using. The device name, HALOIBM.DEV, is the device file located on the default disk drive that names the IBM Color Card. This file is supplied with the HALO Graphics package, assuming you order one for this configuration. If you had a different board, then Media Cybernetics would supply a driver for that one. Notice that the name of the file is given as a constant. Actually, however, the address of that constant is passed to setdev( ).

The call to setdev( ) causes the HALOIBM.DEV file to be loaded into memory, thus giving the environment the proper data to know how to write to the graphics screen. Next, variable x is assigned a value of zero. This is the value which, when used as the argument to initgraphics( ), will cause the graphics screen to be initialized to medium-resolution graphics mode. The next line calls this function, and uses the memory location of the value stored in x as the argument. This argument, then, is a pointer to the value stored in x. This call causes the graphics screen to be cleared and initialized to medium-resolution graphics mode.

The next two lines assign x the value of 160 and y the value of 100. These are the coordinates for the center of the medium-resolution graphics screen. Next, movabs( ) is called with pointers to x and y as its arguments. The movabs( ) function is an acronym for *move absolute*, and causes the invisible graphics cursor to be repositioned at coordinates 160,100.

Now, x is assigned a new value of 60. The pointer to this value is then handed to cir( ) as its argument. The cir( ) function draws a circle on the screen with its center at the current graphic cursor position. The circle is drawn in the default color index of three, which is white. If the circle were to be drawn in another color index, then the setcolor( ) function could have been called with any legal color index as its argument (i.e., a pointer to a legal color index value).

Finally, the value of x is set to two, and a pointer to this value is given as the argument to fill( ). The fill( ) function in HALO Graphics is used to fill simple objects with color in the same manner as the GW-BASIC PAINT statement. The HALO fill( ) function is very fast, but it can only be used to fill simple geometric objects like circles and boxes. When a circle contains other circles or complex polygons are involved, the flood( ) function is often required. This does the same thing as fill, but it is not limited to simple objects. It executes far more slowly than does fill( ).

That's the end of the program. While the only visible result of its execution is a filled circle, you have learned that this program also initialized the graphics screen and moved the text cursor before any information was actually written to the graphics monitor.

In this example, setdev( ) and initgraphics( ) are a part of the initialization function set. The first initializes the screen driver, while the second initializes the actual screen hardware. The movabs( ) function is a part of cursor/coordinate function set that establishes and/or moves the various cursor types to the physical screen, based upon a set of coordinates.

The cir( ) and fill( ) functions are a part of that set of functions that actually write information to the graphics screen. There are also functions that draw lines, boxes, polygons, and every other imaginable geometric shape.

There are variations on all of these functions as well. For instance, the initgraphics( ) function initializes the screen to one of the available graphics modes and then clears that screen. A variation on this function is called startgraphics( ). This one also initializes the graphics screen to a specified mode, but the screen is not cleared, and all previous information on this screen is retained, although it might be altered somewhat by the mode setting if it is different from the current mode in effect.

The following C program is a variation on the previous example. It places the circle radius argument in a *for* loop, producing a series of concentric circles with ever-increasing radii:

```
main()
{

        int x, y;

        setdev("haloibm.dev");

        x = 0;
        initgraphics(&x);

        x = 160;
        y = 100;
        movabs(&x, &y);

        for (x = 10; x <= 80; x += 10)
            cir(&x);

        setprn("haloepsn.prn");
        gprint();
        closegraphics();


}
```

There is nothing especially new about this program. The radius value for the cir( ) function is counted from 10 to 80 in the body of a *for* loop in steps of ten. On each pass of the loop, a circle is drawn on the screen. As x is incremented, the diameter of the circle is increased.

There are a few new functions in this program that are easily explained. The setprn( ) function is another initializer that sets the device driver for the system printer. HALO Graphics offers a very wide assortment of printer drivers. The one used with my system, which uses an Epson MX-80 printer, is haloepsn.prn. When this name is fed to setprn( ), the file named in the argument is used as the printer driver.

The next new function is gprint( ). This one is used without an argument, and simply causes the graphics screen to be "dumped" to the printer. This function must be called after setprn( ) has been successfully executed. Only one call to setprn( ) is necessary during any program.

The last new function is closegraphics( ). This one requires no argument, and simply terminates the HALO environment. This function should be called within a program when no further HALO graphics operations are to be performed. Of course, when a program completes a normal exit, the environment is closed anyway.

This program has displayed its concentric circles on the screen and then dumped the screen to the system printer. Figure 9-1 shows what the screen write looks like.

Notice that the circles are oblong. This is due to the distortion of the medium-resolution graphics screen as produced by the IBM Color Card. This screen consists of a grid of 319 pixels horizontally and 200 pixels vertically. Because the ratio of horizontal to vertical screen elements is not 1:1, distortion will result. The following program adds one more function to the previous program to correct this problem:

```
main()
{

    int x, y;
    float f;

    setdev("haloibm.dev");

    x = 0;
    initgraphics(&x);

    x = 160;
    y = 100;
    movabs(&x, &y);

    f = 0.8;
    setasp(&f);

    for (x = 10; x <= 80; x += 10)
        cir(&x);

    setprn("haloepsn.prn");
    gprint();

    closegraphics();

}
```

The screen write from this program is shown in Fig. 9-2. Notice that the concentric circles in this example are much more uniform. It should be pointed out that a certain amount of distortion takes place when a screen is dumped to the printer as well. While neither circle in Figs. 9-1 and 9-2 is perfectly uniform, the latter one appears to be a perfect circle when viewed on the screen itself. The circle in Fig. 9-1 is more "out-of-round" on the screen than it appears to be in the printed version.

The improved uniformity is due to the new function that is called from

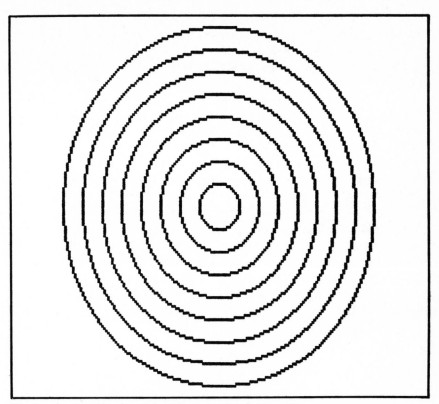

Fig. 9-1. An example of a circle drawn with the cir ( ) function.

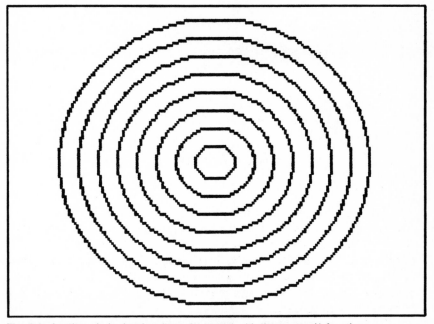

Fig. 9-2. Another circle that has been improved with the setasp ( ) function.

this program. The setasp( ) function, an acronym for *set aspect ratio*, requires a floating-point value as its argument. More specifically, it requires a single-precision floating-point value which, in C, is of type float. Note that double types are not legal in this or any other HALO function. These functions expect to receive a 32-bit value, not the 64-bit values supplied by double types. For this reason, variable f has been declared a float and is assigned a value of 0.8. By experimentation, this was found to be the aspect ratio that produced the best results in medium-resolution graphics mode on my Princeton Graphic Systems HX-10 monitor. Different machine, monitor, and color card combinations will require different aspect ratio values for the most pleasing visual results.

DRAWING LINES

I arbitrarily chose to open the discussion on HALO Graphics using the cir( ) function to produce circles on the graphics screen. However, HALO is capable of far more than circles. The following discussion is concerned with more linear objects, like lines and boxes.

The following program draws a line in color index 2 (cyan) from coordinates 10,15 to 178,100:

```
main()
{

    int c, x, y;

    setdev("haloibm.dev");

    x = 0;
    initgraphics(&x);

    c = 2;
    setcolor(&c);

    x = 10;
    y = 15;
    movabs(&x, &y);

    x = 178;
    y = 100;
    lnabs(&x, &y);

    closegraphics();

}
```

Two new functions are introduced in this program. First of all, setcolor( ), as its name implies, is used to determine the screen foreground color from a palette of four possible colors. Using the IBM Color Card, one of two palettes may be selected via the setpal( ) function. The default palette is 1 which is the one in effect for this program. Setcolor( ) requires an integer argument value of from zero to three. Variable c is assigned a value of two, for color index 2, and a pointer to this value is passed to setcolor( ). When this function is executed, all screen writes will be done in color index 2 (cyan) until setcolor( ) is executed again with a different value.

Next, x and y are assigned the values of the starting point of the line. The movabs( ) function positions the graphic cursor at these coordinates. Now, x and y are assigned the values of the line's ending coordinates.

A new function, lnabs( ), is now called with pointers to x and y as its argument. The lnabs( ) function is an acronym for *line absolute*, and draws a line from the current position of the graphic cursor (10,15) to the point specified by its arguments (178,100). The line is written, but the position of the graphic cursor is still at the original setting of 10,15.

It should be pointed out that functions like movabs( ) and lnabs( ) have alternate equivalents that are movrel( ) and lnrel( ), standing for *move relative* and *line relative*, respectively. These functions are given arguments whose values are relative to the current graphic cursor position, while the functions used in the program examples are given arguments that name the absolute coordinates. You could have used lnrel( ) in place of lnabs( ) in the last program, but the arguments to this function would have to be changed to 168,85.

Remember, these are relative coordinates. With the graphic cursor set to 10 for the x-axis, adding 168 will result in absolute coordinate 178. Likewise, adding the relative coordinate value of 85 to the current y-axis value of 15 results in an absolute coordinate of 100. HALO offers absolute and relative coordinate function for most operations. Generally speaking, the absolute coordinate functions are easier to work with, but there are times when offsets from the current graphic cursor location are advantageous and can be put to more practical uses.

You could draw a box using the lnabs( ) function four times to draw each side. Here, you might also make use of lnrel( ) to draw the remaining three sides in relationship to the first side and to each other. Best of all, however, is the HALO box( ) function, which is also the easiest to use. The following program demonstrates the use of the HALO Graphics box( ) function:

```
main()
{

    int x1, y1, x2, y2, c, m;

    setdev("haloibm.dev");

    m = 0;
    initgraphics(&m);

    c = 1;
    setcolor(&c);

    x1 = 20;
    y1 = 15;
    x2 = 134;
```

```
        y2 = 156;
        box(x1, y1, x2, y2);

        closegraphics();

}
```

The box( ) function draws a box on the screen based upon two sets of coordinates. The first set names the upper left corner of the box, while the second set of coordinates names the lower right-hand corner. The box will be drawn in color index 1, because this was the value pointed to in memory by the argument to setcolor( ). This box may be filled with the same or another color by moving the cursor to a point within the box and making a call to fill( ).

For filled boxes, another function may be called: the bar( ) function in HALO Graphics. This function is used in much the same manner as box( ), except the object will be filled with the current screen foreground color. The following program is identical to the previous example, except the bar( ) function is used to produce a filled box:

```
        main()
        {

            int x1, y1, x2, y2, c, m;

            setdev("haloibm.dev");

            m = 0;
            initgraphics(&m);

            c = 1;
            setcolor(&c);

            x1 = 20;
            y1 = 15;
            x2 = 134;
            y2 = 156;
            bar(x1, y1, x2, y2);

            closegraphics();

        }
```

The bar( ) function may also fill the box with one of several hatching patterns as determined by another HALO function sethatchstyle( ). Prior to calling this function, you would use defhatchstyle( ) to define a particular hatch pattern. These two functions will not be discussed further in this brief overview of HALO Graphics, but they point to the multitude of capabilities available with this excellent graphics package. These are only two of over 150 functions the graphics programmer may choose to work with in HALO Graphics.

Returning to circles for a moment provides the opportunity to talk about a very specialized and very powerful function that HALO Graphics incorporates. The pie( ) function is used for the specific programming of pie charts. There are several adjunct functions that are also used with pie( ) for this purpose. The pie( ) function is used in a format of:

```
pie(radius, ang1, ang2, color)
```

where ang1 and ang2 are the starting and ending angles of a pie slice or section.

The following program demonstrates the use of the pie( ) function as called from Turbo C:

```
main()
{

        int x, y;
        float a, b, f;

        setdev("haloibm.dev");

        x = 0;
        initgraphics(&x);

        x = 160; y = 100;
        movabs(&x, &y);

        f = 0.8;
        setasp(&f);

        x = 2;
        setcolor(&x);

        x = 60;
        y = 1;
        a = 0.5;
        b = -0.5;
        pie(&x, &a, &b, &y);

        x = 25;
        y = 0;
        movrel(&x, &y);

        x = 60;
        y = 2;
        a = -0.5;
        b = 0.5;
        pie(&x, &a, &b, &y);

        closegraphics();

}
```

This program creates the screen image shown in Fig. 9-3, producing two

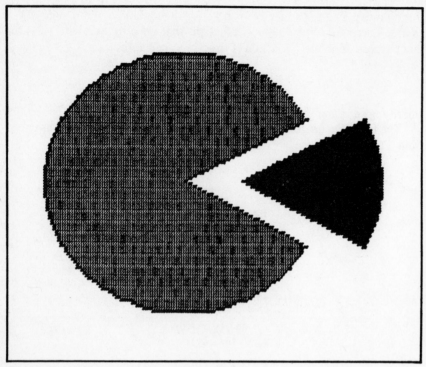

Fig. 9-3. The beginnings of a simple pie chart.

different pie wedges in two different colors on the screen. This program is very simplistic, but shows the basic use of this powerful function. This type of program can serve as the heart of a far more complex program that will accept various values and produce a labeled pie chart based upon these values.

The angle values ranging from 6.28 to −6.28 are expressed in radians, although the setdegree( ) function may be called to allow degree arguments to be accepted instead. Notice that the first call to pie( ) uses arguments of 0.5 and −0.5 respectively. The next call reverses this with −0.5 and 0.5. This means that the second pie section will be the missing portion of the first. The movrel( ) function comes in handy in this usage to shift the center of the circle from which the pie sections are taken by 25 pixels horizontally. This provides the offset for the pie section and makes for a more pleasing appearance.

TEXT GRAPHICS

The HALO Graphics interface with Turbo C also contains a large number of functions that can be used to write graphics text characters to the screen. Figure 9-4 shows a small sampling of what is available from this package. Various font types are loaded from a font file, using the setfont( ) function. It is necessary to create a text cursor so that it may be positioned on the screen and to specify the text attributes. These include height-to-width ratio, color, path (left-to-right, right-to-left, upside down, top-to-bottom, bottom-to-top, etc.), and mode.

220

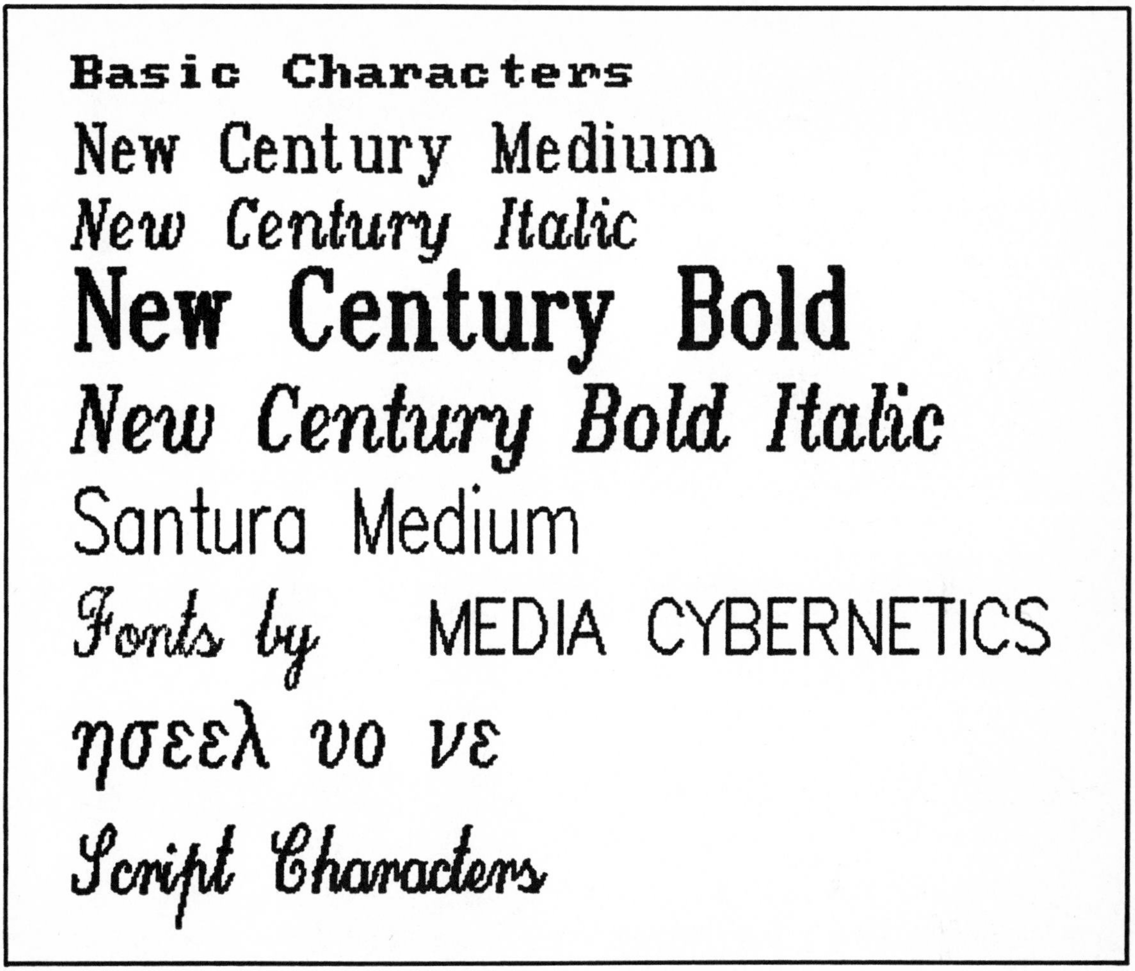

Basic Characters

New Century Medium

New Century Italic

New Century Bold

New Century Bold Italic

Santura Medium

Fonts by MEDIA CYBERNETICS

ησεελ υο νε

Script Characters

Fig. 9-4. Some of the font styles available in HALO.

The following C program calls HALO Graphics functions to write a text graphic to the screen:

```
main()
{
        int a, b, c, d;
        char p[10];

        strcpy(p, "TURBO C");

        setdev("haloibm.dev");

        a = 0;
        initgraphics(&a);

        b = 8;
```

```
            c = 4;
            settext(&b, &c, &a, &a);

            c = 5;
            d = 2;
            inittcur(&c, &d, &a);

            c = 15;
            d = 100;
            movtcurabs(&c, &d);

            btext(p);

            closegraphics();

      }
```

This simple program has been used to display a text graphics of the string "TURBO C" on the screen. Figure 9-5 shows the results when this program is executed.

The settext( ) function is called first, establishing the size and characteristics of the graphics text. In this sample program, b is assigned a value of eight. This is the text height, and is specified in units of eight pixels. This means that the text will be 8 × 8 or 64 pixels high. A value of four is used for the second argument, so the text will be 32 pixels wide. The next argument specifies the path. A value of zero here means that the text will be printed from left to right. The final argument specifies the mode. A value of zero prints borderless text, while a value of one prints text with a border.

After the text specifications have been set, inittcur( ) is called to initialize the text cursor. This sets the size and type of the visible cursor. Next, movtcurabs( ) is called. This function is the equivalent of a locate( ) function, but for the text cursor only. This is set at column 15, row 100. Finally, the btext( ) function is called with its argument being the pointer to the string "TURBO C". This is the value that is displayed on the screen.

Fig. 9-5. Graphic text output of HALO.

MIXING TEXT AND GRAPHICS

There are many other graphics text functions available, as well as over a hundred other functions that address almost everything a graphics programmer could imagine. This last program uses many of the functions discussed and a few new ones to produce a program that will allow you to draw some moderately sophisticated pie charts on the screen, each section containing a text label:

```
main()
{
     int x, y, z, xx, yy, zz, sc, val[45], num;
     int x1, x2, y1, y2, xxx, yyy, zzz, lx, ly;
     float ff, gg[512],ggg[512], hh, ii, tot;
     char *name[25], *malloc();

     tot = 0;

     printf("Number of items in chart is:");
     cscanf("%d", &num);
     if (num < 2)
          exit(0);

     puts("");

     for (yy = 0; yy < num; ++yy) {
          printf("Name of item %d is:", yy + 1);
          gets(name[yy]= malloc(25));
          printf("Value of %s is:", name[yy]);
          cscanf("%d", &val[yy]);
          puts("");
          tot = tot + val[yy];
     }

     for (zz = 0; zz < yy; ++zz)
          gg[zz] = val[zz] / tot;

     setdev("haloibm.dev");
     x = 0;
     initgraphics(&x);
     setapal(&x);

     x = 160;
     y = 100;
     movabs(&x, &y);

     ff = -6.2831;
     ii = 0.8;
     setasp(&ii);

     x = 2;
     setcolor(&x);

     sc = y = 1;
     sethatchstyle(&z);

     x = 80;
```

```
for (zz = 0; zz < num; ++zz) {
    setcolor(&sc);
    sethatchstyle(&y);
    ii = ff + (gg[zz] * 6.2831);
    pie(&x, &ff, &ii, &y);
    hh = ff + ((gg[zz] / 2) * 6.2831);
    arc(&x, &ff, &hh);
    inqarc(&x1, &y1, &x2, &y2);
    xxx = 1;
    inittcur(&xxx, &xxx, &xxx);
    yyy = 2;
    settextclr(&yyy, &xxx);
    yyy = 0;
    settext(&xxx, &xxx, &yyy, &yyy);
    lx = x2;
    ly = y2;

    if (x2 < 160)
        x2 = x2 - (strlen(name[yy]) * 12);
    else
        x2 += 16;
    if (y2 < 50)
        y2 -= 10;

    if (y2 > 160)
        y2 += 10;

    movabs(&lx, &ly);
    lnabs(&x2, &y2);
    lx = 160;
    ly = 100;
    movabs(&lx, &ly);
    movtcurabs(&x2, &y2);
    btext(name[zz]);
    ff = ii;
    ++y;
    if (y == 6) {
        y = 1;
        ++sc;
    }
    if (sc == 4)
        sc = 1;

}
deltcur();

}
```

I won't go into a detailed description of this program, but generally, it gathers names and values for each chart item. The values do not necessarily have to add up to 100 as if they were percentages, because this program adds all values and then determines the appropriate percentage value of each.

Once the values and names have been stored in arrays, the graphics function set is called to establish a piechart. The pie( ) function is used as before, along with arc( ) which draws an arc along the same curve as pie( ). This extra

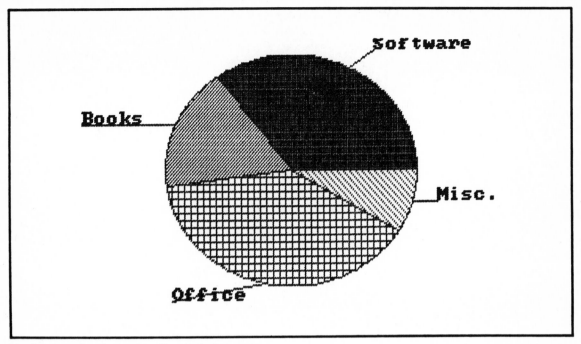

Fig. 9-6. Sample print-out from the piechart program.

function is essentially used to redraw the same arc so that the inqarc( ) function may be called. This allows for the calculation of the coordinate pair naming the exact center of that arc. This is the placement point for the text label that is written via the btext( ) function.

This is a moderately complex exercise in simple chart-making that shows just what can be done with HALO Graphics and Turbo C. Figure 9-6 shows a sample screen write produced by this program.

SUMMARY

By the time you read these words, a HALO Graphics version of Turbo C will be on the market. If you are interested in graphics interfaces for the C programming language, I can give no other graphics environment as high a recommendation as HALO. It is a graphics language unto itself that interfaces well with many languages. Once you understand this language, you can program HALO Graphics via calls from many languages other than C. HALO is very powerful, and has been used by many programmers to produce sophisticated graphic or graphic-enhanced programs that have been on the commercial market for years.

The mating of HALO Graphics with Turbo C is a natural one. The high speed available with HALO, due to the code having been written in Assembler, is called rapidly from the Turbo C environment. Truly, this is the needed environment of the serious graphics programmer. While some simple graphic functions can be written in C, Assembler is required for most of the more

225

complex functions, due to the fast execution speeds needed. When these routines are called from C, you get the best of both worlds: the convenience of programming in a moderately high-level language while calling extremely fast graphic routines.

Appendix

Commented Program Listings

This appendix provides a commented program listing for most of the programs presented in Chapter 7 of this text. When combined with the contents of the chapter, the fullest possible understanding of the programs will be gained.

```
left(a, b, x)   /* Write left x characters in b to a */
char *a, *b;    /* a is target array; b is source string */
int x;          /* x = number of characters in substring */
{
    int i = 0;  /* Start at offset zero */
    x = (x <= strlen(b) ? x : strlen(b);  /* Make sure x <=
strlen(b) */

    while (i++ < x)      /* Count through character offsets */
        *a++ = *b++;     /* copy b to a */

    *a = '\0';           /* Add null character */

}
```

```c
left(a, b, x)    /* Write left x character in b to a */
char a[], b[];   /* a is target array; b is source array */
int x;           /* Number of characters to write */
{

     int i = 0;    /* Start at offset zero (leftmost) */

     while ((a[i] = b[i++]) && i < x) /* Copy all characters
while a[i] != '\0' and while i < x */
          ;

     a[i] = '\0';  /* Add null character */

}
```

```c
char *left(b, x)  /* Return pointer to leftmost x chars in b */
char b[];         /* b is source array */
int x;            /* Number of characters in substring */
{

     char a[250];  /* Array to hold substring */
     int i = 0;    /* Start at character offset 0 */

     while ((a[i] = b[i++]) && i < x)  /* Same as previous
function */
          ;

     a[i] = '\0';  /* Add null character */

     return(a);    /* Return char pointer to a */

}
```

```c
right(a, b, x) /* Write rightmost x chars in b to a */
char *a, *b;   /* a is target array; b is source string */
int x;         /* x = number of rightmost chars to write */
{

     int i, l;

     l = strlen(b);
     x = (x > l) ? l : x; /* Make sure x <= strlen(b) */
     i = l - x;           /* Starting char offset */

     while (*a++ = *(b + i++)) /* Copy all chars including null */
          ;

}
```

```c
mid(a, b, x, y) /* Write y chars in b to a beginning at x */
char *a, *b;    /* a is target array; b is source string */
int x, y;       /* Start at char x and write y characters */
{
```

```
        int l;

        --x;        /* --x is equal to the offset of char x */
        y += x;     /* This gives the offset of the yth char */
        l = strlen(b);

        while (x < y && x <= l) /* loop while x < y and x < strlen(b) */
            *a++ = *(b + x++); /* copy chars from a to b */
        *a = '\0';   /* Add null character */

}
```

```
/* Replace substring from x to x+y in a with string in b */

mids(a, x, y, b)
int x, y;    /* x = starting char; y = substring char length */
char *a, *b; /* a is target string; b is source string */
{

        int l;

        l = strlen(a) - 1;
        y += x;   /* Offset of last char in target string */
        --x;      /* Offset of first char in target string */

/* The following loop cycles while x<=y and x<= the length */
/* of the source string minus 1 and the null character in b */
/* has not been copied */
        while (x <= y && x <= l && *b != '\0')
            *(a + x++) = *b++; /* Copy sequential chars in b */
                              /* to offset in a */

}
```

```
reverse(a) /* rewrite a from right to left */
char a[]; /* source string */
{

        char temp[250];  /* Array to temporarily hold reversed string */
        int x, y;

/* The following for loop counts from the last character offset */
/* to offset zero, writing characters in a to temp */
        for (x = strlen(a) - 1, y = 0; x >= 0; --x, ++y)
            temp[y] = a[x];

        temp[y] = '\0';   /* Add null character */
        strcpy(a, temp);  /* Write reverse string over source */
}
```

```
space(b)  /* Puts spaces between chars in b */
char b[]; /* Source string */
{

        char a[250];   /* Temporary array to hold spaced string */
```

```c
        int x, y;

        x = y = 0;

        while (a[x++] = b[y++])  /* copy char in a to b */
                a[x++] = ' ';  /* Write space character; move to next
offset */

        strcpy(b, a);  /* Write new string over source string */

}
```

```c
space(b)  /* Put spaces between chars in b */
char b[]; /* Source string */
{

        char a[250];  /* Temporary array to hold spaced string */
        int x, y;

/* The following for loop counts through each character offset */
/* and copies characters from b to a, adding a space between */
/* each one */
        for (x = 0, y = 0; a[x] = b[y]; ++x, ++y)
                a[++x] = ' ';

        strcpy(b, a); /* Write spaced string over source string */

}


/* Return char pointer to Roman Numeral string equivalent of d */

char *roman(d)  /* Return char pointer */
int d;          /* Decimal integer value from 1 to 3999 */
{

        int y;
        char temp[100], roman[100];

        /* The following static arrays contain the decimal */
        /* Graduations possible in Roman Numerals and the Roman */
        /* equivalent graduations */

        static int dec[] = {1000, 900, 500, 400, 100 },
                          {90, 50, 40, 10, 9, 5, 4, 1 };
        static char *rom[] = { "M", "CM", "D", "CD", "C", "XC", "L" },
                            { "XL", "X", "IX", "V", "IV", "I" };

        y = 0;
        temp[0] = '\0';
        roman[0] = '\0';

        if (d > 3999 || d < 1) /* If argument too large or too small */
                return("ERROR");  /* Return pointer to "ERROR" */

        while (y < 13) {    /* Count through static array */
                while ((d - dec[y]) >= 0) {  While d contains
graduation */
```

```
                strcat(temp, rom[y]); concatenate Roman equivalent
to temp */
                d -= dec[y];  /* Decrease d by static char value */
            }

        strcat(roman, temp);  /* Copy contents of temp to roman */
        strcpy(temp, "\0");   /* Erase temp */

        ++y; /* Go to next static array element and go through
same routine for next value */
    }

    return(roman);  /* Return pointer to Roman Numeral string */

}
```

```
/* Return the decimal integer equivalent of Roman Numeral */
rom2dec(rn) /* rn contains Roman Numeral string */
char rn[];
{

    int x, y, l, ret;
    char temp[3], roman[20];

/* The following static arrays contain the decimal and Roman */
/* Graduations possible in any value from 1 to 3999 */
    static int dec1[] = { 900, 400, 90, 40, 9, 4 };
    static int dec2[] = {1000, 500, 100, 50, 10, 5, 1 };
    static char *rom1[] = { "CM", "CD", "XC", "XL", "IX", "IV" };
    static int rom2[] = { 'M', 'D', 'C', 'L', 'X', 'V', 'I' };

    strcpy(roman, rn); /* Copy argument to internal array */
    l = strlen(roman); /* Get length of argument */
    ret = 0;

    for (x = 0; x < l; x += 2) {  /* Count through string chars */
        sprintf(temp, "%c%c", roman[x], roman[x + 1]); /* Copy
first two characters in roman[] to temp[] */
            for (y = 0; y <= 5; ++y)  /* Count through static
array elements */
                if (strcmp(temp, rom1[y]) == 0) { /* Look for
Roman character */
                    roman[x] = ' '; /* Write space char over
in roman[] */
                    roman[x + 1] = ' '; /* Write space over
second Roman character */
                    ret += dec1[y];  /* Increment return
variable */
                }

    }

    for (x = 0; x < l; ++x) { /* Count through roman[] */
        if (roman[x] == ' ') /* If a space char */
            continue;        /* Keep on counting */

        for (y = 0; y <= 6; ++y)  /* Count through static array */
            if (roman[x] == rom2[y]) /* If a match is found */
```

```
                    ret += dec2[y]; /* Increment ret by static
array decimal value */
      }

      return(ret);        /* Return decimal value */

}
_____

/* Print enlarged letters from IBM character set */
banner(p)
char p[];  /* String to be enlarged */
{

      int byte, seg, off, x, y;
      char b[10];

      seg = 0xf000;  /* Segment offset of ROM character set */

      for (x = 0; x <= 7; ++ x) { /* 8-bits in each ROM char */
            for (y = 0; y <= strlen(p); ++y) { /* Count thru arg */
                  off = 0xfa6e + (p[y] * 8 + x); /* Get offset of ROM
char byte */
                  byte = peekb(seg, off);  /* Get that byte */
                  dec2bin(b, byte); /* Write a binary string
equivalent of that byte  to b */
                  bigprint(b);    /* call bigprint() */
                  if (y == 8)  /* If more than 8 characters in arg */
                        break;  /* That's all I can take. Break */
            }
            printf("\n");  /* Go to next line */

      }

}
dec2bin(c, x) /* Write 8-bit binary equivalent of x to c */
char c[];
int x;
{

      int a, ct;

      a = 128;
      ct = 0;

      while (a >= 1) {  /* Decrement a until it is less than 1 */
            if ((x - a) >= 0) {  /* If difference is 0 or more */
                  c[ct++] = '1';  /* Write character '1' to c */
                  x -= a;         /* Decrease x by a */
            }
            else                 /* If difference is less than 0 */
                  c[ct++] = '0';  /* Write character '0' to c */

            a /= 2;   /* Go to next lowest binary value */
      }

      c[ct] = '\0';  /* Terminate with null character */

}
```

```
bigprint(a) /* Print blocks and nulls from binary string */
char a[]; /* 8-bit binary string from dec2bin() */
{

     int x;
     for (x = 0; x <= 7; ++ x) { /* Count through 8-bits */
          if (a[x] == 49)        /* if a[x] == '1' */
               printf("%c", 219);/* Print a block (ASCII 219) */
          else                   /* if a[x] == '0' */
               printf("%c", 0);  /* Print the null character */
     }

}
```

```
#include <dir.h>  /* Include header file where ffblk is found */
main()
{

     struct ffblk r;  /* d is a structure of type ffblk */

     if (findfirst("*.*", &r, 0) != 0)  /* Return first general
file */
          exit(0);  /* If findfirst() not equal to 0, exit */
     else             /* If it equal 0 */
          printf("%s\n", r.ff_name); /* Print file name from
struct */

     while (findnext(&r) == 0)  /* Find the next filename */
          printf("%s\n", r.ff_name); /* Print it */

}
```

```
#include <dir.h>
main()
{

     struct ffblk r;
     int x, y;
     char *hold[250], *malloc();

     y = 0;

     if (findfirst("*.*", &r, 0) != 0) /* Get first filename */
          exit(0);
     else
          strcpy(hold[y++] = malloc(20), r.ff_name); /* Copy it to
hold[] */

      while (!findnext(&r))   /* Get next filename */
          strcpy(hold[y++] = malloc(20), r.ff_name); /* Copy it to
hold[] */

     sort(hold, y);    /* Alphabetize the contents of hold[] */

     for (x = 0; x < y; ++x) /* Count through contents of hold[] */
          puts(hold[x]); /* Print each filename */

}
```

```c
sort(x, i)   /* Sort i elements in x in ascending order */
char *x[];   /* An array of pointers to strings */
int i;       /* Total elements in *x[]; */
{

     char *y;
     int a, b, z;

     for (z = i / 2; z > 0; z /= 2)    /* Start at halfway point */
          for (b = z; b < i; b++)      /* count from z to i - 1 */
               for (a = b - z; a >= 0; a -= z) { /* Count from
beginning */
                    if (strcmp(x[a], x[a + z]) <= 0) /* if a[x] <=
x[a + z] */
                         break;   /* Break out of this nested loop */
                    y = x[a];     /* Else, assign y the string in
x[a] */
                    x[a] = x[a + z]; /* x[a] is assigned x[a + z] */
                    x[a + z] = y; /* x[a + z] is assigned the
string originally in x[a] */
               }

}
```

```c
#include <dir.h>     /* Contains struct ffblk */
#include <sort.c>    /* Include source code for sort */
main()
{

     struct ffblk r;
     int c, x, y, z;
     char *hold[250], *malloc();

     y = 0;

     x = findfirst("*.*", &r, 0); /* Get first file */

     while (!x) {          /* While x is 0 */
          strcpy(hold[y] = malloc(20), r.ff_name); /* Copy
filename to hold[]; */
          x = findnext(&r); /* Get next filename */
          ++y;
     }

     sort(hold, y);       /* Sort contents of hold[] */
     x = z = 0;

   while (x < y) {  /* While x < number of elements in hold[] */
     for (x = z; x < y, x <= z + 20; ++x) { /* Format print chain */
       printf("%-15s%c", hold[x], ((y - (20 + z)) <= 0 ) ? '\n' : ' ');
       if ((x + 21) < y)
          printf("%-15s%c", hold[x + 21], ((y - (40 + z)) <= 0) ? '\n' : ' ');
       if ((x + 42) < y)
          printf("%-15s%c", hold[x + 42], ((y - (60 + z)) <= 0) ? '\n' : ' ');
       if ((x + 63) < y)
          printf("%-15s\n", hold[x + 63]);
       if (x >= y)
          break;
```

```
                        printf("\n\nPress Any Key For More");   /* Screen
full */

                        c = getch();           /* Detect keyboard input */
                        printf("\n\n\n");      /* Print three newlines */
                        z += 84;               /* Go to next offset in hold[] */
        }


}
```

```
#include <dir.h>  /* Header file with struct ffblk */
main()
{

        struct ffblk r;
        int c, x, y, z;
        char *hold[250],n[80], e[8], *malloc();

        y = 0;
        x = findfirst("*.*", &r, 0);

         while (!x) {
              strcpy(hold[y] = malloc(20), r.ff_name);
              x = findnext(&r);
              ++y;
        }

        sort(hold, y);
        x = z = 0;

        while (x < y) {
          for (x = z; x < y, x <= z + 20; ++x) { /* Printing
format uses fnsplit to divide filename into separate components */
          fnsplit(hold[x], n, n, n, e);
          printf("%-10s%-8s%c", n, e, ((y - (20 + z)) < 0 ) ? '\n' : ' ');
          if ((x + 21) < y) {
             fnsplit(hold[x + 21], n, n, n, e);
             printf("%-10s%-8s%c", n, e, ((y - (40 + z)) < 0) ? '\n' : ' ');
          }
          if ((x + 42) < y) {
             fnsplit(hold[x + 42], n, n, n, e);
             printf("%-10s%-8s%c", n, e, ((y - (60 + z)) < 0) ? '\n' : ' ');
          }
          if ((x + 63) < y) {
             fnsplit(hold[x + 63], n, n, n, e);
             printf("%-10s%-8s\n", n, e);
          }
          if (x >= y)
             break;
        }

         printf("\n\nPress Any Key For More");
                        c = getch();
                        printf("\n\n\n");
                        z += 84;
        }
```

```
}
sort(x, i) /* New version, sorts based upon extension value */
char *x[];
int i;
{

    char *y, c[30], d[30], q[80];
    int a, b, z;

    for (z = i / 2; z > 0; z /= 2)
        for (b = z; b < i; b++)
            for (a = b - z; a >= 0; a -= z) {
                fnsplit(x[a], q, q, q, c); /* x[a] = extension
of filename */
                fnsplit(x[a + z], q, q, q, d); /* x[a + z] =
extension of filename */
                if (strcmp(c, d) <= 0)
                    break;
                y = x[a];
                x[a] = x[a + z];
                x[a + z] = y;
            }

}
```

```
split(fn, n, e) /* Split filename into name and .extension */
char *fn, *n, *e; /* fn=full filaname; n = target name array; e =
target extension array */
{

    *e = '\0';

    while (*n = *fn) /* Copy filename in fn to n */
        if (*n == '.') { /* When you get the decimal (.) */
            *n = '\0';  /* Terminate n with a null char */
            while (*e++ = *fn++) /* Read extension into e */
                ;
            break;  /* When the null char has been copied, exit
this inner loop */
        }
        else {      /* If there is no extension */
            *n++;  /* Go to next offset in n */
            *fn++; /* Go to next offset in fn */
        }

}
```

```
split(fn, n, e) /* Split filename into name and extension */
char *fn, *n, *e;  /* fn = full name; n = name; e = extension */
{

    *e++ = '.';  /* copy decimal point to front of e */

    while ((*n++ = *fn++) != '.') /* Copy name to n */
        ;

    *--n = '\0';  /* Terminate n with null character */

    while (*e++ = fn++)  /* Copy extension to e */
```

```
                  ;

}


screen(mode, burst)    /* Establish screen mode and burst */
int mode, burst;
{

     union REGS r, *inregs, *outregs;   /* Pointers to union in
dos.h */

     inregs = &r;
     outregs = &r;
     burst = burst % 2; /* Normalize burst value */
     r.h.ah = 15;

     int86(0x10, inregs, outregs);    /* Get current mode */

     if (mode == 0 && r.h.ah > 40)  /* Determine new mode from */
          mode = 2 + burst;           /* Current mode value */
     else if (mode == 0)
          mode = burst;
     else
          mode = (mode == 1) ? 4 + burst : 6;

     r.h.al = mode;      /* Put mode value in al */
     r.h.ah = 0;

     int86(0x10, inregs, outregs); /* Set mode */

}


               pset(x, y, c) /* Set pixel at x, y in color c */
               int x, y, c;
               {

                    /* REGS is found in dos.h */
                    union REGS r, *inregs, *outregs;

                    inregs = &r;
                    outregs = &r;

                    r.x.cx = x; /* cx = x-coordinate */
                    r.x.dx = y; /* dx = y-coordinate */
                    r.h.al = c; /* al = color index */
                    r.h.ah = 12;/* ah = function number */

                    int86(0x10, inregs, outregs); /* Set pixel */

               }


               point(x, y)   /* Return color index of pixel at x, y */
               int x, y;
               {
```

```
                union REGS r, *inregs, *outregs;
                inregs = &r;
                outregs = &r;

                r.x.cx = x; /* cx = x-coordinate */
                r.x.dx = y; /* dx = y-coordinate */
                r.h.ah = 13;/* ah = function number */

                int86(0x10, inregs, outregs);  /* Get color index
to al */

                return((int) r.h.al); /* Return al as an int value */

        }
```

```
     #include <pset.c>   /* Source code for pset() */
     line(x1, y1, x2, y2, c) /* Draw a line from x1, x2 to x2, y2
in color index c */
     int x1, x2, y1, y2, c;
     {

        int a, b;

        double m = (y1 - y2) / (double) (x1 - x2); /* Calculate
slope of line */

        for (a = x1; a <= x2; ++a) {  /* count from x1 to x2 */
            b = m * a;      /* Plot y-axis */
            pset(a, b, c); /* Set pixel along this axis */
        }

     }
```

```
     #include <pset.c>        /* Source code for pset() */
     line(x1, y1, x2, y2, c) /* Draw line from x1, y1 to x2, y2 in
color index c */
     int x1, x2, y1, y2, c;
     {

        int a, b, temp;

        double m = abs(y1 - y2) / (double) abs(x1 - x2); /*
Calculate slope based upon absolute values */
        temp = x2;
        if (x1 > x2) {  /* Determine which coordinate pair is
larger */
            x2 = x1;     /* Swap values to make x1 < x2 */
            x1 = temp;
        }

        for (a = x1; a <= x2; ++a) {    /* Count from low to high */
            b = m * a;     /* Plot y axis */
            pset(a, b, c); /* Write pixel along this axis */
        }

     }
box(x1, y1, x2, y2, c)/* Draw a box with upper left corner at
```

```
x1,y1 and lower right corner at x2,y2 in color index c */
int x1, x2, y1, y2, c;
{

    int a, b, temp;

    temp = x1;
```

```
    if (x1 > x2) {   /* If x1 < x2 */
        x1 = x2;     /* Swap */
        x2 = temp;   /* these values */
    }

    temp = y1;
    if (y1 > y2) {          /* Swap values of y is y1 < y2 */
        y1 = y2;
        y2 = temp;
    }

    a = x1;
    while (a <= x2) {        /* Write parallel horizontal lines */
        pset(a, y1, c);
        pset(a++, y2, c);
    }
    while (y1 < y2) {        /* Write parallel vertical lines */
        pset(x1, y1, c);
        pset(x2, y1++, c);
    }

}
```

```
circle(a, b, r, c) /* Draw circle with center at a,b and radius of
r pixels in color index c */
int a, b, r, c;
{

    int h, i, j, k, m, n, x, y;
    double sin(), cos(), t;
/* Arc conversions */
    h = a + r;
    i = a - r;
    j = b + r;
    k = b - r;

    for (t = 0; t <= 90; t += .025) {/* Count from 0 to 90 in
steps of 0.025 */
        x =  r * sin(t) + a; /* Get x coordinate from sine
formula */
        y =  r * cos(t) + b; /* Get y coordinate from cosine
formula */
        pset(x, y, c);   /* Set pixel in base arc */
        m = k + (j - y); /* Calculate y axis for second arc */
        pset(x, m, c);   /* Set that pixel */
        n = i + (h - x); /* Calculate for third arc */
        pset(n, y, c);   /* Set that pixel */
        pset(n, m, c);   /* Set pixel for fourth arc */
    }

}
```

```c
#include <stdio.h>
main()                /* Make look-up table */
{
     FILE *fp, *fopen();
     double sin(), cos(), t;

     if ((fp = fopen("lookup", "w")) == NULL) /* Open lookup */
          exit(0);

     fprintf(fp, "static double sc[] = {\n"); /* Print static
array declaration and name */

     for (t = 0; t <= 89.975; t += .025) /* Step thru values */
          fprintf(fp, "{ %lf, %lf },\n", sin(t), cos(t)); /*
Write values to file */

     fprintf(fp, "{ %lf, %lf }\n };", sin(t), cos(t)); /*
Write final values */

     fclose(fp); /* Close lookup */

}
```

```c
cls() /* Clear the text screen */
{

          printf("%c[2J", 27); /* ANSI code */

}
```

```c
cls()  /* Clear the current text/graphics screen */
{

    int attr;
    union REGS r, *inregs, *outregs;

    attr = 0;      /* Graphic screen attribute value */
    inregs = &r;
    outregs = &r;

    r.h.ah = 15;  /* Get mode function number */

    int86(0x10, inregs, outregs); /* Get screen mode */

    if (r.h.al == 7 || r.h.al < 4)  /* If al = 7 then the current
mode is monochrome. If al < 4 then mode is text only */
         attr = 7;   /* Change to text mode attribute */

    r.h.ah = 6;        /* Scroll screen function number */
    r.h.bh = attr;     /* by register = attribute value */
    r.h.ch = 0;        /* Upper left screen coordinate pair */
    r.h.cl = 0;        /* See above */
    r.h.dh = 24;       /* Lower right coordinate pair */
    r.h.dl = 79;       /* See above */
    r.h.al = 0;        /* scroll all */

    int86(0x10, inregs, outregs);     /* Scroll screen */
```

```
            r.h.ah = 2;     /* Set cursor function number */
            r.h.bh = 0;     /* Page number */
            r.h.dh = 0;     /* New position coordinates */
            r.h.dl = 0;     /* See above */

            int86(0x10, inregs, outregs);   /* Set cursor */

}
```

```
        locate(x, y)  /* Set text cursor at x, y */
        {

            int attr;
            union REGS r, *inregs, *outregs;

            inregs = &r;
            outregs = &r;

            r.h.ah = 2;    /* Set cursor function call */
            r.h.bh = 0;    /* Page number */
            r.h.dh = x - 1;  /* Normalize coordinate value */
            r.h.dl = y - 1;  /* See above */

            int86(0x10, inregs, outregs); /* Set cursor */

        }
```

```
#include <dos.h>
#include <ctype.h>
main()              /* Look into all of memory */
{
    unsigned char far *l;
    long x, strtol();
    int y, z, zz, off;
    char a[10], val[10], val2[10], c[20], val3[15];

    printf("%c[2J", 27);  /* Clear Screen */

    strcpy(val, "0000:0000");
    locate(21, 35);     /* Position Cursor */
    printf("%s", val);
    locate(21, 35);      /* Reposition to start of window */

    z = 0;
    off = 1;

    while (off) {
        z = 0;
        strcpy(val3, "0x");    /* Copy 0x to front of val3 */
        while (zz = getch()) {   /* Get keyboard characters */
            if (zz == 27) {       /* If ESCape key */
                printf("%c[2J", zz); /* Clear screen */
                exit(0);             /* Exit Program */
            }
            if (zz == 13)       /* If <return> */
                break;          /* Break out of loop */
            zz = toupper(zz); /* Else, make all chars upper
```

```
case */
                if (zz < '0' || zz > 'F') /* If char is out of
range */
                    continue;       /* Go back for another */
                if (zz < 'A' && zz > 57)   /* See above */
                    continue;
                printf("%c", val2[z++] = zz); /* Print keyboard
value in window */
                if (z == 4) /* If cursor at color (:) */
                    locate(21,40);    /* Skip over it */
                if (z == 8) {  /* If full address is input */
                    val2[z] = '\0'; /* Terminate string with null */
                    break;
                }
            }

        locate(1, 1);  /* Position cursor at top of screen */
        if (z < 7) {   /* Has full 32-bit address not been input? */
            zz = z;         /* If so, write captured address to
val[] */
                if (zz == 4)
                    ++zz;
                while (val2[z++] = val[zz++]) /* Write it to val2
preserving the color(:) */
minus the color(:) */
                    if (val[zz] ==':')
                        ++zz;
        }
        strcpy(val, val2);  /* Write the address back to val[] */
        format(val);        /* Call format() */
        strcat(val3, val2); /* Concatenate val2 to val3 */
        x = strtol(val3, c, 0); /* Get the long value in val3 to
x */

        l = (unsigned char far *) x;  /* Set pointer to address */

        for (z = 0; z < 256; z += 16) {   /* Display bytes */
            sprintf(a,"%lx", x);
            format(a);          /* Makes mem locations neater */
            printf("%s  ", a);
            x += 16;            /* Get next offset */
            for (y = 0; y < 16; ++y) {    /* Display 16 bytes
of data */
                zz = *(l + y);
                if (zz < 16)
                    sprintf(a, "0%x", zz);
                else
                    sprintf(a,"%x", zz);

                printf("%c%c " , toupper(a[0]), toupper(a[1]));
            }

            printf(" *");  /* Asterisk separator */

            for (y = 0; y <= 16; ++y) {    /* Display characters */
                zz = *l++;
                printf("%c", (isprint(zz)) ? zz : '.');
            }

            printf("\n");   /* Make new line for next row */
```

```
                }

                locate(21, 35);
        }
}
format(c)     /* Make Hex letters upper case and add colon */
char c[];
{

        int x, y;
        char a[40], b[40];

        x = strlen(c);
        switch(x) {        /* Pad with '0' to make all addresses same
length */
                case 1:
                        strcpy(b, "0000000");
                        break;
                case 2:
                        strcpy(b, "000000");
                        break;
                case 3:
                        strcpy(b, "00000");
                        break;
                case 4:
                        strcpy(b, "0000");
                        break;
                case 5:
                        strcpy(b, "000");
                        break;
                case 6:
                        strcpy(b, "00");
                        break;
                case 7:
                        strcpy(b, "0");
                        break;
                default:
                        strcpy(b, "\0");
                        break;
        };

        x = y = 0;
        strcat(b, c);  /* Concatenate new string to b */
        while (a[x++] = toupper(b[y++]))  /* Make all chars upper
case */
                if (x == 4)   /* Test for colon(:) position */
                        a[x++] = ':';/* Add colon */

        strcpy(c, a);  /* Copy new string to old */

}
locate(x, y)    /* Position text cursor on screen */
int x, y;
{

        union REGS r, *inregs, *outregs;

        inregs = &r;
```

```
        outregs = &r;

        r.h.ah = 2;
        r.h.bh = 0;
        r.h.dh = x - 1;
        r.h.dl = y - 1;

        int86(0x10, inregs, outregs);


}
```